HOW *to* USE

WITHDRAWN

Microsoft®
Windows® XP

Walter Glenn

SAMS

201 W. 103rd Street
Indianapolis, Indiana 46290

Visually in Full Color

How to Use Microsoft® Windows® XP

International Standard Book Number: 0-672-32256-0

Library of Congress Catalog Card Number: 2001090439

Printed in the United States of America

First Printing: September 2001

04 03 02 01 4 3 2 1

Trademarks

All terms mentioned in this book that are known to be trademarks or service marks have been appropriately capitalized. Sams Publishing cannot attest to the accuracy of this information. Use of a term in this book should not be regarded as affecting the validity of any trademark or service mark.

Microsoft and Windows are registered trademarks of Microsoft Corporation.

Warning and Disclaimer

Every effort has been made to make this book as complete and as accurate as possible, but no warranty or fitness is implied. The information provided is on an "as is" basis. The author and the publisher shall have neither liability nor responsibility to any person or entity with respect to any loss or damages arising from the information contained in this book or from the use of programs accompanying it.

Acquisitions Editor
Betsy Brown

Development Editor
Alice Martina Smith

Managing Editor
Charlotte Clapp

Project Editor
Elizabeth Finney

Production Editor
Tony Reitz

Indexer
Eric Schroeder

Proofreader
Juli Cook

Technical Editor
Galen Grimes

Team Coordinator
Amy Patton

Interior Designer
Gary Adair

Cover Designers
Aren Howell
Nathan Clement

Page Layout
Stacey Richwine-DeRome
Mark Walchle

Contents at a Glance

Introduction 1

1 Using the Windows XP Desktop 4

2 Working with Files and Folders 30

3 Printing 60

4 Working on the Internet 78

5 Using Internet E-Mail and Newsgroups 102

6 Working on a Network 122

7 Working Away from the Network 144

8 Having Fun with Windows XP 160

9 Protecting Your Files 176

10 Changing Windows XP Settings 190

11 Using the System Tools 224

12 Installing New Software and Hardware 246

Appendix: Installing Windows XP 258

Glossary 270

Index 278

Table of Contents

Introduction 1

1 Using the Windows XP Desktop 4

How to Log On to Windows XP 6

How to Use Your Mouse 8

How to Display Icons on Your Desktop 10

How to Start a Program 12

How to Arrange Windows on the Desktop 14

How to Switch Between Programs 16

How to Use the System Tray 18

How to Browse Your Disk Drives 20

How to Get Help 22

How to Use the Recycle Bin 24

How to Log Off Windows XP 26

How to Shut Down Your Computer 28

2 Working with Files and Folders 30

How to Use Windows Explorer 32

How to Search for a File or Folder 34

How to Create a Folder 36

How to View Items in a Folder 38

How to Create a File 40

How to Open a File 42

How to Save a File 44

How to Create a Shortcut to a File or Folder 46

How to Rename a File or Folder 48

How to Delete a File or Folder 50

How to Move or Copy a File or Folder 52

How to Format a Floppy Disk 53

How to Format a Floppy Disk 54

How to Send a File to the Floppy Drive 56

How to Open a File with a Certain Program 58

3 Printing 60

How to Print a Document from a Program 62

How to Print a Document from Windows 64

How to Manage Documents Waiting to Print 66

How to Change Printer Settings 68

How to Share a Printer with Others 70

How to Install a Local Printer 72

How to Set Up Your Computer to Use a Network Printer 76

4 Working on the Internet 78

How to Start Internet Explorer 80

How to Get to a Web Site 82

How to Search for a Web Site 84

How to Use the Favorites Menu 86

How to Use the History List 88

How to Make Web Pages Available Offline 90

How to Change Settings for Internet Explorer 92

How to Use MSN Explorer 94

How to Use Windows Messenger 98

How to Publish a File to the Web 100

5 Using Internet E-Mail and Newsgroups 102

How to Send E-Mail with Outlook Express 104

How to Receive E-Mail 106

How to Use the Address Book 108

How to Change Settings for Outlook Express 110

How to Receive an Attached File 112

How to Send an Attached File 114

How to Subscribe to a Newsgroup 116

How to Read a Newsgroup Posting 118

How to Post to a Newsgroup 120

6 Working on a Network *122*

How to Set Up a Small Network   **124**

How to Set Up Additional User Accounts   **128**

How to Share an Internet Connection   **130**

How to Use My Network Places   **132**

How to Add a Network Place   **134**

How to Find a Computer on the Network   **136**

How to Find a File on the Network   **138**

How to Share a File or Folder with Others   **140**

How to Map a Network Drive   **142**

 7 Working Away from the Network *144*

How to Create and Fill a Briefcase   **146**

How to Take a Briefcase with You   **148**

How to Update Files in a Briefcase   **150**

How to Make Items Available Offline   **152**

How to Use Offline Items   **154**

How to Synchronize Offline Items   **156**

How to Change Offline Settings   **158**

 8 Having Fun with Windows XP *160*

How to Play Music and Movies   **162**

How to Record Music   **164**

How to Find Music Online   **166**

How to Make Movies   **168**

How to Work with Pictures   **172**

How to Play Games   **174**

9 Protecting Your Files *176*

How to Set Local Permissions on a Domain-Based Network   **178**

How to Set Shared Permissions on a Domain-Based Network   **180**

How to Encrypt a File or Folder   **182**

How to Lock Your Workstation   **184**

How to Assign a Screen Saver Password   **186**

How to Change Your Logon Password   **188**

 10 Changing Windows XP Settings *190*

How to Change the Volume   **192**

How to Set Up a Screen Saver   **194**

How to Change Your Desktop Theme   **196**

How to Change Your Wallpaper   **198**

How to Change Desktop Appearance   **200**

How to Change Display Settings   **202**

How to Change Mouse Settings   **204**

How to Change Keyboard Settings   **206**

How to Customize the Taskbar   **208**

How to Change Folder Options   **210**

How to Change Power Options   **212**

How to Change System Sounds   **214**

How to Add an Item to the Start Menu   **216**

How to Add an Item to the Quick Launch Bar   **218**

How to Start a Program When Windows Starts   **220**

How to Set Accessibility Options   **222**

11 Using the System Tools *224*

How to Back Up Your Files   **226**

How to Restore Files from a Backup   **228**

How to Use Automated System Recovery   **230**

How to Free Up Space on Your Hard Disk   **232**

How to Defragment Your Hard Disk   **234**

How to Schedule a Task to Occur Automatically   **236**

How to Use the Windows Troubleshooters   **238**

How to Get System Information   **240**

How to Use System Restore   **242**

How to Compress Files and Folders   **244**

12 Installing New Software and Hardware *246*

How to Add a Program to Your Computer   **248**

How to Change or Remove a Program   **250**

How to Add Windows Components from
the CD   **252**

How to Add Windows Components from the
Internet   **254**

How to Find Out About Your Installed
Hardware   **256**

Appendix: Installing Windows XP *258*

How to Upgrade to Windows XP   **260**

How to Install Windows XP on a Blank
Hard Drive   **262**

How to Activate Windows XP   **266**

How to Create Setup Floppy Disks   **268**

Glossary *270*

Index *278*

About the Author

Walter Glenn is an independent writer, editor, and networking consultant. He is a Microsoft Certified Systems Engineer, Internet Specialist, and Certified Trainer. He has been part of the computer industry for about 17 years, working his way from PC repair, to programming, to networking and has written extensively about networking and the Windows operating environment. He lives and works in Huntsville, Alabama.

Dedication

For my kids, Liam and Maya.

Acknowledgments

I want to thank the team at Sams Publishing, including Betsy Brown, Alice Martina Smith, Elizabeth Finney, Galen Grimes, Tony Reitz, and the production team. Thanks also to Kristen Pickens and Neil Salkind of StudioB for their guidance and support.

Tell Us What You Think!

As the reader of this book, *you* are our most important critic and commentator. We value your opinion and want to know what we're doing right, what we could do better, what areas you'd like to see us publish in, and any other words of wisdom you're willing to pass our way.

You can e-mail or write me directly to let me know what you did or didn't like about this book—as well as what we can do to make our books stronger.

Please note that I cannot help you with technical problems related to the topic of this book, and that because of the high volume of mail I receive, I might not be able to reply to every message.

When you write, please be sure to include this book's title and author as well as your name and phone number. I will carefully review your comments and share them with the author and editors who worked on the book.

Email: **consumer@samspublishing.com**

Mail: Mark Taber
           Associate Publisher
           Sams Publishing
           201 West 103rd Street
           Indianapolis, IN 46290 USA

The Complete Visual Reference

Each chapter of this book is made up of a series of short, instructional tasks, designed to help you understand all the information that you need to get the most out of your computer hardware and software.

Click: Click the left mouse button once.

Double-click: Click the left mouse button twice in rapid succession.

Right-click: Click the right mouse button once.

Drag: Click and hold the left mouse button, position the mouse pointer, and release.

Pointer Arrow: Highlights an item on the screen you need to point to or focus on in the step or task.

Selection: Highlights the area onscreen discussed in the step or task.

Type: Click once where indicated and begin typing to enter your text or data.

Drag and Drop: Point to the starting place or object. Hold down the mouse button (right or left per instructions), move the mouse to the new location, and then release the button.

Drag   **Drop**

Each task includes a series of easy-to-understand steps designed to guide you through the procedure.

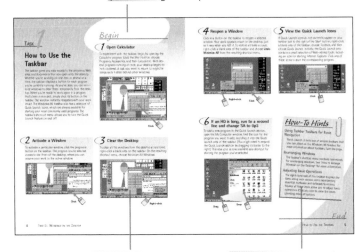

Each step is fully illustrated to show you how it looks onscreen.

Extra hints that tell you how to accomplish a goal are provided in most tasks.

 Key icons: Clearly indicate which key combinations to use.

Menus and items you click are shown in **bold**. Words in *italic* are defined in more detail in the glossary. Information you type is in a **special font**.

If you see this symbol, it means the task you're in continues on the next page:

Continues

Introduction

*L*et's face it. Most of you have better things to do than become a computer expert; a complex operating system such as Windows XP can be pretty intimidating when your boss or administrator plops it on your desk and says, "This is what you'll be using from now on." Fortunately, Windows XP is designed to be easy to use, and this book is designed to make it even easier. Whether you are completely new to Windows, or feel at home clicking your way through all those dialog boxes, you are likely to have questions:

- How do you search for a file when you don't know its name?
- How do you install a network printer?
- How do you manage documents that are waiting to print?
- How do you work with files on the network?
- How do you make a movie?
- How do you set permissions on a file?
- How do you change the way your mouse works?

How to Use Windows XP provides easy-to-follow, step-by-step, and visual instructions for performing all of these common (and some not-so-common) tasks. This book uses actual pictures of the Windows XP screens to show you what you'll see at each step of a task. With each picture, a written explanation shows you the details of performing the task in simple, jargon-free language. Using the pictures with the text is a great way to learn and accomplish the tasks the first time. Later, you can refresh your memory simply by scanning the pictures.

Windows XP comes in two different editions: Windows XP Home Edition and Windows XP Professional (actually, there is a third edition—Windows XP 64-bit Edition—which will debut later and is for high-end technical workstations). You can find out which edition you have by looking at your Windows XP CD-ROM. If you have

already installed Windows XP, you can find out which edition you have by watching the screen when Windows is starting. You can also find out by pressing **Ctrl+Alt+Del** simultaneously while Windows is running; the window that opens tells you which edition you have.

For the most part, Windows XP Home Edition and Windows XP Professional are identical. They look and feel the same and come with all the same functionality and programs. Windows XP Professional does include a few extra features that Windows XP Home Edition does not; these features are intended to make Windows XP Professional more suited to a corporate environment:

- Windows XP Professional supports computers with multiple processors (CPUs) for higher performance. Windows XP Home Edition supports only one processor.
- Windows XP Professional supports extra security measures, such as the ability to assign detailed permissions to files and folders. These permissions, which specify the rights other people on a network have to use your files, are covered in Part 9 of this book, "Protecting Your Files."
- Windows XP Professional is designed to work more efficiently on a domain-based network that uses powerful server computers running Windows 2000 or 2002 Server.

If you use Windows XP at home or in a small business (and maybe on a small network), these extra features provided by Windows XP Professional will have little added value.

This book is primarily intended for the home or small business user, although the tasks are equally well-suited for the professional user. For the most part, all the tasks in this book can be applied to both editions of Windows XP. The few instances where this is not true, or where subtle differences might trip you up, are prominently pointed out.

Each task described in this book is a specific action you will use in Windows XP, such as changing the volume on your computer or backing up files. Most tasks are described in no more than seven steps. Many tasks also include special "How-To Hints" that provide information related to the task. Finally, tasks are arranged in the following groups, making it easy to learn related sets of skills without hunting through the book:

- Using the Windows XP Desktop
- Working with Files and Folders
- Printing
- Working on the Internet
- Using Internet E-Mail and Newsgroups
- Working on a Network
- Working Away from the Network
- Having Fun with Windows XP
- Protecting Your Files
- Changing Windows XP Settings
- Using the System Tools
- Installing New Software and Hardware
- Installing Windows XP

Whatever your level of expertise and for whatever reason you use Windows XP, you will find this book a useful tool. Whether you read it cover to cover, or set it aside for reference when you come across a specific task with which you need help, this book provides you with the information you need to complete the task and get on with your work. Enjoy!

Task

1 How to Log On to Windows XP   6

2 How to Use Your Mouse   8

3 How to Display Icons on Your Desktop   10

4 How to Start a Program   12

5 How to Arrange Windows on the Desktop   14

6 How to Switch Between Programs   16

7 How to Use the System Tray   18

8 How to Browse Your Disk Drives   20

9 How to Get Help   22

10 How to Use the Recycle Bin   24

11 How to Log Off Windows XP   26

12 How to Shut Down Your Computer   28

PART 1

Using the Windows XP Desktop

*T*he Windows desktop works much like its real-world counterpart; it is a place where you organize files, run programs, and coordinate your work. When you run a program or open a folder, these items open in a window on the desktop. You can keep multiple windows open at once, arrange them how you like, and switch between them easily.

In the following tasks, you will explore some of the basic features of the Windows desktop—features that you will use daily. You will learn how to log in and out of Windows, how to use a mouse, how to run a program, and how to get help when you need it. You will also learn techniques for arranging windows and switching between open programs. Finally, you will learn the proper way to shut down your computer.

How to Log On to Windows XP

Windows XP is a *secure system*. If more than one user account is configured on your computer, or if your computer is on a network, you must *log on* (supply a username and password) so that Windows knows who you are and what you are allowed to do on the computer and network. If your computer is on a network, your logon information is supplied by your network administrator. When you install Windows XP on your own computer, you supply the information during setup. Depending on how your computer is set up, you may see the new Windows XP logon screen (shown in Steps 1–3) or the traditional logon screen (shown in Steps 4–7).

Begin

1 Select the User Account

From the list of available users, click the user account with which you want to log on. If a password is not assigned to the account (that is, if the password field was left blank when Windows was installed), you will enter directly into Windows. Otherwise, you'll be asked for a password.

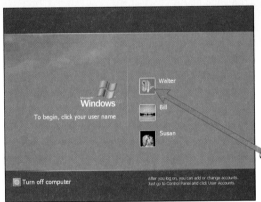

Click

2 Enter Your Password

Type your password in the box that appears. As you type, the characters you enter appear as dots or asterisks. This prevents people looking over your shoulder from discovering your password. Note that the password is case-sensitive.

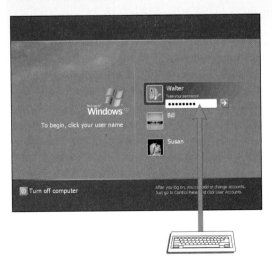

3 Log On

Click the arrow next to the password box (or press the **Enter** key on your keyboard) to submit the password and log on to Windows. After you log on, the desktop appears, and you can begin using Windows.

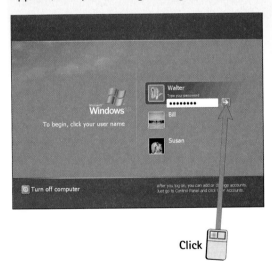

Click

4 Press Ctrl+Alt+Del

An alternative way to log on to Windows is to use the traditional logon screen. To get to the main logon screen, you must press the **Ctrl**, **Alt**, and **Del** keys all at once. This special key combination informs Windows that you want to enter a username and password.

5 Enter Your Username and Password

Type your username and password into the appropriate boxes. As you type the password, the characters you enter appear on the screen only as asterisks. Passwords are case-sensitive. You must enter the correct combination of uppercase and lowercase characters and numbers.

6 Show Extra Login Options

Most of the time, a username and password are enough for you to log on to Windows XP. However, you can click the **Options** button for more choices, including choosing a different domain and logging on to just the computer instead of a network. For more information on domains and networking, see Part 6, "Working on a Network."

7 Shut Down

You can also shut down your computer from the logon screen. Clicking the **Shutdown** button opens a dialog box from which you can choose to shut down or restart the computer. These options are great when you need to shut down the system but don't want to wait through the logon process.

End

How to Use Your Mouse

Your mouse allows you to get many common tasks done quicker than with the keyboard. Sliding the mouse on your desk moves the pointer on the screen. The pointer usually appears as an arrow pointing up and to the left—just point it to the item you want to select. The pointer shape changes as you move over different areas of the screen—a vertical bar shows where you can enter text, for example. The shape also changes to indicate system status. An hourglass means that Windows is busy doing something. An hourglass with an arrow means that Windows is working on something but that you can continue to do other things in the meantime.

Begin

1 Point to an Object

An *object* refers to an item on your screen, usually an icon, that represents a program, file, or folder. You can point to an object by sliding the mouse so that the tip of the mouse pointer arrow is over that object.

2 Click an Object

Clicking your left mouse button one time selects an object. When you select the object, its icon and text become highlighted with a dark blue background. Then you can perform another action on the object, such as deleting it.

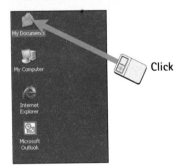

Click

3 Double-Click an Object

Double-clicking means to move the mouse pointer over an object and click the left mouse button twice in quick succession. Double-clicking an object on your desktop *launches* it. Double-clicking a folder opens it; double-clicking a program runs it.

Double-click

The folder you double-clicked opens

4 Right-Click an Object

When you click once on an object with the right mouse button, a shortcut menu pops up that lets you perform various actions associated with the object. The command in boldface is the action that would be performed by double-clicking the object.

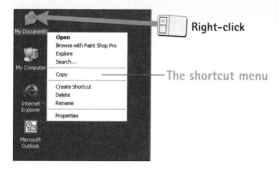

Right-click

The shortcut menu

5 Drag an Object

To drag an object, point to the item, click and hold the left mouse button, and move the mouse to reposition the item. Release the mouse button to drop the object. The drag-and-drop approach is the way to move files to new folders and to move whole windows on your desktop.

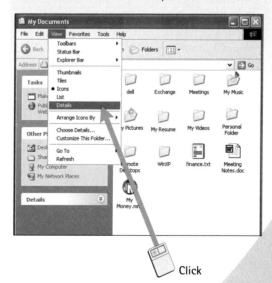

Drag   Drop

6 Open a Menu

Many windows, such as open folders and programs, have menus that provide access to different commands for working in the window. To open a menu, click the menu's name once.

Click

7 Select a Menu Command

After a menu is open, you can click any command on the menu to have Windows perform that action.

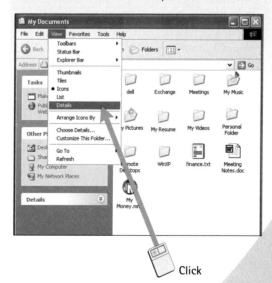

Click

End

How to Display Icons on Your Desktop

In previous versions of Windows, icons representing important parts of your system (such as the **My Computer** and **My Documents** icons—which you'll learn about later) were always shown on your desktop. Depending on your situation, this may or may not be the case with Windows XP. If you buy a copy of Windows XP and install it yourself (using the procedures covered in the Appendix), your desktop will be empty except for the **Recycle Bin**. If you buy your computer with Windows XP already installed, the icons may or may not be on the desktop, depending on the manufacturer of your computer. Throughout this book, many tasks assume that these icons are displayed on the desktop. If you don't see them on your desktop, you can find them on the **Start** menu. You can also tell Windows to show the icons on the desktop using the following steps.

Begin

1 Open the Start Menu

The **Start** menu is the centerpiece of the Windows XP desktop and lets you access all your programs and most of the Windows settings available for configuration. The first time you start a computer with Windows XP, the **Start** menu opens for you automatically. After that, you must open it yourself by clicking its button once.

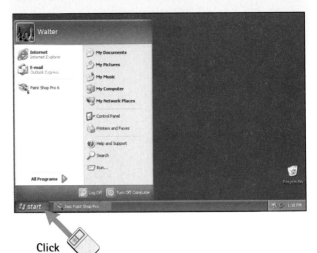

Click

2 Find the Icon You're Looking For

All the icons that used to appear on the Windows desktop now appear in the upper-right part of the **Start** menu.

3 Click an Icon to Open Its Window

To open the window for any of the icons in the **Start** menu, just click the icon once with the left mouse button. The **Start** menu closes and a window opens on your desktop.

Click

4 Open an Icon's Shortcut Menu

Right-click any icon to open a shortcut menu with special commands for working with that icon.

 Right-click

5 Show the Icon on the Desktop

Click the **Show on Desktop** command in the shortcut menu to have that icon appear on the Windows desktop. (The icon will still appear on the **Start** menu, as well.) If you decide you don't want the icon on your desktop after all, open the **Start** menu, right-click the icon in the menu, and choose **Show on Desktop** again to remove the icon from the desktop.

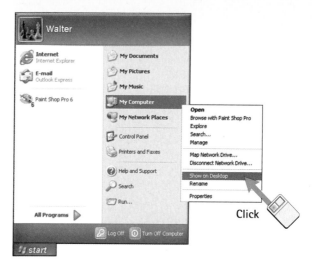

Click

6 Open the Desktop Icon

After the icon is shown on your desktop, double-click it to open it.

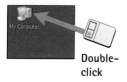

Double-click

7 Turn on Other Icons

Each of the icons shown in the upper-right portion of the **Start** menu can appear as icons on your desktop. Just right-click each one in turn and choose the **Show on Desktop** command from the shortcut menu.

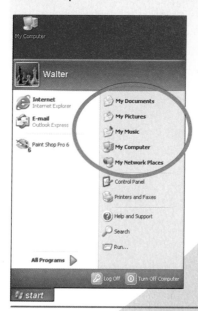

End

TASK 4

How to Start a Program

The real reason you bother with Windows is so that you can run programs that let you get your work done (and play an occasional game of Solitaire). Windows XP provides several ways to run your programs. To begin with, all your programs are conveniently located on the **Start** menu. This menu includes some simple programs that come with Windows (such as a calculator and a notepad) and any other programs you have installed.

1 Click the Start Button

Click the **Start** button to open the **Start** menu. Directly under your logon name, you'll find shortcuts to your Web browser and e-mail program (Internet Explorer and Outlook Express, by default). Under these shortcuts, you'll find shortcuts to any programs you've run recently. On the right side of the **Start** menu, you'll find shortcuts to various important folders on your system and access to the help and search features.

2 Click the More Programs Button

If you don't see the program you are looking for on the **Start** menu, click the **All Programs** button to see a list of all the programs installed on your computer. Some might be listed in folders within the **My Programs** folder; just point to a subfolder to open it. Programs that have recently been installed are highlighted. When you find a program you want, click the shortcut to run it.

3 Click a Quick Launch Shortcut

Some programs have shortcuts on the **Quick Launch** toolbar, just to the right of the **Start** button. Click any of these shortcut buttons to launch the program. The program opens in a new window on the desktop.

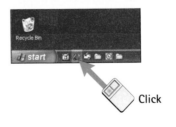

4 Maximize a Program Window

Click the **Maximize** button to make the program window take up the whole screen (except for the space occupied by the taskbar).

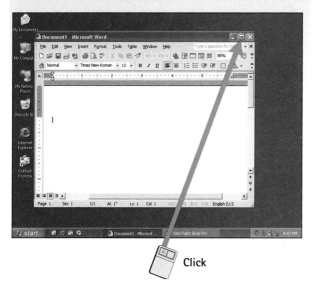

Click

5 Restore a Program Window

After a window is maximized, the **Maximize** button turns into a **Restore** button. Click the **Restore** button to shrink the window back to its previous size.

Click

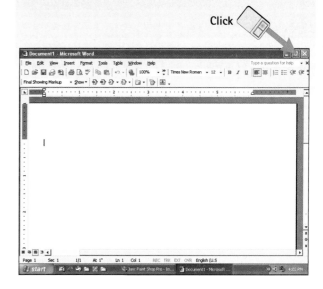

6 Minimize a Program Window

Click the **Minimize** button to remove the window from the desktop but leave the program running. You can tell the program is still running because its button remains in the taskbar at the bottom of the screen. Click the taskbar button to restore the window to the desktop.

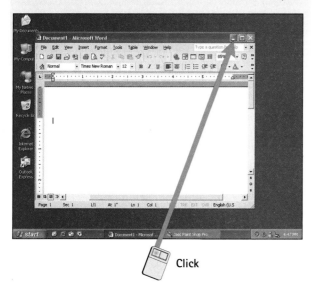

Click

7 Close a Program Window

Click the **Close** button to end the program and remove its window from the desktop. The program displays a dialog box asking you to save any unsaved work before it closes. You can also close a program by choosing the **Exit** command from the **File** menu.

Click

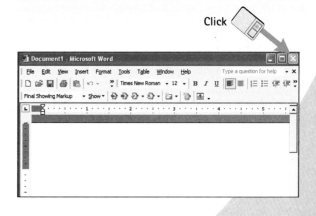

End

How to Arrange Windows on the Desktop

Windows offers the ability to keep many windows, whether program windows or folder windows, open at the same time. Although having multiple windows open at the same time provides the ability to easily move between tasks, using multiple windows can become confusing. Fortunately, Windows offers some clever tools for working with and arranging the windows on your desktop.

Begin

1 Resize a Window

When you move your pointer to the outer edge or corner of a window, the pointer changes into a double-headed arrow. When the pointer changes, click and drag the edge of the window to change its size.

2 Move a Window

You can move an entire window to a different location on the desktop by dragging its title bar. You can even move the window off the edges of your screen.

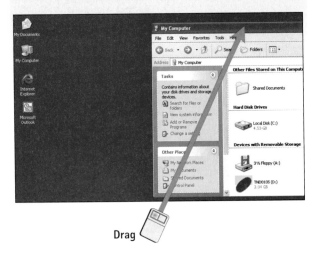

Drag

3 Cascade Windows

When you have a number of windows open at once, you can line them up in a cascade by right-clicking the taskbar and choosing **Cascade Windows** from the shortcut menu.

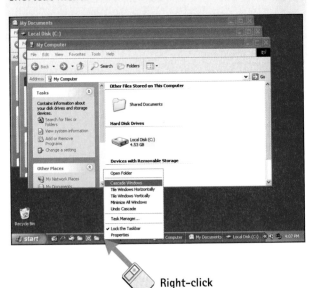

Right-click

4 Tile Windows Vertically

Another way to arrange multiple windows on your desktop is to *tile* them, which means that Windows tries to fit them all on the screen at once. Right-click the taskbar and choose **Tile Windows Vertically** to arrange them from left to right on your screen.

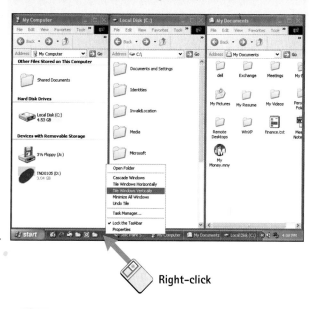

Right-click

5 Tile Windows Horizontally

You can also tile windows horizontally, meaning that Windows fits them all on your screen from top to bottom. Right-click the taskbar and choose **Tile Windows Horizontally**.

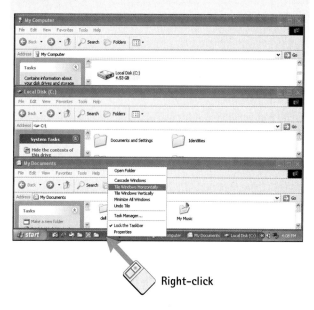

Right-click

6 Minimize All Windows

You can minimize all open windows on your desktop at once (and thus clear them from your desktop) by right-clicking the taskbar and choosing **Minimize All Windows**. This is a great way to get to your desktop quickly.

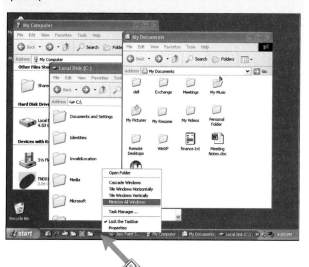

Right-click

How-To Hints

Showing the Desktop

A better way to get to your desktop quickly instead of using the **Minimize All Windows** command is to use the **Show Desktop** button on the **Quick Launch** toolbar. This button effectively minimizes all windows, even if some windows are showing dialog boxes (something the **Minimize All Windows** command can't do). Click **Show Desktop** again to reverse the action and return all the minimized windows to their previous states.

End

How to Switch Between Programs

When you run several programs at once, you must be able to switch between these programs easily. Windows offers three great methods for switching between open applications—two using the mouse and one using the keyboard.

Begin

1 Click the Program's Window

The easiest way to switch to an open program is simply to click the program's window, if some portion of the window is visible. Inactive windows have a slightly dimmer title bar than the active window. Clicking anywhere on an inactive window brings it to the front and makes it active.

Click to make the inactive window active

The active window

2 Click a Program's Taskbar Button

When you can't see the window you want, the simplest way to switch to it is to click that window's button on the taskbar. This action brings that window to the front of the desktop in whatever size and position you left it.

Click

3 Resize the Taskbar

When there are a lot of open windows, the buttons on the taskbar might get too small to be of much value in determining which window is which. You can hold your pointer over a button to see its full description, or you can drag the top edge of the taskbar up to make it bigger.

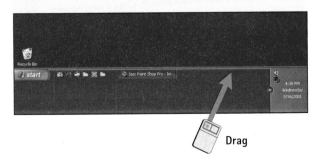

Drag

4 Use Grouped Taskbar Buttons

When more than one window is open for a single program, Windows XP groups those windows using a single taskbar button instead of multiple taskbar buttons. For example, you may be looking at a few different Web sites in different windows using Internet Explorer. A single taskbar button for Internet Explorer is displayed and the number of active Internet Explorer windows (five in the example shown here) is shown on the button. Click the button once to open a menu from which you can choose a specific window to activate.

5 Press Alt+Tab

You can also switch between open windows using your keyboard. Press and hold the **Alt** key and then press the **Tab** key once (without letting go of the **Alt** key). A box appears, displaying icons for each window. Press the **Tab** key to cycle through the windows. When you get to the window you want, release the Alt key to switch to it.

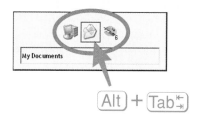

How-To Hints

Getting Out of Alt+Tab

If you use **Alt+Tab** to open the box that lets you switch between windows and then decide that you don't want to switch, just press **Esc** while you're still holding down the **Alt** key. The box disappears and puts you right back where you were.

Unlocking the Taskbar

If you find that you cannot resize the taskbar, it is probably locked. A locked taskbar cannot be resized or moved. Some people prefer to keep their taskbar locked so that no accidental changes are made to it. Others prefer to leave it unlocked so that they can easily resize it. Right-click anywhere on the taskbar and click the **Lock the Taskbar** command to deselect that command and unlock the bar.

End

How to Use the System Tray

The *system tray* is the part of the taskbar at the far right side that holds your clock and probably several other small icons. These icons show information about programs that are running in the background on your computer. Some of the icons provide access to certain functions of the programs they represent. For example, the speaker icon lets you set your system's volume and configure audio properties.

Begin

1 Expand the System Tray

The system tray collapses automatically to show only the clock and any recently used icons. To view the entire system tray, click the button with the double-left arrow at the left side of the system tray. A few seconds after you move your pointer away from the area, the system tray collapses again.

Click

2 Viewing the Date

Hold the mouse pointer over the clock for a moment to view a pop-up balloon with the current date.

3 Setting the Clock

Double-click the clock to open a dialog box that lets you set the current date and time, as well as configure time-zone settings.

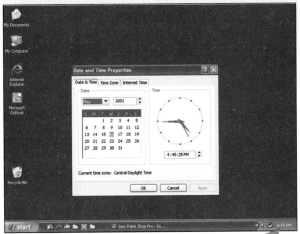

Double-click

4 Setting the Volume

Click the speaker icon in the system tray to open the volume control. Slide the control up or down to change the volume of your system. A beep sounds to let you know how loud the volume is set.

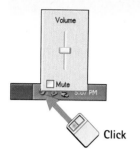

Click

5 Using Other System Tray Icons

Unfortunately, the system tray icons for different programs behave in different manners. Sometimes, right-clicking or left-clicking the icon once opens a dialog box for configuration of some sort (as was the case with the volume control). Sometimes, right-clicking the icon opens a shortcut menu with program options. You'll have to experiment or read the documentation for the appropriate program.

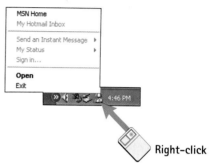

Right-click

How-To Hints

Keeping the System Tray Open

To keep the system tray open and showing all its icons all the time, right-click the taskbar and choose **Properties**. On the **Taskbar** tab of the dialog box that opens, disable (that is, remove the check mark next to) the **Hide inactive icons** option.

Turning Off Icons

You can turn off some icons in the system tray by right-clicking the icon and choosing the **Exit** command, if one exists. There also might be a command for setting options or preferences. Sometimes these settings contain an option for permanently turning off the icon. Another place you might look is in the **Startup** folder on your **Start** menu. Often, programs that are configured to start with Windows place icons on the system tray. For more about using the **Startup** folder, see Part 10, "Changing Windows XP Settings."

Updating the Clock Automatically

If you have Internet access and are not behind a firewall, Windows XP can update your clock automatically. Double-click the clock. In the dialog box that opens, select the **Internet Time** tab. Select the **Automatically synchronize with an Internet time server** option and then choose an available server.

End

How to Browse Your Disk Drives

Your disk drives hold all the information on your computer: all the files, folders, and programs, as well as all your documents. The **My Computer** window gives you access to these drives, whether they are hard drives, floppy drives, CD-ROM drives, or something else. **My Computer** also provides a shortcut to the Windows **Control Panel**, which is discussed more in Part 10, "Changing Windows XP Settings."

Begin

1 Open My Computer

Double-click the **My Computer** icon on the desktop to open the **My Computer** window.

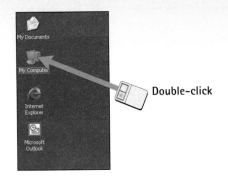

Double-click

2 Select a Disk Drive

The **My Computer** window shows any drives present on your computer. Click the icon for the drive you want to investigate to select it. Your floppy drive is usually named **A:** and your main hard drive is usually named **C:**. Information about the capacity and free space on any selected drive is shown in the **Details** pane to the left.

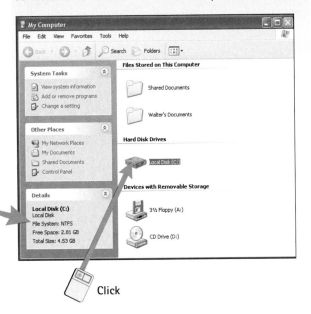

Click

3 Open a Drive

Double-click the drive icon to open that drive.

Double-click

4 Open a Folder

Objects on a drive are organized into folders. *Folders* can contain both files and other folders. Double-click a folder to open it.

5 Open a File

When you select a file, a description of that file appears on the left side of the window. Double-click a file to launch the program that created the file (that is, the program *associated* with the file) and open that file within the program.

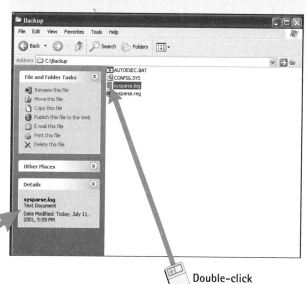

Double-click

6 Navigate Folders

Click the **Back** button in the toolbar at the top of the folder window to go back to the folder you just came from. Click the down arrow next to the **Back** button to view a list of previous locations you can jump back to.

Click

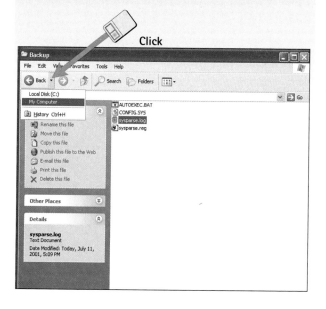

How-To Hints

Browsing Your Computer

Click the down arrow to the right of the **Address** bar (just beneath the window's toolbar) to open the drop-down list. Use this list to browse a hierarchical list of the drives and open folders on your computer.

Going Up One Level

Use the **Up One Level** button (it looks like a folder with an arrow pointing up) to go to the parent folder of the folder you are presently viewing.

Program Associations

Some files might not have a program associated with them. In this case, you'll be given the chance to choose the program you want to use to open the file. See Part 2, "Working with Files and Folders," for more information on this topic.

End

How to Get Help

Windows XP boasts a comprehensive Help system that lets you get details on Windows concepts and performing specific tasks. You can browse the contents of Windows Help, search for specific terms, or even ask questions in plain English.

Begin

1 Open Help

To open the Windows Help system, click the **Start** button and then choose **Help and Support**. The **Help and Support Center** window opens.

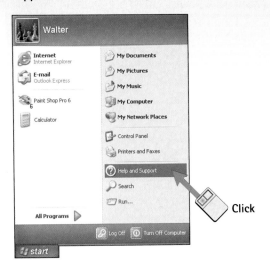

Click

2 Enter a Search Term

If you know what topic you are looking for help about, type a word, phrase, or even a question in the **Search** box and click the **Search** button.

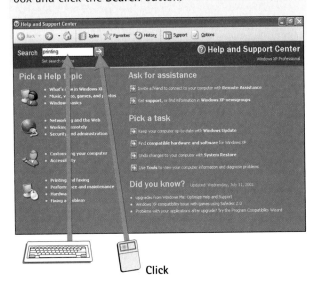

Click

3 Select a Result

Windows shows a list of all articles that match your search words. Click one of the result terms in the left pane to view the article in the right pane. Buttons above the article let you print the article or add it to a list of favorites.

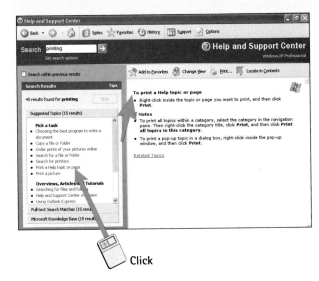

Click

4 Pick a Help Topic

If you are not sure what the name of the topic you're looking for is, or if you just want to browse the Help system, click the link for a help topic on the main **Help and Support Center** page.

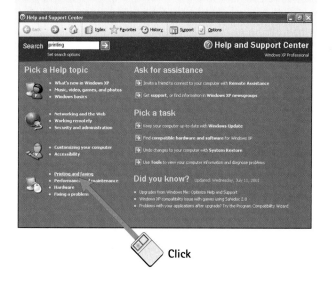

Click

5 Pick a Category

In the left pane, Windows displays the categories for the topic you selected in Step 4. Click a category to display a list of help articles related to that category in the right pane.

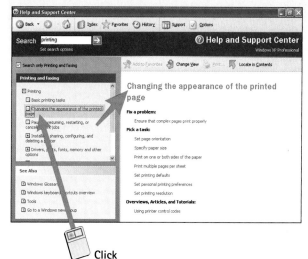

Click

6 Pick an Article

Click the article in the list you want to view. Windows opens the selected article in a new window. When you're done reading the article, click the window's **Close** button to close the window and return to the **Help and Support Center** window.

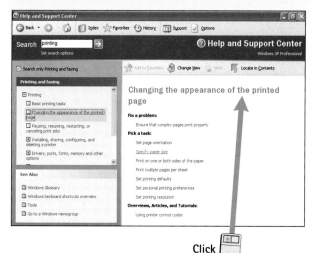

Click

How-To Hints

Using the F1 Key

Press the **F1** key at any time while using Windows to open a help page related to your current activity. Many programs also support the F1/Help feature.

Using the Index

Click the **Index** button on the help window's toolbar to view a searchable index of all help articles. Some people find it easier to browse the Help system this way.

End

How to Use the Recycle Bin

You can delete files, folders, and programs from your computer at any time. However, when you delete an item, Windows does not immediately remove it from your computer. Instead, the item is placed into the **Recycle Bin**. You can restore an item from the **Recycle Bin** later if you decide you would rather not delete it. When the **Recycle Bin** becomes full (depending on the amount of disk space allocated to it), Windows deletes older items permanently to make room for newer items. You can think of the **Recycle Bin** as sort of a buffer between your files and oblivion.

Begin

1 Drag an Object to the Recycle Bin

The easiest way to delete an object is to drag it to the **Recycle Bin**. You can drag an item from the desktop or from any open folder. You can also delete a file by selecting it and pressing the **Delete** key on your keyboard.

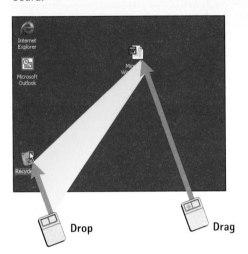

Drop   Drag

2 Confirm the Deletion

When you try to delete an object, Windows asks you to confirm that you really want to delete it. Click **Yes** if you're sure; click **No** if you made a mistake and don't want to delete the named object.

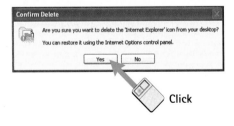

Click

3 Open the Recycle Bin

Double-click the **Recycle Bin** icon on the desktop to open it. All files in the **Recycle Bin** are listed with their original locations and the date on which they were deleted.

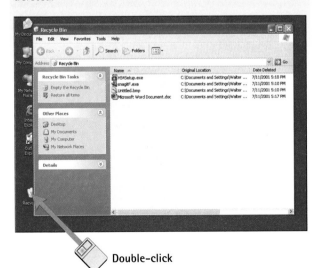

Double-click

4 Restore Files

To remove a file from the **Recycle Bin** and restore it to its original location, select the file and click the **Restore this item** link that appears on the left.

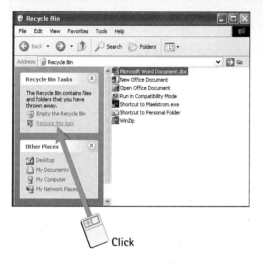

Click

5 Delete Files

Right-click a file in the **Recycle Bin** list and choose **Delete** from the shortcut menu to permanently delete that file from your hard disk.

Right-click

6 Empty the Recycle Bin

To permanently delete all the files from the **Recycle Bin** (which you might want to do to regain some disk space), make sure that no files are selected and click the **Empty Recycle Bin** link on the left.

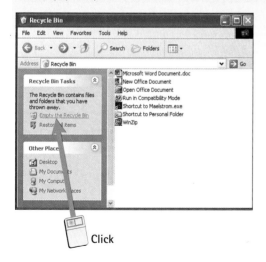

Click

How-To Hints

Another Way to Empty the Bin

You can empty the **Recycle Bin** without opening it by right-clicking its icon on the desktop and choosing **Empty Recycle Bin** from the shortcut menu.

Allocating Recycle Bin Space

By default, 10% of your hard drive space is reserved for use by the **Recycle Bin**. You can change the amount of space used by right-clicking the **Recycle Bin** and selecting the **Properties** command from the shortcut menu. On the **Global** tab of the **Recycle Bin Properties** dialog box, drag the slider to change the maximum size of the **Recycle Bin**.

End

How to Log Off Windows XP

As you learned earlier in this part, logging on (providing Windows with your username and maybe a password) tells Windows who is using the computer. Logging off tells Windows that you are finished with your computer session. You should log off whenever you plan to be away from the computer for a length of time (such as for lunch or at the end of the day).

Begin

1 Click Log Off

Click the **Start** button and then choose **Log Off**.

Click

2 Switch User

If you are not finished using Windows and just want to let someone else use the computer for a short time, you can simply switch users. Click the **Switch User** button if you want to leave all your programs running and your documents open while the other person uses the computer. The logon window (shown in Task 1) opens so that the other person can log on. When that person logs off, you can switch back to your account and continue working.

Click

3 Log Off

Logging off closes any running programs. Although Windows usually gives you the chance to save any unsaved documents before it actually logs off, you should save your files manually before you log off to make sure that your data is safe.

Click

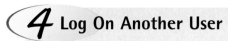

4 Log On Another User

As soon as you log off, Windows presents the logon screen. You can now log back on as described in Task 1.

How-To Hints

Using a Screen Saver Password

Screen saver passwords let your computer automatically lock itself whenever the screen saver activates. To access the computer again, you'll have to type the password to deactivate the screen saver. For more on this feature, see Part 9, "Protecting Your Files."

End

TASK *12*

How to Shut Down Your Computer

While running, Windows keeps a lot of its information in *system memory*—memory that is not sustained when the computer is turned off. For this reason, you should never simply turn your computer off using the power button. You should always use the **Shut Down** command to allow Windows to gracefully shut itself down.

Begin

1 Click Turn Off Computer

Click the **Start** button and then choose **Turn off computer**. The **Turn Off Computer** window opens.

Click

2 Choose the Turn Off Option

Click the **Turn Off** button. Windows closes all open programs (giving you the opportunity to save unsaved documents) and tells you when it is safe to turn off the power. This is the option you will likely choose at the end of the day or when the computer will be unused for a lengthy period.

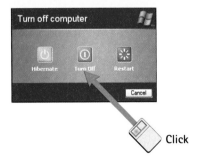

Click

3 Choose the Restart Option

Click the **Restart** button to have Windows shut itself down and then automatically restart the computer. After the computer is restarted, you can log on to Windows again. Restarting your computer is the first thing you should try if you find that Windows, another program, or a hardware component isn't working as you think it should.

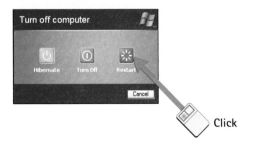

Click

4 Choose Hibernate or Standby

Some computers offer additional logoff options, including **Hibernate** and **Standby**. The **Hibernate** option saves all the information in your computer's memory to hard disk and then shuts the computer down. When you restart the computer, all your programs and windows are restored to the same state in which you left them. The **Standby** option turns off the power to most of the components of your computer, but keeps enough power going to your computer's memory so that it can remember its current state. When you restore a computer from **Standby** (usually by pressing the power button, but different computers can vary in the method), the computer returns to the state in which you left it.

5 Save Any Open Files

If you attempt to shut down Windows while programs are running with unsaved documents, you are given the chance to save those documents before shut-down proceeds. Choose **Yes** if you want to save the changes to the named document; choose **No** if you don't want to save the changes; choose **Cancel** if you want to abort the shut-down process altogether.

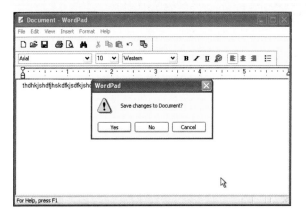

How-To Hints

Other Active Users

Because Windows XP now allows multiple user accounts to be logged on at the same time, you may find that when you try to shut down or restart the computer, other user accounts are still logged on. Windows XP informs you that the accounts are still active and gives you a chance to cancel your request to log off. You should log off the other accounts (or have the people to whom the accounts belong log off); if you don't, any documents open in those accounts will be lost. Windows does not give you the option of saving other people's files the way it lets you save your own when shutting down or restarting.

Task

1 How to Use Windows Explorer 32

2 How to Search for a File or Folder 34

3 How to Create a Folder 36

4 How to View Items in a Folder 38

5 How to Create a File 40

6 How to Open a File 42

7 How to Save a File 44

8 How to Create a Shortcut to a File or Folder 46

9 How to Rename a File or Folder 48

10 How to Delete a File or Folder 50

11 How to Move or Copy a File or Folder 52

12 How to Format a Floppy Disk 54

13 How to Send a File to the Floppy Drive 56

14 How to Open a File with a Certain Program 58

PART 2

Working with Files and Folders

*E*verything on your computer is made up of *files* on your hard disk. Windows itself is really just thousands of different files that interact with one another to present what you've come to know as the Windows desktop. The applications you use from day to day are also collections of many files that interact with one another and with Windows files. Finally, all the documents you create are themselves files that are loaded by the applications you use to create them. For example, when you save a document in Microsoft Word, that document is saved as a file on your disk.

On your disk, files are organized into folders. Like its real-world counterpart, a *folder* is just a place to keep things. In Windows, a folder can contain files and other folders. For example, suppose your C: drive contains a folder named **Backup**, which in turn holds a folder named **July**, which in turn holds a file named **smith.jpg** (a picture file). The name of a file can be up to 256 characters long and usually has a three-character extension (the three characters after the dot) which identifies the type of file it is. The file extension **.jpg** indicates that the file contains a type of picture file called a JPEG. By default, extensions are not shown for file types your system knows about.

In Windows, the full description of the location of a file on a drive is called a *path* and includes the name of the disk drive, the names of each folder, and the name of the file—each name separated by a backslash (\). For the **smith.jpg** document mentioned earlier, the path would be **C:\Backup\July\smith.jpg**.

How to Use Windows Explorer

Part 1, "Using the Windows XP Desktop," explained how to use the **My Computer** window to browse through the folders and files on a disk drive. In truth, you can use the **My Computer** window to get to any file on your computer and do anything you want with it. However, Windows offers another utility, **Windows Explorer**, that you might find more useful for working with the files and folders on your computer. It's really a matter of personal style.

Begin

1 Open Explorer

You run Windows Explorer just like you do any other program. Click the **Start** button and select **All Programs, Accessories, Windows Explorer**.

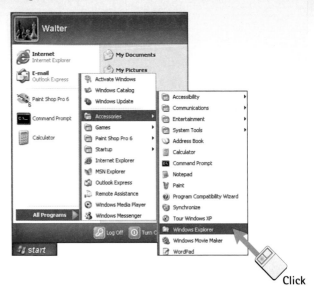

Click

2 Browse Folders

The left pane of the Explorer window shows a hierarchy of all the drives, folders, and desktop items on your computer. A drive or folder that contains other folders has a plus sign to the left of the icon. Click the **plus sign** to expand it and see the folders inside.

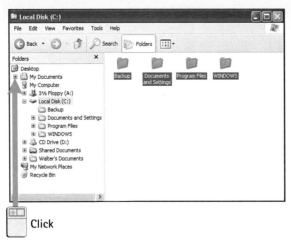

Click

3 Open a Folder

Click any folder in the list in the left pane; all the files and folders in that folder are shown in the right pane.

Click

4 Open a File

The right pane works the same way as the **My Computer** window. You can double-click any file or folder in this pane to open it.

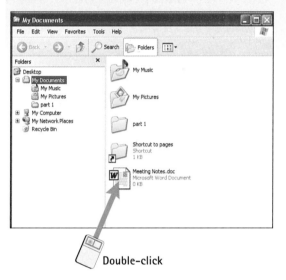

Double-click

5 Move a File to Another Folder

One of the advantages of using Windows Explorer is that you can easily move a file to any other folder on your computer. Drag a file from the right pane and drop it on any folder icon in the left pane to move the file there.

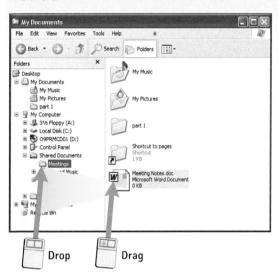

Drop   Drag

6 Copy a File to Another Drive

Copying a file to another drive is as easy as moving it. Just drag a file from the right pane to another disk drive (or a folder on another drive) to copy it there. Notice that the icon you are dragging takes on a small plus sign to let you know that the file will be copied, but not moved.

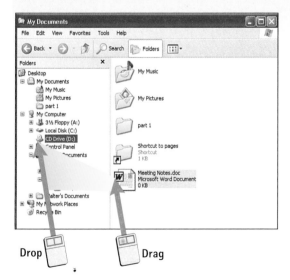

Drop   Drag

How-To Hints

Auto-Expanding

When you move a file to another folder in Windows Explorer, the folder doesn't have to be visible already. While dragging the file, hold the mouse pointer over a folder's plus sign for two seconds to automatically expand that folder.

Auto-Scrolling

While dragging a file, hold the mouse pointer at the top or bottom of the left pane for two seconds to automatically scroll up or down.

Copying or Moving to Other Locations

For more on how to move or copy files between folders and drives, see Task 11, "How to Move or Copy a File or Folder," later in this part.

End

How to Search for a File or Folder

Using Windows Explorer is great if you know where the file or folder you want is located. Sometimes, however, it's hard to remember just where you put something. Fortunately, Windows has a great search function built right in that helps you find files and folders. You can search for folders by all or part of their names, by text they might contain, or by their location. You can even search using all three of these criteria at once.

Begin

1 Open the Search Window

Click the **Start** button and select **Search**. You'll also find a **Search** button on the toolbar of most windows that performs the same function. A search window opens.

Click

2 Select the Type of Document

The left pane holds the interface you will use for searching. Results of any search you perform are displayed in the right pane. Choose the type of document you want to search for from the list in the left pane. The pane changes to show additional search questions based on the type of file you choose.

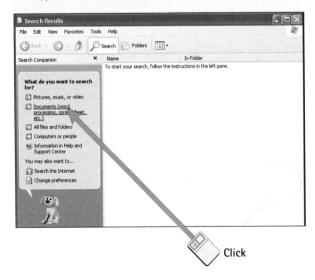

Click

3 Type the Document Name

Type all or part of the name of the file or folder you want to search for in the text box. When you search, Windows shows all of the file and folder names that contain the text you enter.

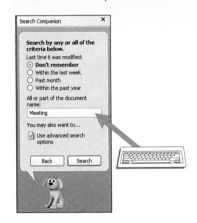

4 Select a Time Frame

If you know approximately when the document was last modified, select one of the time options. If you don't remember, just leave the **Don't remember** option selected.

Click

5 Click Search

After you have entered your search criteria, click **Search** to have Windows begin the search.

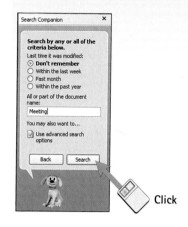

Click

6 View the Results

The results of your search are displayed in the right pane. You can double-click a file to open it right from the search window.

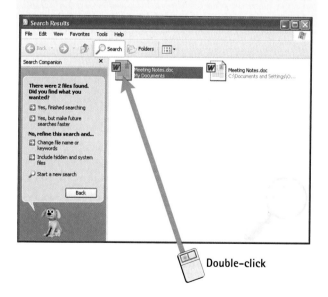

Double-click

How-To Hints

Advanced Search Options

On the page where you enter the name of the document to search for, click **Use advanced search options** to open a window that lets you specify additional search criteria, such as the dates files were created or modified, the drives to search, the size of files, and the type of files to search for.

Quickly Open a File's Folder

You can quickly open the parent folder of a file you've found by right-clicking the file in the results pane and choosing **Open Containing Folder** from the shortcut menu.

End

How to Create a Folder

Folders help you organize your files. You create a folder using the **My Computer** window or **Windows Explorer**. You can create a folder in any existing disk drive or folder or on the Windows desktop itself.

Begin

1 Find the Place to Make the Folder

The first step in creating a folder is to decide where you want to create it. Use the **My Computer** window or **Windows Explorer** to find the place you want to be.

2 Create the New Folder

In the **Tasks** list, select **Make a new folder**. Alternatively, pull down the **File** menu and select **New, Folder**.

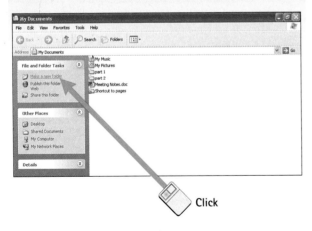

Click

3 Rename the Folder

The new folder appears in the current location with the default name **New Folder**. The name is already high-lighted; you can rename it by typing the name you want and pressing **Enter** or clicking somewhere outside the name field (here I've named the folder **Personal Folder**). You can also rename the folder later by select-ing it and choosing **File, Rename** and then typing the new folder name. Note that renaming the folder does not affect any files contained in that folder.

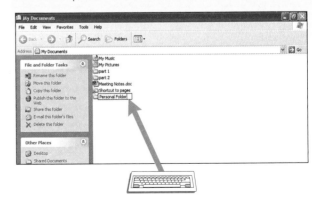

4 Create a Folder on the Desktop

To create a new folder directly on your desktop, right-click any empty area of the desktop. Point to **New** on the shortcut menu and then choose **Folder**.

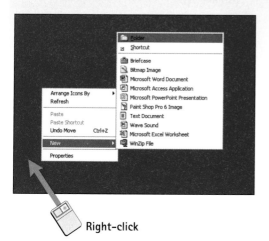

Right-click

5 Name the New Folder

As you did in Step 3, type a new name for the folder (its default name is **New Folder**) and press **Enter**.

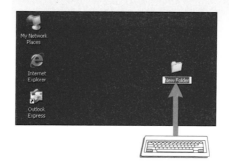

How-To Hints

Saving a Document

Some programs let you create a new folder from the same dialog box you use to save a document. There is usually a button named **Create New Folder**. Just click the button, name the new folder, and open it to save your document there.

Creating a Folder in the Start Menu

The **Start** menu is really a folder on your hard disk; you can create new folders in it to help organize your files. Right-click the **Start** button, choose **Open** from the shortcut menu, and create the folder in the window that opens using the methods described in this task. The new folder appears on your **Start** menu. For more on customizing your **Start** menu, see Part 10, "Changing Windows XP Settings."

End

How to View Items in a Folder

Normally, both the **My Computer** window and **Windows Explorer** show you the contents of a folder as large icons that represent other folders and files. This is a friendly way to view folders, but not always the most useful, especially if a folder contains large numbers of files or many files with similar names. You can also view the contents of a folder as small icons, as a list, as a list with file details, or even as thumbnails.

Begin

1 Open a Folder

First, you need to find a folder to view. You can do this in either the **My Computer** window or in **Windows Explorer**. In this **Windows Explorer** example, notice that the regular large icon view looks pretty cluttered.

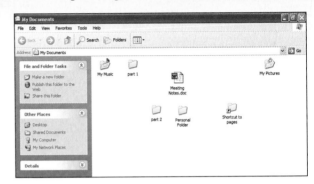

2 Change to List View

Choose **View, List** to view the folder contents as a list. The contents are listed in alphabetical order. You can also use the **View** button on the toolbar to change views.

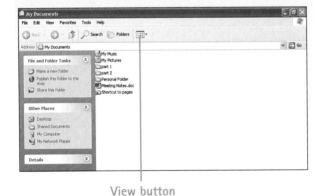

View button

3 Change to Details View

The **Detail** view is perhaps the most useful way to view the contents of a folder. Choose **View, Details**. Contents are presented in a list with columns that include file details, such as the size and type of the file and when the file was last modified.

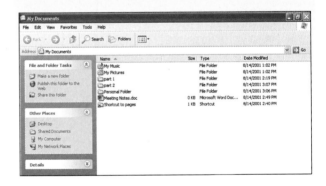

4 Change to Thumbnail View

Thumbnail view presents the contents of a folder as small *thumbnails*, or previews, of the actual documents. Only certain file types, such as JPEG images, support this type of viewing. Choose **View, Thumbnail** to display the folder contents as thumbnails. Other types of documents are displayed as larger versions of their normal icons.

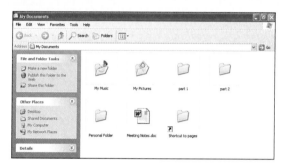

5 Arrange Icons

In addition to choosing how to view the contents of a folder, you can also choose how those contents are arranged. Choose **View, Arrange Icons By** and then choose **Name, Type, Size,** or **Modified** (the date the files were last modified) to order the contents of the folder. You can also have the folder arrange the icons automatically.

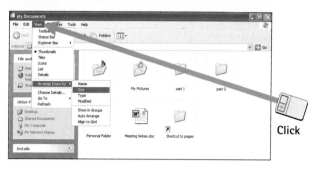

Click

How-To Hints

Arranging in Details View

You can easily arrange the contents of a folder in the **Details** view by clicking the column heading by which you want to order the contents. For example, click the **Type** column heading to group the files in the current folder by type. You can choose the columns that are shown in **Details** view by choosing **View, Choose Columns** from the menu bar. A window opens with lots of different choices for columns to display. Just select the ones you want.

Other Arrangements

Select **View, Arrange Icons By, Show in Groups** to divide a folder's window into different sections that show different types of items, such as folders, drives, and files. Within each group, icons are arranged according to your other settings on the **View** menu. The **Auto Arrange** option on the same menu automatically arranges the icons in a window by alphabetic and numerical order and groups them together at the beginning of a window. The **Align to Grid** option gives you the freedom to arrange your icons as you like, while making sure that they all uniformly align to an invisible grid in the window.

Cleaning Up Your Windows

Many users find that the common tasks shown on the left side of most windows take up too much space and really aren't that useful anyway. You can turn the task list off for all folders by going to **Start, Control Panel, Folder Options.** On the **General** tab of the **Folder Options** dialog box, choose the **Use Windows classic folders** option. To turn the task list back on, come back to the **Folder Options** dialog box and choose the **Show common tasks in folder** option. Unfortunately, you cannot enable the list for some folders and disable it for others.

End

How to Create a File

Most of the time, you will create new documents from within a particular program. For example, you usually use Microsoft Word to create a new Word document. However, Windows does offer the ability to quickly create certain types of documents without opening the associated program at all. This can be quite useful when you are creating a large number of new documents that will be edited later.

Begin

1 Locate the Parent Folder

First, you must find the folder in which you want to create the new file. You can create a file directly in any folder on your computer. Here I used **Windows Explorer** to navigate to the new **Personal Folder** folder I created in Task 3, "How to Create a Folder."

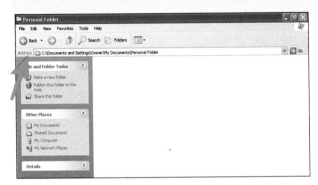

2 Create the File

Choose **File, New,** and then select the type of file you want to create. Note that the list of file types presented in the submenu covers basic Windows objects (such as folders, shortcuts, and text files) and objects that depend on additional software you have installed (such as Microsoft Word documents).

Click

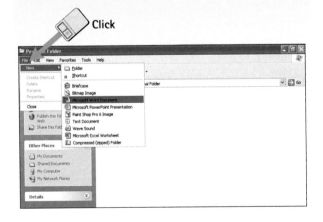

3 Locate the New Document

The new document appears in the selected folder with a generic name, such as **New Microsoft Word Document.** If you don't see the new file immediately, use the window's scrollbars to find it.

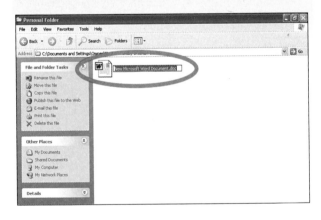

4 Rename the File

The new file appears with the name already high-lighted. Just start typing to enter a new name for the file. When you're done, press **Enter** or click somewhere outside the text box.

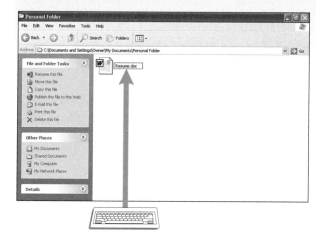

5 Open the File to Edit

After you have created and renamed your new file, double-click it to launch the appropriate program and open the new file with it. Now that the file is open in the appropriate application, you can work with it just as you would any other file created in that application.

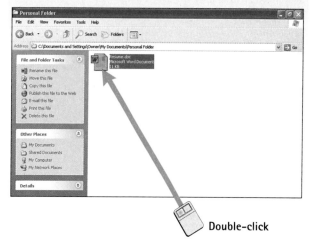

Double-click

How-To Hints

Renaming Files

Files can have names of up to 256 characters, including spaces. There are several special characters you cannot use in your file's name, including \ / : * ? " < >

Preserving the File Type

When you create a new file, Windows automatically gives it the right three-letter file *extension* (the three letters after the dot) to indicate the file type. If your Windows settings allow you to see the file extension (by default, they don't), be sure that you don't change the extension when you rename the file. If you do, the file won't open with the right program. Windows warns you if you try to change the file extension.

Populating a Folder Quickly

In **Windows Explorer** or **My Computer**, you can create as many new documents as you need and then go back and rename them later. To create files even more quickly, create one file, copy it by selecting it and pressing **Ctrl+C**, and then paste as many new files in the same folder as you need by pressing **Ctrl+V**. Each new file has the text **Copy of** and a number prepended to the filename to distinguish it from its siblings (for example, if the original file is named **resume.doc**, the first copy is named **Copy of resume.doc**; the second copy is named **Copy [2] of resume.doc**, and so on).

End

How to Open a File

There are several different ways to open a file in Windows. One way is to locate the file in the **My Computer** window or **Windows Explorer** and open it from there. You can also open a file from within the program that created it. Windows even keeps track of the files you have opened recently so that you can reopen these in one simple step using the **Start** menu.

Begin

1 Double-Click the File

Find the file you want to open by using the **My Computer** window or **Windows Explorer**. Double-click the file to launch the file's program and open the file with it. Here, the file **Resume.doc** will open in Microsoft Word.

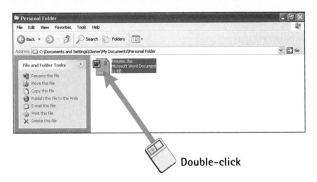

Double-click

2 Open a Recently-Used File

Windows keeps track of the most-recent 15 documents you have opened. To open any of these documents, click the **Start** button and point to the **My Recent Documents** option to see a list of the documents most recently opened on your computer. Select the document you want to open. If the **My Recent Documents** option does not show up on your **Start** menu, see Part 10, "Changing Windows XP Settings," for details on how to add it.

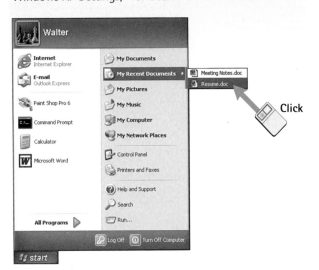

Click

3 Run a Program

Yet another way to open a file is from within the program that created it. The first step is to run the program. Click the **Start** button, point to **More Programs**, and find the program you want to run in the submenus that appear.

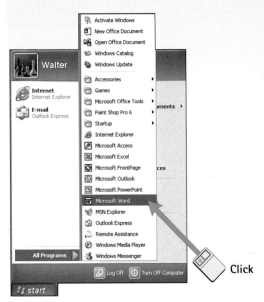

Click

4 Choose Open from the File Menu

After the selected program opens, choose **File, Open** from the menu bar. The **Open** dialog box appears.

Click

5 Find the File to Open

For most programs, the **Open** dialog box works a lot like the **My Computer** window. Navigate through the folders on your computer system to find the file you want to open, select it, and click **Open**.

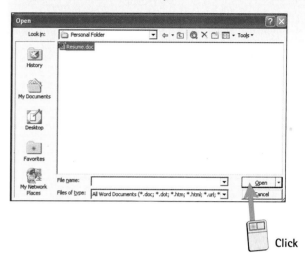

Click

How-To Hints

Removing Recently Used Files

You can clear the list of recently used files from the **Recent Documents** folder by right-clicking the taskbar and choosing **Properties** from the shortcut menu. In the Properties dialog box that opens, click the **Start Menu** tab and then click **Customize**. In the dialog box that opens, click the **Advanced** tab and then click **Clear List**.

Searching for Files

When you search for files using the **Search** command on the **Start** menu, you can open any of the files you find just by double-clicking them. For more information about searching for files, see Task 2, "How to Search for a File or Folder," earlier in this part.

End

How to Save a File

Saving your work is one of the most important things you'll do on your computer. After all, if you don't save your work, what's the point of doing it in the first place? Saving a file is always done while you are working on it within a program. There are two save commands in most programs. **Save As** lets you choose a location and name for your file. The **Save** command simply updates the file using its current location and name. The first time you save a new file, the program actually uses the **Save As** function no matter which command you choose.

1 Open the Save As Dialog Box

If you want to save a file using a particular name or to a particular location, click the **File** menu and then choose **Save As**. Note that you can use this command to save a copy of the file you are working on with a new name or to save versions of a file. The **Save As** dialog box opens.

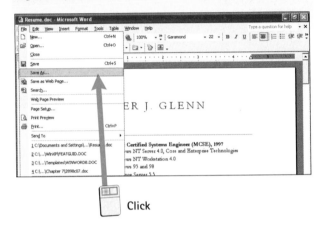

Click

2 Choose a Location

The **Save As** dialog box works just like the **My Computer** window. Choose the disk drive to which you want to save the file using the **Save in** drop-down list. After you choose the drive, navigate to the desired folder just as you do in the **My Computer** window.

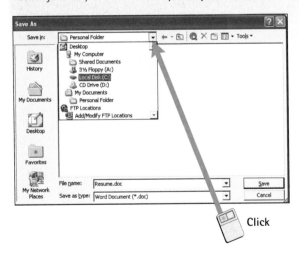

Click

3 Choose a Favorite Place

Instead of using the drop-down list, you can choose a favorite place by clicking the icon for a folder in the bar on the left of the dialog box. For example, clicking the **My Documents** button opens the **My Documents** folder in the **Save As** dialog box. You can then save your file in that folder or browse to another folder inside the folder.

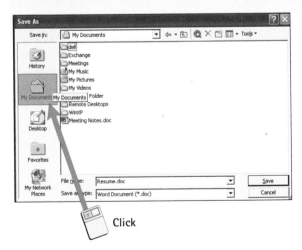

Click

4 Create a New Folder

If you want to save the file you're working on in a new folder, navigate to the folder in which you want to store the new file, then click the **Create New Folder** button in the **Save As** dialog box toolbar. Type a name for the new folder and press **Enter**. Open the new folder by double-clicking it.

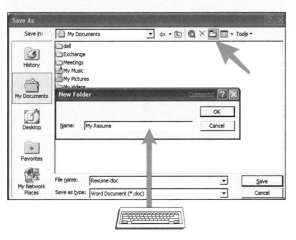

5 Name the File

Type the name for the document in the **File name** box. Note that, in most applications, you do not have to include the file extension when you type the filename. The application supplies the extension for you. If you do include an extension, the application accepts it.

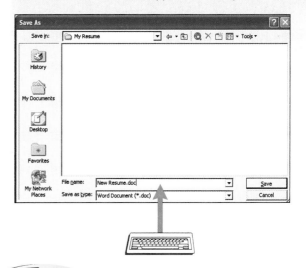

6 Save the File

Click **Save** to save the new file in the selected folder with the name you specified.

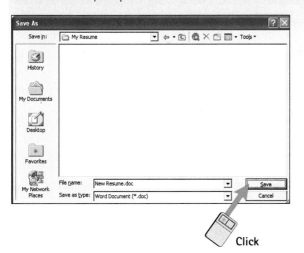

Click

7 Save the File as You Work

Periodically as you work, save any changes to your document using the **Save** button on the program's main toolbar (or the **Save** command on the **File** menu). If you click **Save** and it is the first time you are saving a new document, the **Save As** dialog box opens and prompts you for a filename. Otherwise, the file is saved in the current location with the current filename, overwriting the last version of the file you had saved.

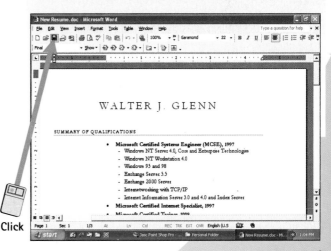

Click

End

How to Create a Shortcut to a File or Folder

A *shortcut* is an icon that points to a file or folder somewhere on your computer. The shortcut is merely a reference to the actual object and is used to access the object without having to go to the object's location. For example, on your desktop you could place a shortcut to a frequently used document. You could then double-click the shortcut to open the file without having to go to the folder where the actual file is stored.

Begin

1 Open Windows Explorer

The first step in creating a new shortcut is to use the **My Computer** window or **Windows Explorer** to find the file or folder to which you want to make a shortcut. To open Windows Explorer, click **Start** and select **All Programs, Accessories, Windows Explorer**.

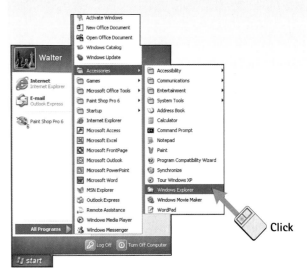

Click

2 Select a File or Folder

In Windows Explorer, navigate to the object to which you want to make a shortcut. In this example, I want to create a shortcut to my new **Personal Folder** folder.

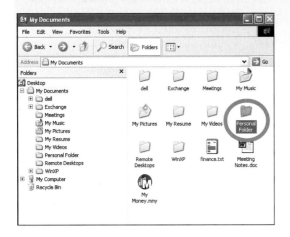

3 Drag the File to Your Desktop

Click and hold the *right* mouse button and drag the object to a blank space on the desktop. Release the right mouse button to drop the icon on the desktop.

Drop

Right-drag

4 Choose Create Shortcut Here

When you release the right mouse button, a shortcut menu appears. Choose **Create Shortcuts Here**.

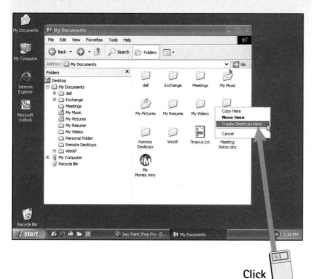

Click

5 Rename the Shortcut

Notice that the shortcut icon has a small arrow on it, indicating that it is a shortcut. You can rename the shortcut to anything you like by right-clicking the shortcut icon and choosing **Rename** from the shortcut menu.

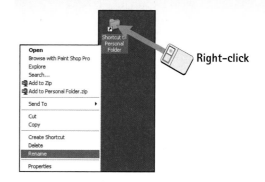

Right-click

6 Double-Click the Shortcut

To open the original object to which you made the shortcut, double-click the shortcut icon. In this example, double-clicking the **Shortcut to Personal Folder** shortcut opens the **Personal Folder** folder in Windows Explorer.

Double-click

How-To Hints

Finding Out a Shortcut's Target

If you find a shortcut and can't remember what object it's pointing to, just right-click the shortcut and choose **Properties** from the shortcut menu. In the **Properties** dialog box, the **Target** text box tells you the path to the original object.

End

How to Rename a File or Folder

In Windows XP, you can name files or folders just about anything you want. Names are limited to 256 characters, including spaces, but there are a few special characters you are not allowed to use, including the following: \ / : * ? " < >. You can rename files and folders at any time. Note that you should be very careful to rename only those files and folders that you created in the first place. Windows and Windows programs are composed of many folders and files that have special names. Changing the names of these files can often cause a program, or even Windows itself, to malfunction.

1 Select the File

To rename a file in the **My Computer** window or **Windows Explorer**, first select the file with a single click.

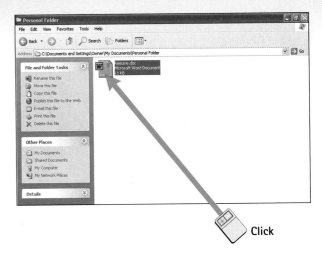

Click

2 Choose Rename from the File Menu

From the menu bar, choose **File, Rename**. A box appears around the name of the file or folder you selected in Step 1 and the filename itself is highlighted.

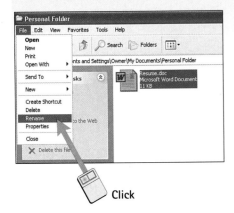

Click

3 Type a New Name

Type a new name for the selected file. Note that as you type, the highlighted filename is replaced by the text you type. If you want to edit (and not replace) the current filename, use the arrow keys or mouse pointer to position the insertion point, then add and delete characters from the filename as desired. When you're done with the filename, press **Enter**.

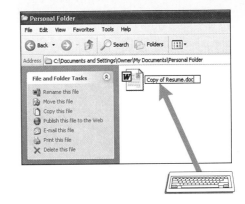

4 Click the Name Twice Slowly

A quicker way to rename a file (and one that also works on files on the desktop) is to first select the file with a single click and then click the name of the file a second later—not so fast as to suggest a double-click. You can also select the file and press the **F2** key. When the file-name is highlighted, you can then type a new name.

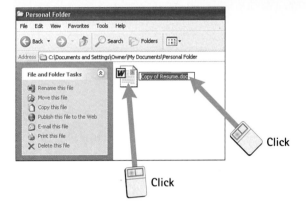

Click

Click

5 Right-Click the File

Yet another way to rename a file is to right-click the file and choose **Rename** from the shortcut menu. You can then type a new name as explained in Step 3.

Right-click

How-To Hints

Keeping Names Simple

Although you can create very long filenames in Windows, it is usually better to keep them short and simple. The reason for this is that when you view the contents of a folder, file-names are often cut off after the first 15–20 characters so that you can view more files in the folder. Keep the filenames short so that you can view the contents of a folder without having to switch to details view and adjust the default column size to see the entire filename. For more on adjusting window views, see Task 4, "How to View Items in a Folder."

End

How to Delete a File or Folder

When you delete a file or folder in Windows, the object is not immediately removed from your computer. It is first placed into the **Recycle Bin**, where it is kept temporarily before being permanently deleted. The **Recycle Bin** gives you the chance to recover files you might have accidentally deleted. For more information about the **Recycle Bin**, see Part 1, Task 9, "How to Use the Recycle Bin." There are a few ways to delete objects in Windows, including dragging them to the Recycle Bin or deleting them directly using the keyboard or Windows Explorer.

Begin

1 Select a Group of Files

Place the mouse pointer in a blank spot near a group of objects you want to delete. Click and hold the left mouse button and drag the pointer toward the objects. A dotted rectangle (named the *lasso*) appears behind the pointer. Drag the lasso over all the objects to select them all at once.

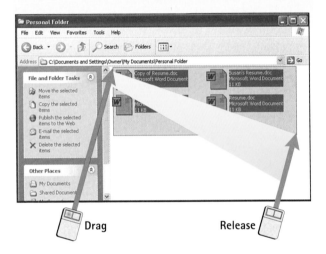

Drag   Release

2 Drag to the Recycle Bin

After you have selected a group of files, drag them to the **Recycle Bin** by clicking any single selected file and holding the mouse button while you drag the pointer over the **Recycle Bin**. Release the mouse button when the **Recycle Bin** icon becomes highlighted to drop the selected files into the **Recycle Bin**.

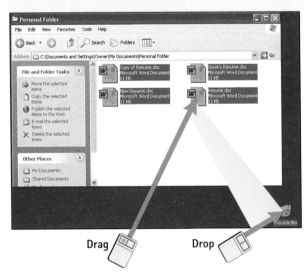

Drag   Drop

3 Select a File

It is also easy to delete files without using the **Recycle Bin**, which is helpful when you can't see your desktop. First, select the file you want to delete by clicking it once.

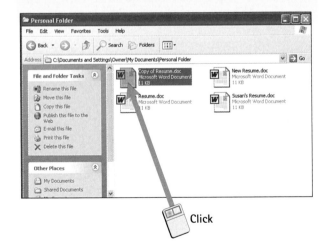

Click

4 Use the Delete Key

Press the **Delete** key on your keyboard to send the selected file (or files) to the **Recycle Bin**.

[Del]

5 Choose Delete from the File Menu

After a file is selected, you can also open the **File** menu and choose **Delete** to send the file to the **Recycle Bin**.

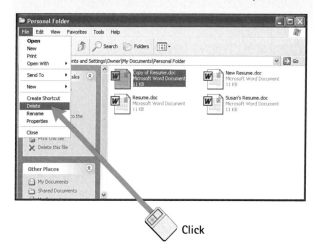

Click

How-To Hints

Disabling the Recycle Bin

If you would rather not use the **Recycle Bin**, right-click the **Recycle Bin** icon on the desktop and choose **Properties** from the shortcut menu. Select the **Do not move files to the Recycle Bin** option. Be careful, though. When this option is selected, files that you delete are permanently removed from your system, giving you no chance to recover them.

Changing the Recycle Bin Settings

There are several ways you can customize the operation of your **Recycle Bin**. For more information on this, see Part 1, "Using the Windows XP Desktop."

End

TASK 11

How to Move or Copy a File or Folder

Most people move objects around from folder to folder by simply dragging them using the left mouse button. This usually works fine; but it might not provide the exact results you want. Depending on where you drag an object, you can move the object or you can copy it to the new location. For better results, try using the right mouse button instead of the left when you drag files to a new location.

Begin

1 Find the Parent Folder

Use the **My Computer** window or **Windows Explorer** to find the folder that contains the object you want to move or copy.

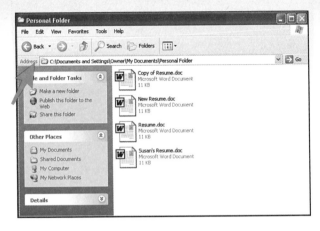

2 Locate an Object

Locate an object you want to move. The object can be a file or a folder. Note that if you move a folder, you move the contents (all the files and folders contained in that folder) as well. If you copy a folder, you copy the contents of the folder as well.

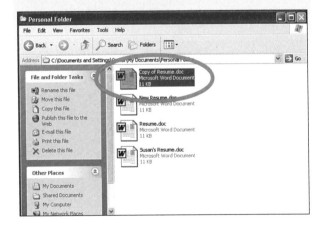

3 Drag the File to a New Location

Place the mouse pointer over the object, click and hold the right mouse button, and drag the object to the target location. In this example, I am dragging the document file to the desktop. Release the right mouse button to drop the object in its new location.

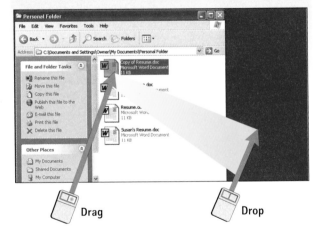

Drag

Drop

52 PART 2: WORKING WITH FILES AND FOLDERS

4 Choose Copy Here

When you release the right mouse button, a shortcut menu appears. Choose **Copy Here** to place an exact copy of the selected item in the new location and keep the original object in the old location.

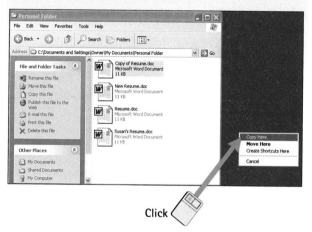

Click

5 Choose Move Here

Choose **Move Here** from the shortcut menu to move the object to the new location and remove it from the old location.

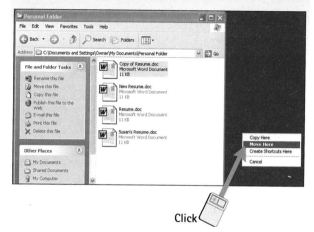

Click

How-To Hints

Left-Dragging

When you use the left mouse button to drag a file, the icon you drag changes to reflect what action will be performed. If the icon has a small plus sign on it, the file will be copied when you release the mouse button. If the icon has a small arrow, a shortcut will be created. If the icon has nothing extra on it, the object will be moved.

Right-Dragging

A much better way to move files is to drag them using the right mouse button instead of the left button. When you release a file or folder you have dragged with the right button, a menu pops up asking whether you want to copy, move, or create a shortcut.

Dragging with Keys

When you drag using the left mouse button, you can hold down the **Shift** and **Ctrl** keys to get different effects. For example, holding down the **Shift** key while dragging a file that would normally be copied causes the file to be moved instead. Holding the **Ctrl** key down while dragging a file that would normally be moved causes it to be copied instead.

End

How to Format a Floppy Disk

When you buy floppy disks from a store, they are usually formatted. Make sure that you buy disks formatted for your system. The package should read "**IBM Formatted**" if the floppy disks are to work with Windows. If you have an unformatted disk, it is easy enough to format in Windows. Formatting is also a quick way to erase all the files that you don't need anymore from a disk. Before you start the steps in this task, insert the floppy disk to be formatted in your floppy drive.

Begin

1 Open My Computer

Double-click the **My Computer** icon on your desktop to open the **My Computer** folder.

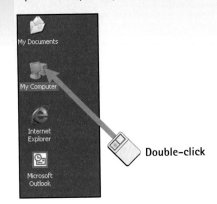

Double-click

2 Right-Click the Floppy Drive

Right-click the drive labeled **3½ Floppy (A:)** and select the **Format** command from the shortcut menu. The **Format** dialog box opens.

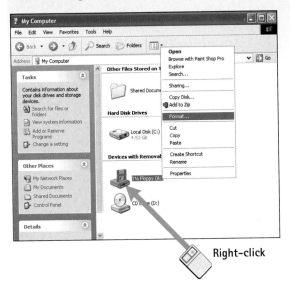

Right-click

3 Choose a Capacity

Almost all computers today use 1.44MB floppy drives, which is the default choice in this dialog box. If you are formatting an older floppy (or one for an older computer), choose the 720K size from the **Capacity** drop-down list.

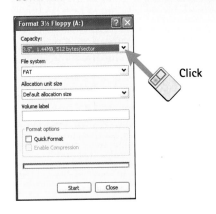

Click

4 Enter a Volume Label

Type a label into the **Volume Label** box. The *volume label* is the name of the floppy disk. You can leave this blank if you do not want a label (most people do leave this field blank).

5 Perform a Quick Format

If you are formatting a disk that has been previously formatted by Windows (as you would do when erasing a disk), choose the **Quick Format** option to significantly shorten the time needed to format the disk.

Click

6 Format the Disk

Click **Start** to begin formatting the disk. A progress indicator at the bottom of the dialog box shows the formatting progress. Another dialog box opens to inform you when the format is done.

Click

How-To Hints

Be Careful When Selecting a Drive

The **Format** dialog box lets you select any drive on your system to format, including floppy drives, hard drives, and some rewriteable and recordable CD-ROM drives. Be sure that the correct drive is selected before formatting. Formatting a hard drive erases all its contents!

End

How to Send a File to the Floppy Drive

Floppy disks are often used to back up files or transfer files to another computer. In Windows, the floppy drive is always labeled **A:** in the **My Computer** window and **Windows Explorer**. As with most other tasks, Windows offers a couple different ways to send files to a floppy disk. Before you begin this task, make sure that a properly formatted floppy disk is in the floppy disk drive.

Begin

1 Open My Documents

Double-click the **My Documents** icon on your desktop to open the **My Documents** folder. If you don't see the **My Documents** icon on your desktop, you can find it on the **Start** menu or add it to your desktop as explained in Part 1, "Using the Windows XP Desktop."

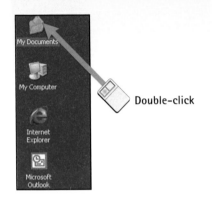

Double-click

2 Open My Computer

Double-click the **My Computer** icon on your desktop to open the **My Computer** window.

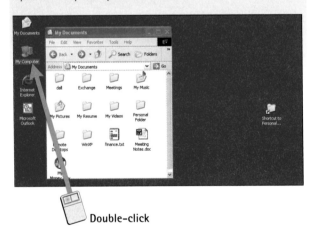

Double-click

3 Tile Your Windows

Right-click the taskbar and choose **Tile Windows Vertically** so that you can see both the **My Computer** and the **My Documents** windows at the same time.

Right-click

4 Drag the File to the Floppy Drive

Place the mouse pointer over the file in the **My Documents** window that you want to copy. Click and hold the left mouse button while dragging the file to the floppy drive icon in the **My Computer** window.

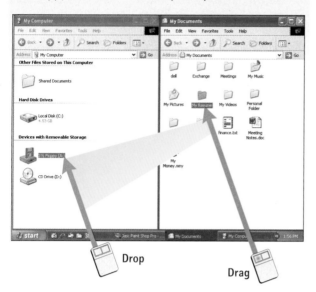

Drop

Drag

5 Copy the File

Release the left mouse button to drop the file on the floppy drive icon. A dialog box appears to track the progress of the copy operation.

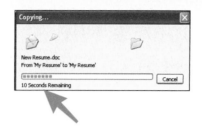

6 Select a File

Another way to send a file to the floppy drive is to choose a command rather than dragging and dropping the file. Start by selecting the file (click it once).

Click

7 Choose Send to Floppy Drive

Right-click the selected file, point to the **Send To** command on the shortcut menu, then choose the floppy drive option. Windows copies the file to the floppy disk in the drive.

Right-click

End

How to Open a File with a Certain Program

Files usually have a certain program *associated* with them, normally the program that created them. A text file, for example, is associated with Notepad. Windows knows what program to use to open a file because of the three-character extension following the file's name. For example, a text file might be named **Groceries.txt**. Windows knows that files with the **.txt** extension should be opened in Notepad. Sometimes, however, you might want to open a file with a different program or even change the program associated with the file altogether.

Begin

1 Right-Click the File

Right-click the file you want to open with a special program and choose **Open With** from the shortcut menu. The **Open With** dialog box opens.

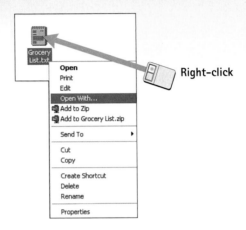

Right-click

2 Choose the Program

Select the program you want to use to open the file.

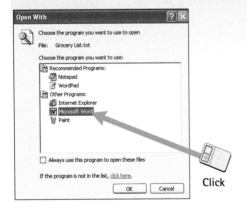

Click

3 Find Another Program

If the program you want to use does not appear in the list, click the **Click Here** link to find the program file on your computer yourself. Most of the programs installed on your computer are located in the **Program Files** folder on your C: drive. If you don't find the program there, consult the documentation for the program to get more information.

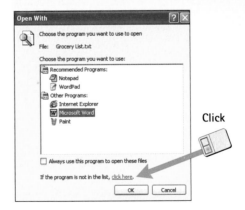

Click

4 Make It the Default Choice

If you want to change an extension's association (that is, to make all files of that type open with the new program you've selected from now on), enable the **Always use this program to open these files** option.

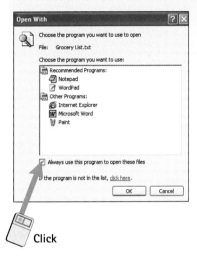

Click

5 Open the File

Click **OK** to open the file in the selected program.

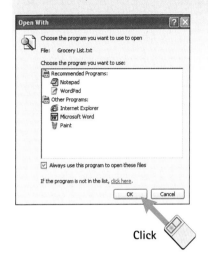

Click

How-To Hints

Viewing File Associations

You can view a complete list of file associations in Windows. Click **Start** and choose **Control Panel**. In the **Control Panel** window, double-click **Folder Options**. In the dialog box that appears, click the **File Types** tab. All associations are listed here. You can create new associations and change existing ones.

End

Task

1   How to Print a Document from a Program   62

2   How to Print a Document from Windows   64

3   How to Manage Documents Waiting to Print   66

4   How to Change Printer Settings   68

5   How to Share a Printer with Others   70

6   How to Install a Local Printer   72

7   How to Set Up Your Computer to Use a Network Printer   76

3

Printing

*P*rinting is one the basic functions you will perform with your computer. Windows XP makes printing as easy as it has ever been, coordinating all the mechanics in the background so that you can focus on your work.

In the tasks in this part, you learn how to print a document from within the program that created it and also from the Windows XP desktop. You also learn how to manage various printer settings, such as how to set your default printer, paper source, and paper size. You learn how to install a printer attached to your own computer and how to set up your computer to use a *shared printer*—one that's available on the network. Finally, you learn how to share your own printer with others on the network. ●

How to Print a Document from a Program

Most of the time, you print documents directly from the program you used to create them, whether that program is a word processor such as Microsoft Word, or a drawing program such as Paint. Because most programs designed for Windows follow similar guidelines, you will find that the process of printing from any Windows program is very similar to the following steps. Many Windows programs also offer a **Print** button on the main toolbar. This button usually prints one copy of the document using all the default printer settings. If you print this way, you bypass the **Print** dialog box described in this task altogether.

Begin

1 Open the File

Open the file you want to print using the **File, Open** command of the program used to create the file. In the program's **Open** dialog box, navigate to the folder where the file is stored, select the file, and click **Open**. Here I am opening a document in Microsoft Word.

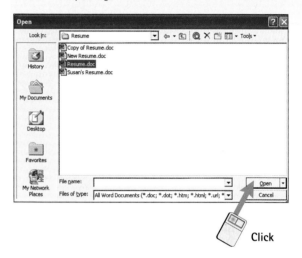

Click

2 Choose the Print Command

When you are ready to print the open document, choose **File, Print** from the program's menu bar. The **Print** dialog box opens, which allows you to specify which pages of the document as well as how many copies you want to print.

Click

3 Choose the Printer to Use

If you have access to more than one printer, use the **Printer** drop-down menu to select the printer you want to use.

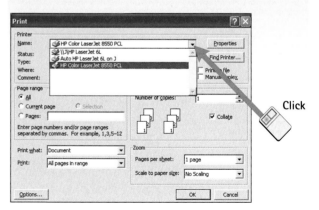

Click

4 Choose Printing Options

Some programs let you set special printing options that are specific to the program you are using. This is usually done by clicking an **Options** button in the **Print** dialog box. For example, some programs allow you to print a document in *draft mode*, which can save a lot of time and printer ink because it prints characters in a lighter text.

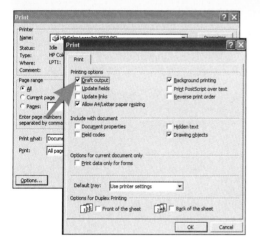

5 Choose Pages and Number of Copies

Almost every Windows program lets you specify the range of pages you want to print. You can use the program's **File, Print Preview** command to see a preview of what the document will look like when printed so that you can determine which pages of a lengthy document you want to print. In the **Number of copies** box, type the number of copies of the document you want to print.

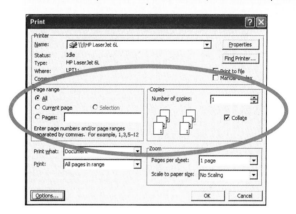

6 Print the Document

After you have selected your printer, specified the pages and number of copies you want to print, set any extra options, and click **OK** to print. Most programs allow you to continue working while your document is being printed.

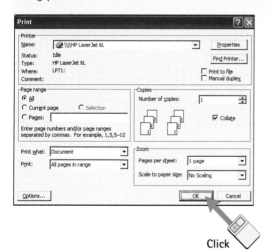

Click

End

How to Print a Document from Windows

Most of the time, you print documents from within programs. However, Windows offers a few ways to print documents straight from the desktop without first opening the document's program. This is a great way to dash off quick copies of documents, or even to print multiple documents at once.

Begin

1 Find the Document You Print

The first step to printing a document in Windows is to find the document. You can use the **My Computer** folder, the **My Documents** folder, or **Windows Explorer**—whichever you prefer. Here, a document named **Resume** is selected in a folder named **Personal Folder**. You learn more about navigating in Windows in Part 2, "Working with Files and Folders."

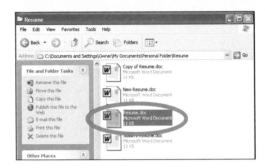

2 Right-Click and Choose Print

To quickly print the document using your default printer and the default settings of the document's program, right-click the document (or select multiple documents and right-click any one of them) and choose **Print** from the shortcut menu. Windows prints one copy of each document. Windows opens the associated program just long enough to print the document and then closes the program again. Note that this trick does not work with all programs—just with programs that have included this feature.

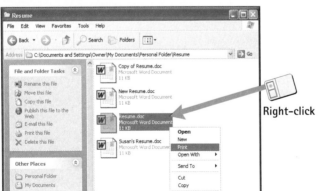

Right-click

3 Open Your Printers Folder

Another way to print a document in Windows is to drag the document onto a printer icon. To perform this action, both the folder holding the document you want to print and your **Printers** folder must be open. To open the Printers folder, click **Start** and select **Printers and Faxes**.

Click

4 Select Documents to Print

Using **My Computer** or **Windows Explorer**, find the folder with the document or documents you want to print and select those document icons.

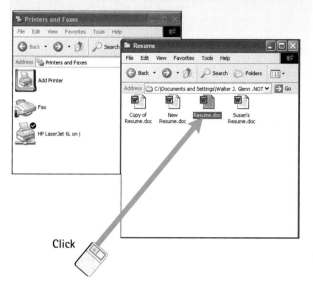

Click

5 Drag a Document to a Printer Icon

Drag any document (or group of documents) from the folder and release it on the icon for the printer you want to use. Windows prints the documents using the default settings for the program that created the documents. This method is the same as using the **Print** toolbar button mentioned in Task 1, but lets you choose the printer you want to use.

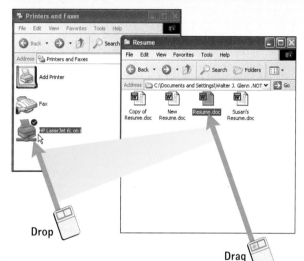

Drop

Drag

How-To Hints

Don't See Printers and Faxes on the Start Menu?

If you don't see the **Printers and Faxes** shortcut on the **Start** menu, open the **Control Panel** instead. You'll find the **Printers and Faxes** folder inside. You can add the **Printer and Fax** shortcut to your **Start** menu by right-clicking the taskbar and choosing **Properties**.

Dragging Multiple Files

You can drag multiple documents to a printer icon in one step: Hold down the **Ctrl** key while you left-click documents in the **My Computer** window. Each document you click while holding down the **Ctrl** key is added to your selection.

Creating a Printer Shortcut on Your Desktop

If you frequently drag files to a printer icon and don't want to keep your **Printers** folder open all the time, you can create a shortcut to the printer on your desktop: Drag the desired printer icon to your desktop and release it. When Windows offers to create a shortcut for you, click **OK**.

Adding a Printer to the Send To Menu

An even better solution than adding a shortcut icon to your desktop is to add the shortcut to the **Send To** menu you can access whenever you right-click a file. This way, you can send a document to any printer just by using the document's context menu. For information on how to add items to the **Send To** menu, see Part 10, "Changing Windows XP Settings."

End

How to Manage Documents Waiting to Print

Whenever you print a document, that document enters a print *queue*, a line of documents waiting for their turn at the printer. A printer icon appears in your system tray next to the clock to let you know that the queue is active. You can open the print queue and do some document management. Some of the things you can do in the print queue depend on whether you are using a printer hooked up directly to your computer or a network printer. Network printers are usually shared by many users; you can manage only the documents that belong to *you*. You cannot affect other user's documents or the print queue itself, unless you are the administrator of the printer.

Begin

1 Open the Print Queue

To open the print queue, double-click the printer icon in the system tray when it appears. Right-clicking the printer icon opens a shortcut menu that lets you open the print queue for any printer on your system, not just the actively printing one.

Double-click

2 View Documents Waiting to Print

The print queue shows a list of documents waiting to print in the order in which they are to be printed. For each document, details such as owner, number of pages, document size, and time of submission are also shown.

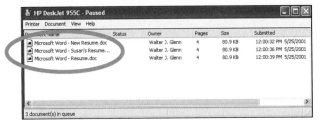

3 Cancel the Printing of a Document

To remove a document from the print queue—that is, to stop it from being printed—right-click the document and choose **Cancel** from the shortcut menu. Be sure that you choose the correct document because Windows does not ask whether you are sure that you want to remove the document.

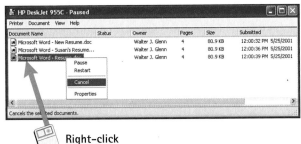

Right-click

4 Pause the Printing of a Document

If you *pause* a document, it remains in the print queue but does not print until you choose to resume printing. Other documents waiting in the queue continue to print. To pause a document, right-click the document and choose **Pause** from the shortcut menu; the status of the document in the print queue window changes to **Paused**. Choose **Resume** from the document's shortcut menu when you are ready for the document to continue printing.

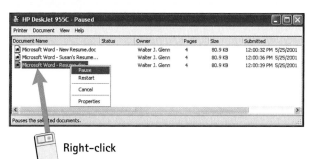

Right-click

5 Restart the Printing of a Document

When you *restart* a paused document, it begins printing again from the beginning. This can be useful if, for example, you start to print a document and then realize the wrong paper is loaded in the printer. You can pause the document, change the paper, and then restart the document. To restart a document, right-click the document and choose **Restart** from the context menu.

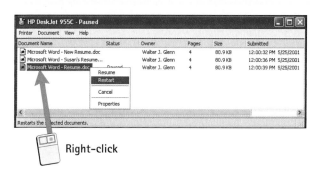

Right-click

6 Change a Document's Priority

A document's *priority* governs when it prints in relation to other documents in the print queue. By default, all documents are given a priority of 1, the lowest priority available. The highest priority is 99. Increasing a document's priority causes it to print before other waiting documents. Double-click the document to open its **Properties** dialog box. Then drag the **Priority** slider to set a higher priority.

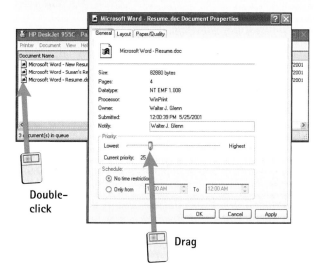

Double-click

Drag

7 Pause the Whole Print Queue

Pausing the entire print queue keeps *all* documents from printing. This can be useful if you suspect a problem with your printer (perhaps it's low on toner). You can pause the queue, fix the problem, and then restart the queue. To pause the queue, open the **Printer** menu and choose **Pause Printing**. The title bar for the print queue window changes to indicate that the printer is paused. To resume printing, choose the **Pause Printing** command again.

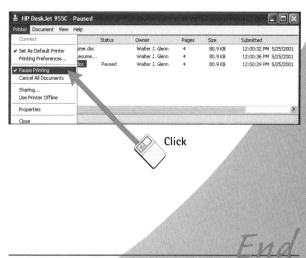

Click

End

How to Change Printer Settings

When you first install a printer in Windows XP, common settings are configured for you. The settings include which printer is used by default, whether pages are printed vertically or horizontally, what kind of paper is being used, and where that paper comes from. After you use your printer for a while, you might find that you need to change those printer settings.

Begin

1 Open the Printers Folder

Click the **Start** button and select **Printers and Faxes**. The **Printer and Faxes** window opens.

Click

2 Set the Default Printer

The *default printer* is the printer that programs print to unless you specify a different printer. In the **Printers and Faxes** window, the default printer has a small check by it. Here, the **Fax** device is the default printer. To set a different printer as the default, right-click its icon and choose **Set as Default Printer** from the shortcut menu.

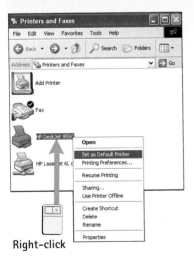

Right-click

3 Open Printer Preferences

To specify your preferences for the printing options that a particular printer uses, open its **Printing Preferences** dialog box. Right-click a printer and choose **Printing Preferences** from the shortcut menu.

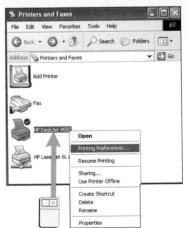

Right-click

4 Change the Page Layout

Select the orientation of the pages to be printed. You can choose to print the pages in **Portrait** format (normal vertical orientation) or **Landscape** (horizontal orientation).

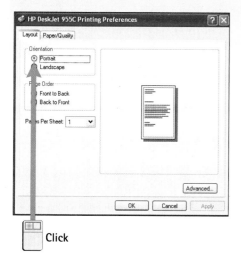

Click

5 Change the Paper Source

Click the **Paper/Quality** tab to see more preferences. Click the **Paper Source** drop-down list to choose a different tray on your printer. The options you see in this list vary based on the printer you are configuring.

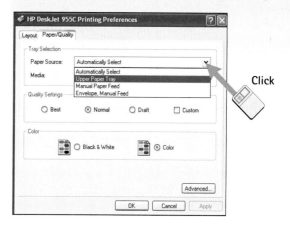

Click

6 Change the Media Type

Click the **Media** drop-down list to choose the type of paper you want to print to. Some printers can use special kinds of paper (such as glossy paper for photos or presentation graphics, transparencies, and even slides). Those printers print differently depending on the kind of paper being used.

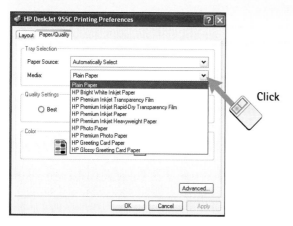

Click

7 Change the Print Quality

Choose the quality of print you want. Better quality uses up more ink and takes more time. Draft quality prints quickly and uses less ink. When you're done setting preferences for this printer, click **OK** to close the dialog box and put these options into effect.

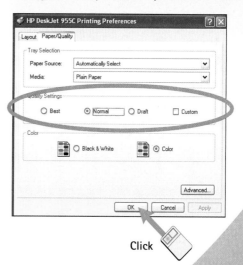

Click

End

How to Share a Printer with Others

When you share a printer, it becomes accessible to other users on your network. By default, all users on the network can see and print to your printer. You can change this so that only particular users or groups of users can use your printer. To share your printer, your computer must be properly configured on a network.

Begin

1 Open the Sharing Dialog Box

In the **Printers and Faxes** window, right-click the printer you want to share and choose **Sharing** from the shortcut menu. The **Properties** dialog box for the selected printer opens.

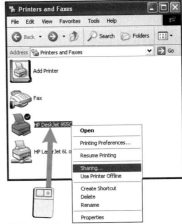

Right-click

2 Share the Printer

On the **Sharing** tab, enable the **Share Name** option and type a name for the shared printer. This is the name others on the network will see when they look for a printer.

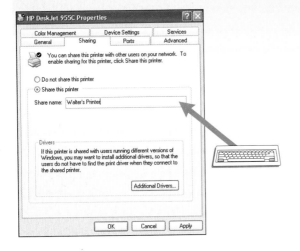

3 Click the Security Tab

If you are using Windows XP Professional on a domain-based network (as you might in a large company), Windows also provides a **Security** tab that lets you limit the users who can access your printer. Click the **Security** tab of the **Properties** dialog box to bring that sheet to the front.

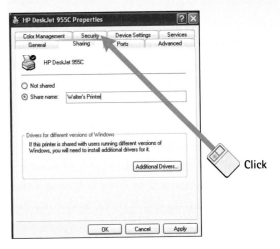

Click

4 Remove the Everyone Group

Select the group named **Everyone** and click **Remove**. This action removes the permissions for all users to access the printer. At this point, no one on the network can print to this printer.

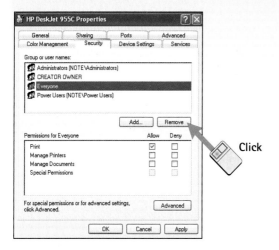

Click

5 Add New Users

Click **Add** to give a new user or group of users permission to access the printer. The **Select Users or Groups** dialog box opens.

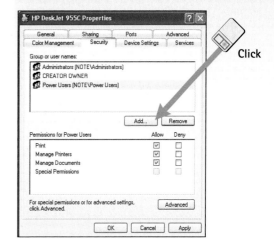

Click

6 Select a User to Add

Select a user from the list at the bottom of the dialog box and click **OK** to add that person or group to the list of users who can use the printer. You return to the printer's **Properties** dialog box.

Click

7 Apply the New Permissions

Select the exact permissions each user should have using the check boxes. The **Print** permission allows the user to print to the printer. **Manage Printers** allows the user to change printer settings. **Manage Documents** allows the user to move, pause, and delete documents waiting to print. Click **OK** to grant the new users you have added access to your printer.

Click

End

How to Install a Local Printer

In Windows lingo, the actual piece of hardware you usually think of as the printer is called the *print device*. The *printer* is the icon you install in the **Printers and Faxes** folder that represents the print device. After you have attached the print device to a computer, it is relatively easy to install the printer to the **Printers and Faxes** folder. In fact, Windows will normally find the print device automatically and configure a printer icon for you. If Windows doesn't find it, use the steps in this task to add the printer yourself.

Begin

1 Run the Add Printer Wizard

In the **Printers and Faxes** folder, click the **Add a Printer** link to launch the **Add Printer Wizard**. When you see the **Welcome** screen, click **Next**.

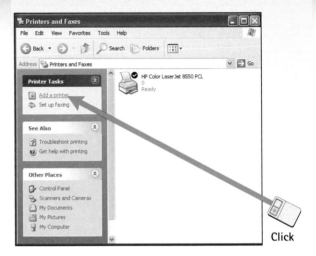

Click

2 Choose Local Printer

On the first page of the wizard, enable the **Local printer** option. A *local printer* is attached directly to your computer (it's not a printer that you reach over the network). A local printer is located in your office; it will not be the printer in the company's printer room or the one attached to Jonnie's computer that you have permission to use.

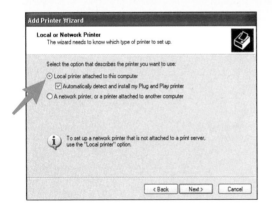

3 Don't Detect the Printer Automatically

Disable the option to automatically detect the printer. If Windows didn't find it automatically already, it probably won't now. If you leave this option selected, Windows will attempt to find the printer itself and figure out what kind it is. If Windows does not find the printer, the wizard will continue as described in this task. If Windows does find the printer, it will set it up for you.

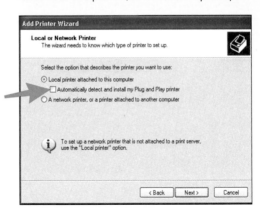

4 Go to the Next Page

Whenever you finish with the options on one wizard page, just click **Next** to go to the next page.

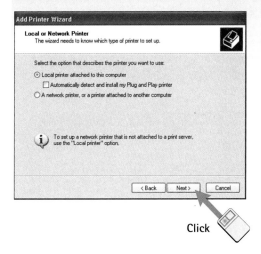

Click

5 Choose a Port

Choose the port on your computer to which the print device is attached. The first print device on a computer is usually on the LPT1 port (the first parallel port). The second print device is usually on the LPT2 port (the second parallel port). When you've selected the port, click **Next** to go on.

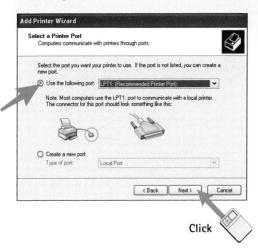

Click

6 Choose a Manufacturer

On the left side of this page is a list of common printer manufacturers. Choose the manufacturer for the print device you are installing.

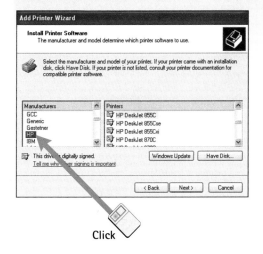

Click

7 Choose a Model

After you choose a manufacturer from the left side of the page, the list on the right changes to display printer models made by the selected manufacturer. Choose the model of the print device you are installing. Click **Next** to go on.

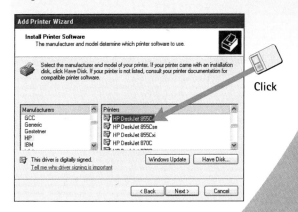

Click

Continued

8 Name the Printer

By default, Windows creates a name for your print device based on its manufacturer and model number (for example, **HP DeskJet 855C**). If you want the printer icon to have a different name, type a new name in the **Printer name** text box.

9 Make It the Default Printer

If you want your new printer to be the default printer used by programs on your computer, click **Yes.** If you prefer to preserve an existing default printer, click **No.** Click **Next** to go on.

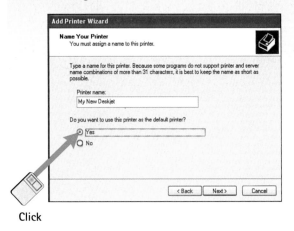

Click

10 Share the Printer

If you want to share the new printer with other users on the network, enable the **Share name** option. Windows creates a share name for you based on the printer name you selected in Step 8 of this task. If you want, you can type a different share name. For more on sharing a printer, see Task 5, "How to Share a Printer with Others." Click **Next** to go on.

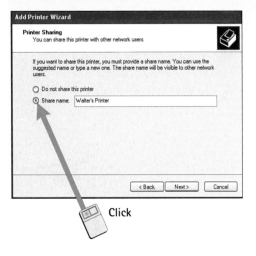

Click

11 Enter a Location and Description

Optionally, you can enter a location and description for the printer to help identify it to others who may use it. You won't see this screen if you did not choose to share the printer in Step 10. Whether you fill in these fields or not, click **Next** to go on.

12 Print a Test Page

Click **Yes** if you want Windows to print a test page to ensure that your new printer is working properly. If the test doesn't work, you are shown how to troubleshoot the installation. Click **Next** to go on.

Click

13 Finish the Installation

Review the configuration of your new printer. If you discover any problems or errors in this information, click **Back** to go back through the steps of the installation. If you are satisfied with the information displayed here, click **Finish**.

Click

How-To Hints

Creating a Share Name

When you create a share name for your printer, it is best to keep the name under eight characters in length. Older programs (those created for use with pre-Windows 95) can recognize only eight-character names. If you are at all unsure whether any users of older programs will print to your printer, keep the name short.

Installing a Printer More Than Once

Each icon in the **Printers and Faxes** folder represents a real printer. You can install more than one icon for a single printer by running the **Add Printer** Wizard again, choosing the same printer and port during setup, and giving the new icon a new name. You may want to do this to configure each icon with different settings. For example, your printer may have two paper trays: one for letter-size paper and one for legal-size paper. You could name one icon **Letter Printer** and configure it to use paper from the letter-size paper tray. You could name the other icon **Legal Printer** and configure it to use the legal-size paper tray. You can also set up additional printer icons to use different print quality, paper types, or whatever other configurations you desire.

End

How to Set Up Your Computer to Use a Network Printer

A *network printer* is often one that is attached to another computer on the network; that computer's user has shared the printer with other users on the network. Some network printers are attached directly to the network and are not on a computer at all. Either way, setting up your computer to print to a network printer requires that you know basically where on your network the printer is located. This means knowing the name of the computer the printer is attached to (if it is attached to a computer) or the name of the printer itself (if it is attached directly to a network) and maybe the workgroup that the computer or printer is part of.

Begin

1 Run the Add Printer Wizard

In the **Printers and Faxes** window, click the **Add a Printer** link to launch the **Add Printer Wizard**. Click **Next** to skip the **Welcome** page.

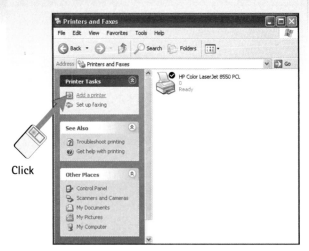

Click

2 Choose Network Printer

On the fist page of the wizard, enable the **A network printer, or a printer attached to another computer** option.

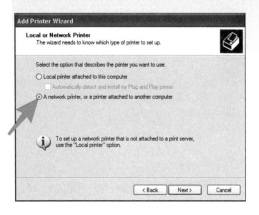

3 Go to the Next Page

When you finish with the options on one wizard page, just click **Next** to go to the next page.

Click

4 Find the Printer

If you know the exact name of the printer you want to connect to (including the network path to that printer), you can enter it in the **Name** text box. You can also connect to an Internet-based printer by entering its address in the **URL** box. If you don't know the name or address (which is usually the case), leave the **Find a printer in the directory** option selected and click **Next** to browse the network for the computer.

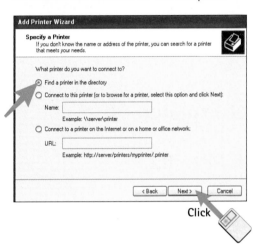

Click

5 Choose the Printer

The **Browse for Printer** page of the wizard shows a hierarchical view of the workgroups and computers on your network. All shared printers are listed at the top. Choose the printer you want to set up and click **Next**.

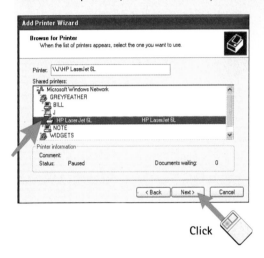

Click

6 Make It the Default Printer

If you want this new printer to be the default printer used by programs on your computer, click **Yes**. If you prefer to preserve an existing default printer, click **No**. Click **Next** to go on.

Click

7 Finish the Installation

Review the configuration of your new printer. If you discover any problems or errors in the information shown here, click **Back** to go back through the steps of the installation. If you are satisfied with the information displayed, click **Finish**.

Click

End

Task

1. How to Start Internet Explorer 80

2. How to Get to a Web Site 82

3. How to Search for a Web Site 84

4. How to Use the Favorites Menu 86

5. How to Use the History List 88

6. How to Make Web Pages Available Offline 90

7. How to Change Settings for Internet Explorer 92

8. How to Use MSN Explorer 94

9. How to Use Windows Messenger 98

10. How to Publish a File to the Web 100

Working on the Internet

The Internet is made up of lots of networks all connected together into one giant network. The most popular part of the Internet today is the World Wide Web, which provides pages that contain text, graphics, and multimedia to programs called *Web browsers*. Over the past few years, the Internet (and especially the Web) has become an important business tool, allowing you to find information on just about anything—businesses, investments, travel, weather, news, healthcare, technology, and more. Microsoft provides a Web browser, called Internet Explorer, as an integral part of Windows XP.

When you visit a Web site, the main page of that site is called the home page. On the home page, there are usually links you can click to visit other pages in the site. Sometimes, links on one site take you to pages in other Web sites. It is this complex manner of linking pages together that gives the Web its name.

Each page on the Web has a specific address, sometimes called a URL (uniform resource locator), that tells your Web browser how to find it. The URL contains such information as the name of the computer and the name of the folder on that computer in which the page can be found, as well as the name of the page itself. For example, the URL **www.microsoft.com/windows/default.asp** tells a browser to find a file named **default.asp** in a folder named **windows** on a computer named **www** in the **microsoft.com** domain.

How to Start Internet Explorer

If you are on a network, your administrator has probably already configured your computer to use the company's connection to the Internet. If you are not on a network (or if your company does not have an Internet connection), you need a modem of some sort and you must sign up for an account with an Internet service provider (ISP). The ISP provides software and instructions to get you connected. When connected, your first task is to get to know your Web browser, Internet Explorer.

Begin

1 Open Internet Explorer

Click **Start** and then **Internet Explorer** to open Internet Explorer. You can also click the **Internet Explorer** icon on the **Quick Launch** bar.

Click

2 Connect to the Internet

If you connect to the Internet using your company's network or using a DSL or cable modem, you should connect to a Web page immediately. If you connect using a regular modem, an extra dialog box might pop up asking you to dial your ISP. If it does, just click **Connect** or **Dial**. Your ISP should provide you with instructions on how to set up the dial-up networking connection.

Click

3 View a Web Page

A Web browser works like any other program you use in Windows. Along the top of the window, you find a menu bar and a couple of toolbars. The **Address** bar lets you enter the address of a page to visit. Use the scrollbar to move through and view the page.

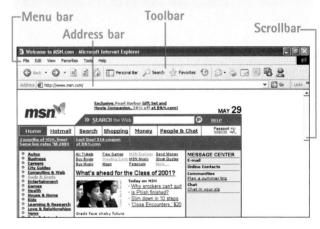

Menu bar   Toolbar
Address bar   Scrollbar

4 Select a Link

On a Web page, *links* to other pages are typically underlined and in blue text, although different pages use different schemes. Links to pages you have visited recently often appear underlined and in red text. When you move your pointer over a link, it turns into a hand pointing its index finger. Just click once to jump to that page. Normally, the page opens in the same window, replacing the page you linked from. Sometimes, pages open in windows of their own.

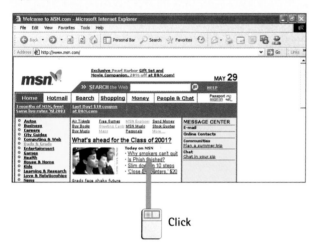

Click

5 Refresh a Page

Some pages change frequently, especially if they contain images that are updated regularly, such as a site that has weather radar images. You can load a page in your browser again by clicking the **Refresh** button on the toolbar.

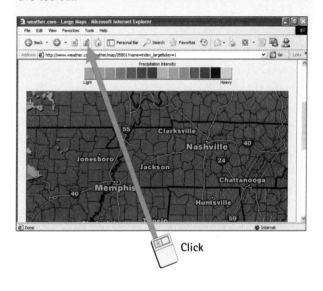

Click

6 Stop a Page from Loading

If a page is taking too long to load or is having problems loading, you can stop it from loading by clicking the **Stop** button on the toolbar. Your browser displays whatever part of the page has already loaded.

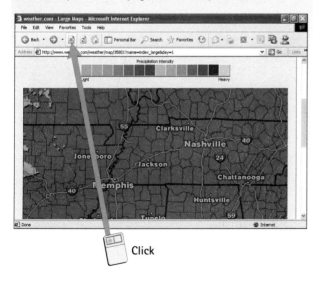

Click

How-To Hints

Viewing a Web Tutorial

Microsoft has a tutorial for using the Web on its Web site. You can access it quickly by choosing the **Tour** command from the Internet Explorer **Help** menu.

Viewing a Page Fullscreen

You can see more of a page at once by viewing it fullscreen. Just select the **Fullscreen** command from the **View** menu. To get back to the regular view, press **F11**.

End

How to Get to a Web Site

If you know the address for a Web page, you can enter it into Internet Explorer's **Address** bar. But there are often easier ways to get to a page. You can keep favorite pages on a special **Favorites** menu or on a **Link** toolbar. You can also use your browser to quickly move backward and forward through pages you've already visited.

Begin

1 Enter the Address

If you know the URL of the site you want to visit, just type it in the Internet Explorer **Address bar** and press **Enter**. As you type, Internet Explorer tries to complete the address for you based on addresses you've entered before. Internet Explorer loads the page if it can find the address.

2 Open the Address List

To view a list of recently visited sites, click the down arrow next to the **Address** box, and click one of the addresses in the list to go to that page.

Click

3 Choose a Link Button

Double-click the **Links** button to slide open the **Links** bar. Click any button on the **Links** bar to jump to that Web page.

Links button

Click

4 Choose a Favorite Site

Internet Explorer lets you keep a list of your favorite Web sites (see Task 4, "How to Use the Favorites Menu," later in this part to learn how to add favorites). Click the **Favorites** menu to open it, and then click any page in the list to jump to that page.

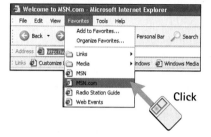

Click

5 Go to Your Home Page

The top page of a Web site is called its *home page*. The default Web page that loads whenever you open Internet Explorer is also called a home page (it's often called *your* home page). Return to your home page at any time by clicking the **Home** button.

Click

6 Go Backward and Forward

As you use Internet Explorer, you can go backward and forward to the last pages you visited by clicking the **Back** and **Forward** buttons on the toolbar. Click the down arrows next to these buttons to open a history of sites you've visited in this online session.

How-To Hints

Adding a Link Button

You can add a button for the page you are viewing to your **Links** bar by simply dragging the icon for the page from the **Address** bar to the **Links** bar.

Making a New Home Page

You can make the page you are viewing your home page by dragging its icon from the **Address** bar to the **Home** button on the toolbar.

End

How to Search for a Web Site

If you don't know the address for a Web site you want to visit, you can often find it just by guessing. Try entering the name of the company (or whatever) you're looking for followed by a three-letter domain suffix. For example, if you want to find Microsoft's Web site, you can just type **microsoft.com** into the **Address** bar. Internet Explorer does the rest. Sometimes, however, you need to search for the information you need.

Begin

1 Open the Search Window

In Internet Explorer, click the **Search** button on the toolbar to open the **Search Companion** on the left side of the window.

Click

2 Enter Some Keywords

Type some keywords to define what you are looking for. If, for example, you want to find Web pages that have to do with tigers in India, type **tiger india**.

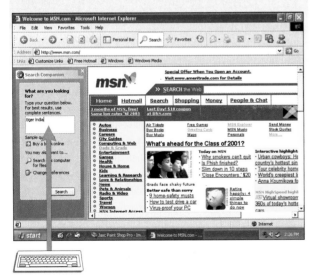

3 Click Search

After you have typed the criteria, click **Search** to begin.

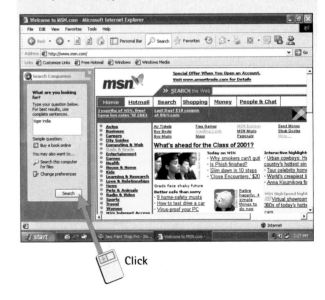

Click

4 Scroll to View Results

Internet Explorer uses the MSN search engine to perform your search and then displays the results in the main browser window. Scroll down to view the results of the search.

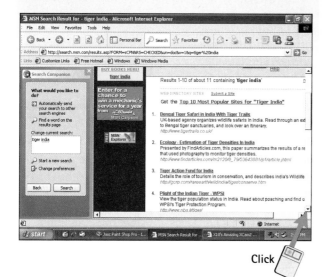

Click

5 Select a Link

Hold the mouse pointer over a link for a moment to view a pop-up window that shows the first several lines of text from the Web page the link represents. When you find a link you want to explore further, click it to jump to that Web page.

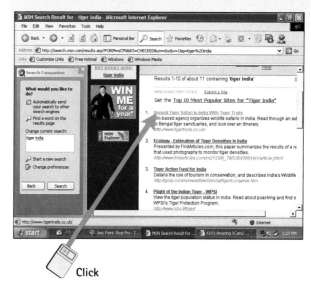

Click

How-To Hints

Using Previous Searches

Internet Explorer remembers searches you've already performed and will automatically display them as you begin to type search terms.

Customizing the Search Procedure

From the main **Search Companion** window, click the **Change Preferences** link to open a window that lets you display advanced options to use while searching. You can change whether the **Search Companion** automatically completes words for you as you type and whether your search is automatically sent to other major Internet search engines (the default setting). If you do not want multiple search engines selected, you can choose which search engine you want the **Search Companion** to use. Choices include MSN, AltaVista, Google, and others. You may find that using only one engine speeds up your searches.

End

How to Use the Favorites Menu

To jump to a page on your list of favorites, all you have to do is open the **Favorites** menu in the Internet Explorer menu bar and choose the page you want to visit from the list. Adding a page to the Favorites list is easy. The first step is to open the page you want to add in Internet Explorer.

Begin

1 Add a Page to the Favorites Menu

To add the Web page you are viewing to your list of favorite pages in the **Favorites** menu, open the menu by clicking it once and then click **Add to Favorites**. The **Add Favorite** dialog box opens.

Click

2 Make Available Offline

If you want the page to be made available for viewing while you are not connected to the Internet, click the **Make available offline** option. Check out Task 6, "How to Make Web Pages Available Offline," for more information on doing this.

Click

3 Rename the Page

Type a different name for the page in the **Name** box if you want. This is the name that will appear in your **Favorites** menu.

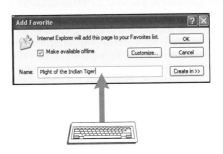

4 Create in a Specific Folder

You can organize your **Favorites** menu into folders. To add the page to a specific folder, click the **Create in** button. If you do not want to put this page in a folder, just click **OK** to add the page to the main **Favorites** menu.

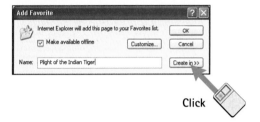

Click

5 Choose a Folder

Click the folder to which you want to add this Web page. You can create a new folder on the menu by clicking the **New Folder** button.

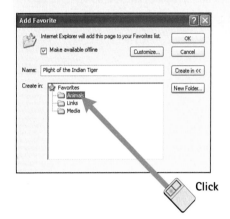

Click

6 Add the Favorite

After you have configured all the previous options you want, click **OK** to add the page to your **Favorites** menu.

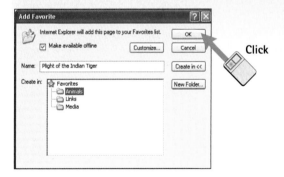

Click

How-To Hints

Organizing Your Favorites Menu

If you want to move, delete, or remove pages on your **Favorites** menu, just open the menu and choose the **Organize Favorites** command.

End

How to Use the History List

Internet Explorer keeps track of all the pages you have visited recently (for the past 20 days, by default). When you can't remember the exact address of a site or a page you've visited before, you can use the **History** list to quickly find it.

Begin

1 Open the History Window

Click the **History** button on the Internet Explorer tool-bar to open the **History** window on the right side of the browser screen.

Click

2 Choose a Time Frame

By default, the **History** window is organized by days and weeks. To look for a site, just click the day when you think you visited it.

Click

3 Choose a Site

From the list of sites you visited on the selected day, find the site you want to explore by clicking it once.

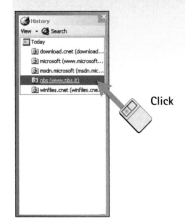

Click

4 Choose a Page

From the list of visited pages on the site, jump to a page by clicking it once.

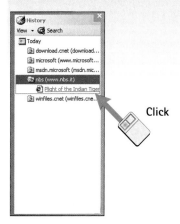

Click

5 Change the View

You can view the **History** window in different ways. Click the **View** button to organize visited pages **By Site**, **By Most Visited**, or **By Order Visited Today**.

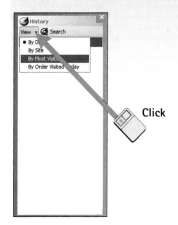

Click

6 Close the History Window

Close the **History** window by clicking the × button in the upper-right corner.

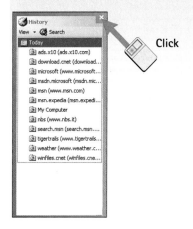

Click

How-To Hints

Searching Your History

Click the **Search** button at the top of the **History** window to search the pages in your **History** list by keyword.

Changing History Settings

See Task 7, "How to Change Settings for Internet Explorer," later in this part for information on how to change your Internet Explorer **History** settings.

History of Local Files

In addition to keeping track of Web pages, Windows keeps track of the files you've opened on your own computer. These files also appear in the **History** list. Windows and Internet Explorer share the same **History** list.

End

How to Make Web Pages Available Offline

Occasionally, you might want to access information on Web pages when you are not connected to the Internet. This can be useful if you are charged for connection time or if you carry your computer around with you. Internet Explorer lets you mark pages for offline viewing, which basically means that the pages are copied to your computer so you can view them without being on the Internet. You can also configure when and how the pages are updated.

Begin

1 Make It Available Offline

First, browse to the page you want to make available offline and choose the **Add to Favorites** command from your **Favorites** menu. In the **Add Favorite** dialog box, enable the **Make available offline** option and click the **Customize** button. This launches the **Offline Favorite Wizard**.

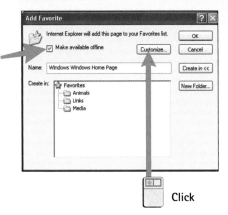

Click

2 Make Links Available Offline

You can choose to make only the current page available or to make pages that the current page links to available as well. If you want to make links available, click the **Yes** option.

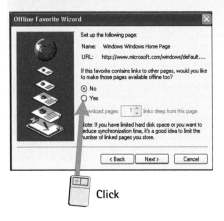

Click

3 Select the Link Depth

Choose how many links deep from the current page you want to make pages available. For example, choosing **3** makes available all pages that the current page links to and all pages that each of those pages links to. Click **Next** to go on.

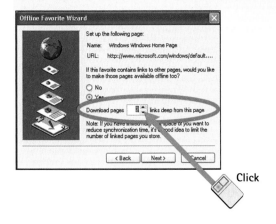

Click

4 Schedule Offline Updates

Synchronizing updates the temporary copies of offline pages on your computer with the most recent copy from the Internet. By default, pages are synchronized only when you choose the **Synchronize** command from the **Tools** menu of Internet Explorer. Create a new synchronization schedule by enabling the appropriate option. Click **Next** to go on.

Click

5 Set Up a Schedule

Choose how often (in days) and at what time of the day you want the page to be automatically updated. You can also name your schedule. Click **Next** to go on.

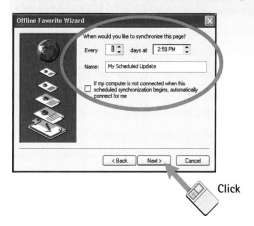

Click

6 Enter a Username and Password

If the page you are making available offline requires that you enter a username and password (as do many news sites or services you might have subscribed to), enable the **Yes** option and supply that information here. When you're done, click **Finish**.

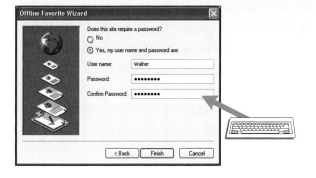

How-To Hints

Changing Offline Settings

You can change the offline settings for a page at any time by choosing **Organize Favorites** from the **Favorites** menu. Select the page from the list and click the **Properties** button to change the offline settings.

End

How to Change Settings for Internet Explorer

After you have played with Internet Explorer for a while, you might want to experiment with some of the ways in which you can customize the program using the **Internet Options** dialog box. The seven tabs on this dialog box present a lot of options. Some of the more useful ones are discussed here.

Begin

1 Open Internet Options

In Internet Explorer, open the **Tools** menu and choose the **Internet Options** command. The **Internet Options** dialog box opens.

Click

2 Enter a New Home Page

The page that Internet Explorer first opens to is called the home page. You can change the home page by typing a new URL in the **Address** box.

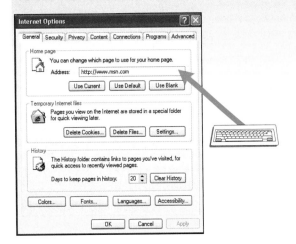

3 Delete Temporary Files

As you browse, Internet Explorer temporarily saves pages and graphics to your hard drive. When you open a previously visited page, Internet Explorer checks to see whether the page has changed. If it hasn't, the temporary files are opened; this way, the page loads faster. You can delete these temporary files to make room on your hard disk by clicking **Delete Files**. The **Delete Files** dialog box that opens also has an option for deleting offline files stored on your drive.

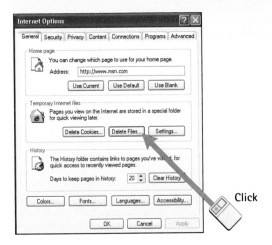

Click

4 Change Temporary Settings

Click the **Settings** button to open the **Settings** dialog box. Here, you can change how often Internet Explorer checks for new versions of the pages stored as temporary files.

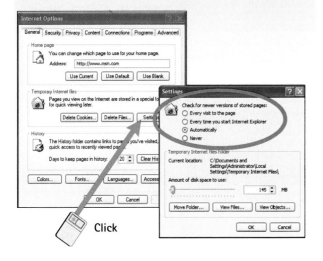

Click

5 Reduce Disk Space Used

Temporary files use up disk space—by default, as much as 2% of your hard disk. On larger drives, this can amount to quite a lot of space. However, storing more temporary files can mean quicker loading of some Web pages. Change the disk space used for temporary files by dragging the slider or by entering a specific value in megabytes.

Drag

6 Change History Setting

By default, Internet Explorer keeps track of the Web pages and local files that you have opened in the last 20 days. You can change this value using the **Days to keep pages in history** scroll buttons.

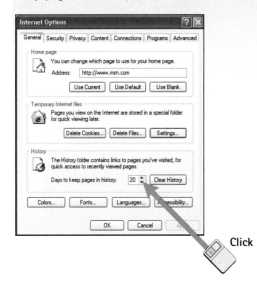

Click

7 Open the Colors Dialog Box

Click the **Colors** button at the bottom of the **General** tab of the **Internet Options** dialog box to change the colors of the text and background of Web pages you visit. Click one of the color buttons to open a palette from which you can choose a new color.

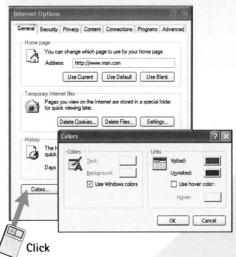

Click

End

How to Use MSN Explorer

Most people find Internet Explorer fairly easy to use and pretty powerful once they get used to it. Windows XP also comes with another program named MSN Explorer that features a Web browser and several other options bundled into one simple interface. To use MSN Explorer, you must be a subscriber to the Microsoft Network (MSN) or set up a free e-mail account with Microsoft's Hotmail. The first time you use the program, MSN Explorer walks you through the process of setting up.

Begin

1 Start MSN Explorer

On the **Quick Launch** bar at the bottom of the screen, click the shortcut for **MSN Explorer**. If you don't find it on your **Quick Launch** bar, you'll find it on the **Start** menu under **All Programs**. If you've not yet set up an account with MSN, you'll be guided through that process now.

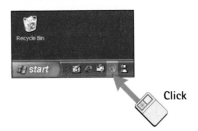

Click

2 Select a User

You can set up multiple MSN accounts. This is useful when multiple family members use the same computer. Whenever you start MSN Explorer, log in to your account by clicking the icon next to your MSN user name.

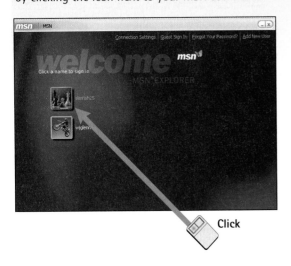

Click

3 Enter Your Password

In the text box that appears, type your password and then click **Sign In**. If you want MSN Explorer to remember your password so that you don't have to type it in each time you log in, enable the **Remember password check box**.

4 Browse the Web

After you sign in, a window opens that looks like a fancy Web browser. You can browse the Web using many of the same techniques you learned for Internet Explorer earlier in this part. Click a link, type an address, and even access your list of Web-page favorites.

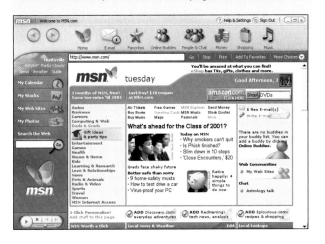

5 Check Your Calendar

Click the **My Calendar** link to create your own personal calendar. You can enter appointments, set reminders, keep track of tasks you have to do, and more.

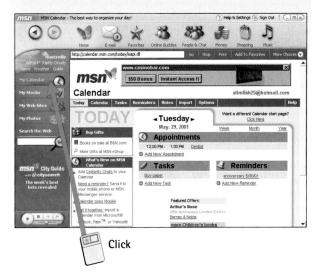

Click

6 Check Your Stocks

MSN Explorer lets you enter all your stocks and then track stock prices and company news. If you have a MoneyCentral portfolio, you can show it on this page. When you click the **My Stocks** link, a separate window opens with a simple list of your stocks. A link in that window takes you to the MoneyCentral site shown here.

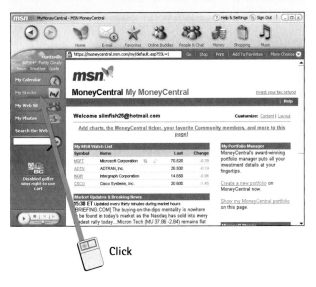

Click

7 Create a List of Web Sites

Click the **My Web Sites** link to open a small window that lists favorite MSN sites, personal Web pages you've created, and files you've put in storage on MSN. A link in the **My Web Sites** page takes you to the **Communities** page shown here.

Click

Continued

8 Store and Share Digital Photos

With your MSN account, you get storage space to which you can upload your digital photos and share them with family and friends. Just click the **My Photos** link to get started. You'll find complete instructions on the **PictureIt!** page.

Click

9 Check Your E-Mail

Click the **E-mail** button to manage your Hotmail account. You can read, write, and send e-mail messages using a simple Web-based interface.

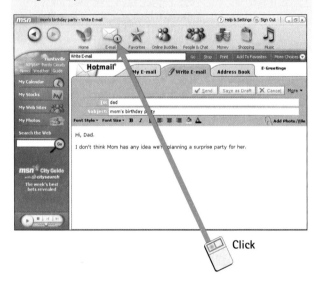

Click

10 Find and Talk to People

Click the **People & Chat** button to jump to the **People & Chat** page of MSN. From here, you can find online discussions on almost any subject. You'll also find links for playing online games and watching live videos.

Click

11 Manage Your Finances

Click the **Money** button to visit **MSN MoneyCentral**, where you can create and manage stock portfolios, investigate online banking, and research almost any financial decision.

Click

12 Shop

Click the **Shopping** button to visit MSN's **eShops**, where you can find almost anything you'd ever want to buy.

Click

13 Find Music

Click the **Music** button to visit **WindowsMedia.com**, where you can find, download, and listen to thousands of different songs.

Click

How-To Hints

Why Use MSN Explorer?

Why should you use MSN Explorer instead of Internet Explorer (or another Web browser) and Outlook Express? After all, you can get to many of the same places (such as MoneyCentral, Hotmail, shopping, and so on) by using any simple Web browser. The answer to this question is really one of taste. MSN Explorer offers all this stuff in one, simplified interface—much like the interface AOL offers with its service. If you use MSN Explorer, you can browse, check stocks, check mail, and so on all in one window without having to type in addresses.

MSN Explorer is also very easy to set up so that other people who use your computer can use it without getting in each other's way. For example, each member of your family can have his or her own account, stock list, and online photos. Many people new to using the Internet also find MSN Explorer's simplified interface a comforting introduction to all things online. Although advanced users usually find the flexibility and customizability of a regular Web browser such as Internet Explorer and an e-mail program such as Outlook Express more to their liking, MSN Explorer just offers another way to access the Internet.

End

How to Use Windows Messenger

Windows XP comes with its own instant messaging program called **Windows Messenger**. It works much like its counterparts from other companies, including AOL Instant Messenger and ICQ. To use it, you must have a Hotmail or Passport account. Windows Messenger walks you through setting up an account the first time you use it.

Begin

1 Start Messenger

On the **Quick Launch** bar, click the shortcut for **Windows Messenger**. If you don't find it on your **Quick Launch** bar, you'll find it on the **Start** menu under **More Programs**. If you've not yet set up your account, you'll be guided through that process now.

Click

2 Check Your Status

The main **Windows Messenger** window shows the name of the account you are signed in with and how many messages you have in your Hotmail or Passport e-mail account. The window also shows a list of all the contacts you've set up, divided into those who are online and those who are offline.

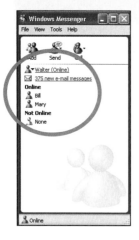

3 Add a Contact

Click the **Add** button to launch a short wizard that lets you add a new contact to your list. You'll be asked for the e-mail address of the contact. You can also search the MSN directory for the contact you want to add. Note that to send instant messages to this person, the contact must also be using Windows Messenger.

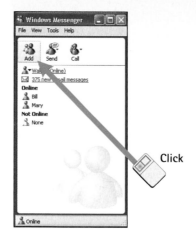

Click

4 Send an Instant Message

Click the **Send** button and choose a contact from the menu that drops down to open a window. Type a message to that contact, and click the **Send** button. If the contact is online, you can chat together in real time. If the contact is offline, that person will receive the message when he or she comes online again.

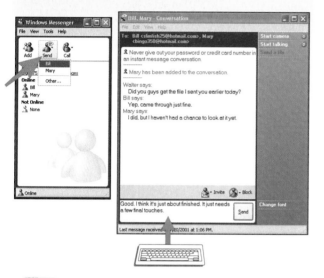

5 Invite Another Contact to Join You

Use the **Invite** button to select another contact to join the conversation. The **Invite** button also lets you invite the contacts you are currently chatting with to start an audio-and-video chat (if you all have the appropriate equipment installed on your computers), run NetMeeting for collaborating on a shared document, or ask for remote assistance.

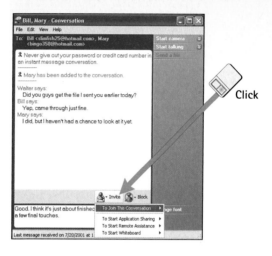

Click

6 Block a Contact

Sometimes, you'll come across people who are sending you instant messages that you'd rather not have to address. Click the **Block** button to block the person who last sent you an instant message from contacting you or even seeing your name in the MSN directory in the future.

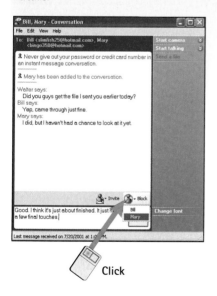

Click

7 Set Your Status

At times during your online session, you may find it inconvenient to receive instant messages. You can change your online status to prevent people from interrupting your work online. Right-click the **Windows Messenger** icon in the system tray and point to the **My Status** command to set your current status. When you're ready to receive instant messages again, don't forget to set your status back to **Online**.

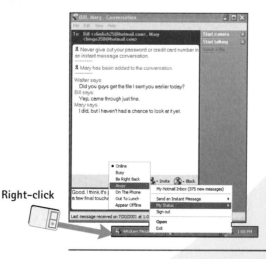

Right-click

End

How to Publish a File to the Web

Many people maintain their own Web sites, whether those sites are served from personal space on a service, such as MSN, a business Web site, or a portion of a company intranet. Windows makes it easy to send (or *publish*) files to a Web site. To publish a file, you must be connected to the Internet. If you connect using a modem, Windows prompts you to make the connection if you are not already connected.

Begin

1 Find the File to Publish

In the **My Computer** window or **Windows Explorer**, find the file you want to publish to the Web and select it by clicking it once. From the **File Tasks** list on the left side of the window, click the **Publish this file to the Web** link.

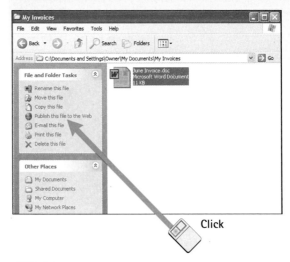

Click

2 Click Next

The **Web Publishing Wizard** starts. Click **Next** to go past the welcome page.

Click

3 Choose a Network Destination

Choose the destination for your file. MSN offers free space in which you can store files. If you want to publish to another location—such as a personal Web site, an intranet, or a network location—choose **Other Network Location**. The publishing process works the same for all three options. For each option, you may be asked for a username and password to publish to the site.

Click

4 Choose a File Destination

Choose the location on the chosen server where you want to publish your file. This location is usually a folder you or a storage service, such as MSN, has created for your use. Make a selection and click **Next** to publish the file.

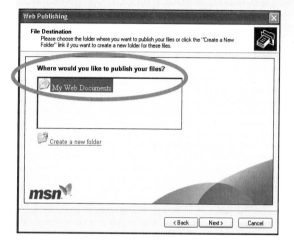

5 Finish

After the file has been published, click **Finish** to exit the wizard. A browser opens to display the file you have just uploaded; note that you are viewing the file from the remote server, not from your local server. Make a note of the URL that is displayed in the **Address** bar for this page so that you can share it with your co-workers and friends.

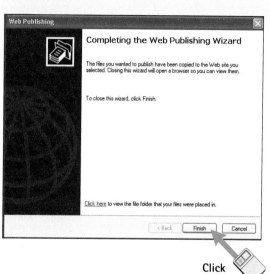

Click

How-To Hints

Creating a Network Place

Publishing to Web sites is easier if you create Network Places for each site you want to publish your files to ahead of time. For details on how to do this, see Part 4, "Working on a Network."

End

Task

1 How to Send E-Mail with Outlook Express **104**

2 How to Receive E-Mail **106**

3 How to Use the Address Book **108**

4 How to Change Settings for Outlook Express **110**

5 How to Receive an Attached File **112**

6 How to Send an Attached File **114**

7 How to Subscribe to a Newsgroup **116**

8 How to Read a Newsgroup Posting **118**

9 How to Post to a Newsgroup **120**

PART 5

Using Internet E-Mail and Newsgroups

Over the past few years, e-mail has become so popular that it's difficult to find people who don't use it. If you're on a company network, it's almost a sure bet that you use e-mail to communicate with other employees. If your network is hooked up to the Internet, or if you have a computer at home, the chances are that you can exchange e-mail with other Internet users.

The tasks in this part cover using Outlook Express, a program that comes with Windows XP, to send Internet e-mail. If you are on a company network, you might use a program other than Outlook Express to send and receive company e-mail—and maybe Internet e-mail, too. Outlook (not to be confused with Outlook Express) is a part of Microsoft Office and is one such alternative program. Whatever program you use to send and receive e-mail, you'll find that the steps for performing the basic e-mail operations are pretty similar.

In the following tasks, you will learn to send and receive a message, use the built-in Address Book, and find e-mail addresses for people. You will also learn to send and receive file attachments with an e-mail message. Finally, you will learn how to subscribe to and use Internet newsgroups. Internet *newsgroups* are message forums open to the public in which many people post and reply to messages. There are literally tens of thousands of newsgroups available on the Internet on just about any topic you can think of. Outlook Express acts as a *newsreader*, a program that lets you read and reply to posts in these newsgroups. ●

How to Send E-Mail with Outlook Express

Sending a message with Outlook Express requires that you know only one thing before you start—the e-mail address of the person you want to send mail to. This address usually takes a form such as **username@company.com**. If you don't know a person's address, the easiest way to find it out is to call them on the phone and ask.

Begin

1 Start Outlook Express

Double-click the **Outlook Express** icon on your desktop to start Outlook Express. If you use a modem to connect to the Internet, Outlook Express launches the connection to sign you on. If you don't see the icon on your desktop, you'll find it on your **Start** menu.

Double-click

2 Compose a New Message

To start a new message, click the **Create Mail** button on the Outlook Express toolbar. This action opens a new window for the message.

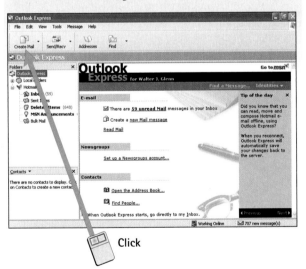

Click

3 Type an Address

In the **To** box, type the e-mail address for the person you want to send mail to. You can enter multiple addresses by separating them with a comma or semi-colon.

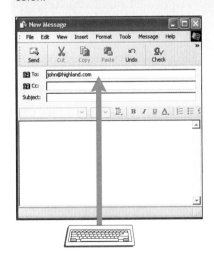

4 Type a Subject

Type a subject for your message in the **Subject** box. Although you do not have to enter a subject to send the message, it is considered good form to do so. The subject line will appear in the recipient's list of new mail to identify the topic of your message.

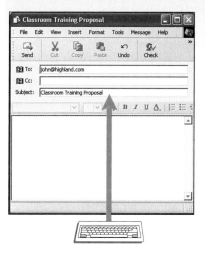

5 Write Your Message

Type the body of your message in the main window. Note that the toolbar above this window has standard tools for formatting your message. Use the **Font**, **Font Size**, **Bold**, **Italic**, and **Underline** tools as you would in a word processing program to format your text; use the **Numbered List** and **Bulleted List** buttons to create lists; use the **Indent** and **Outdent** buttons to move a block of text relative to the left and right margins.

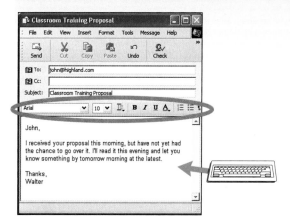

6 Send It

When you are done addressing and typing your message, click the **Send** button on the message window's toolbar to send the message.

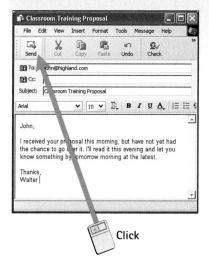

Click

How-To Hints

Your Outbox

When you send a message, it actually goes into your **Outbox** first. Depending on your settings, Outlook Express might send the message immediately or the message might sit in the **Outbox** until you click the **Send/Receive** button on the main Outlook Express toolbar. You can tell that messages are in your **Outbox** when the folder name becomes boldfaced.

Checking Your Spelling

You can spell-check your message before you send it by clicking the **Check** button on the message window's toolbar. You can also set up Outlook Express to automatically check spelling on all messages as they are sent. This process is described in Task 4, "How to Change Settings for Outlook Express."

End

How to Receive E-Mail

Whenever you start Outlook Express, it automatically checks to see whether you have new mail. If you use a modem to connect to the Internet, Outlook Express starts the connection for you. By default, it also checks for new messages every 30 minutes while the program is open. You can force it to check for new messages at any time by clicking the **Send/Receive** button on the main toolbar.

Begin

1 Switch to Your Inbox

When you start Outlook Express, it opens to the Outlook Express home page, which shows an overview of your e-mail and newsgroups. To see new messages, switch to your **Inbox** by clicking it once.

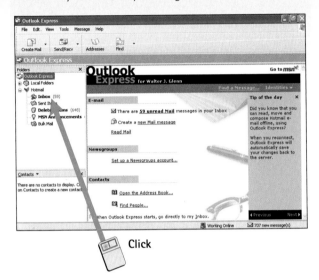

Click

2 Select a Message

All new messages are delivered to your **Inbox**. Columns indicate who each message is from, the subject of the message, and the date the message was received. To select a message, just click it once. The contents are displayed in the preview pane under the message list.

Click

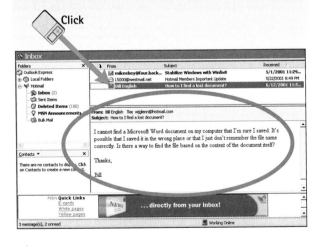

3 Open a Message

You can also open a message in a separate window by double-clicking any message in the message list. Use the **Previous** and **Next** buttons on the toolbar to view other messages in the same window.

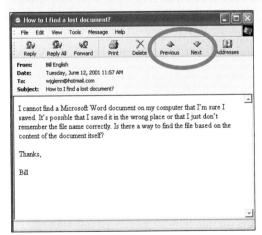

4 Reply to a Message

To reply to the sender of a message, select the message from the list and click the **Reply** button on the toolbar. A new message window appears that includes the e-mail address, subject, and content of the original message. Just type a reply message and click **Send**.

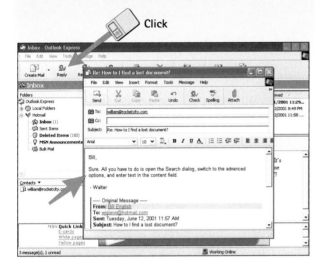

Click

5 Forward a Message

You can also forward a message that you received from one person to one or more other people altogether. Just select the message and click the **Forward** button on the toolbar. A new message window appears that includes a subject and the original message. Enter an e-mail address, type a new message if you want, and click **Send**.

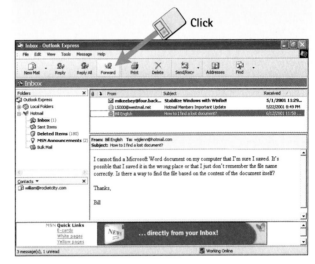

Click

6 Delete a Message

To delete a message from your **Inbox**, select the message and click the **Delete** button on the toolbar. Deleted messages are placed in the **Deleted Items** folder, where you can retrieve them later if needed. Right-click the **Deleted Items** folder and choose **Empty Deleted Items Folder** from the shortcut menu to permanently delete the messages inside.

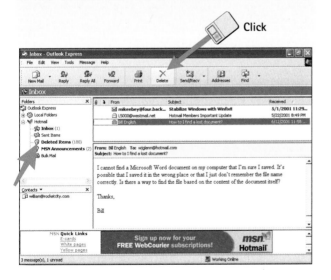

Click

How-To Hints

Creating New Folders

If you like to save old messages, you can organize them by creating new folders to store them in. Select the **Local Folders** item by clicking it once, then choose **File, New Folder** from the menu bar to create and name a new folder. After the folder is created, you can simply drag messages from your **Inbox** to the new folder to move messages to more meaningful storage places.

End

How to Use the Address Book

The Outlook Express **Address Book** is a handy tool that lets you store the e-mail addresses of people you mail regularly so that you don't have to remember addresses and type them in each time you send a message. You also can use the **Address Book** to store other personal information for people, such as postal addresses and telephone numbers.

Begin

1 Open the Address Book

To open the **Address Book**, click the **Addresses** button on the Outlook Express toolbar.

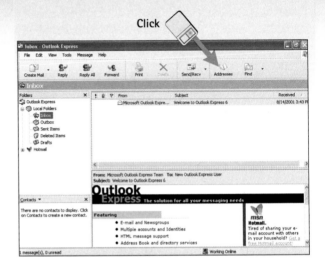

Click

2 Select an Address

The **Address Book** displays a list of contacts, e-mail addresses, and phone numbers. Select any contact by clicking it once.

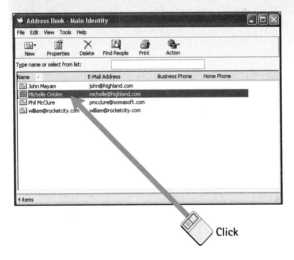

Click

3 Send a Message

You can send an e-mail message to any selected contact by clicking the **Action** button on the toolbar and choosing **Send Mail** from the menu that drops down. This command opens a new message window with the address already filled in.

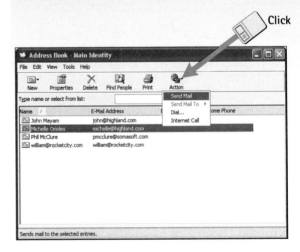

Click

4 Add a New Contact

Whenever you send or reply to a message in Outlook Express, the e-mail address you are sending to automatically is added to your **Address Book**. You can add a new contact to your **Address Book** manually by clicking the **New** button on the toolbar and choosing **New Contact**.

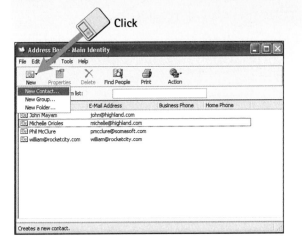

Click

5 Fill in Personal Information

Fill in the first, middle, and last names of your new contact. You can also enter a nickname, if you want, which you can enter into the **To** box of a new message to quickly address new messages.

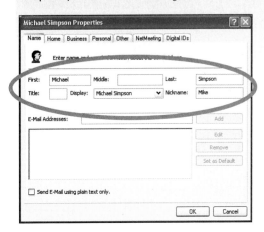

6 Enter an Address

Type the e-mail address for your new contact in the **E-Mail Addresses** box, then click the **Add** button to add the address to your **Address Book**. You can even enter extra e-mail addresses if your contact has more than one. Click the other tabs of this dialog box to enter information such as home and business addresses and phone numbers.

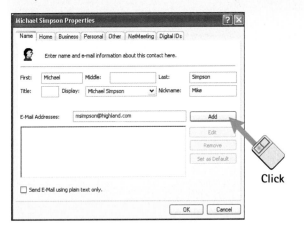

Click

How-To Hints

Using the To Button

In a new message window, move the mouse pointer over the word **To:**, which is next to the **To** box; a button appears. Click the button to open the **Address Book** and choose a contact to send the message to.

Using the Contacts List

Underneath the **Folders** list in the **Outlook Express** window is the **Contacts** list of the same contacts that appear in your **Address Book**. Double-click any name to start a new message to that contact.

End

How to Change Settings for Outlook Express

There are a lot of things you can customize in Outlook Express, including the way mail is received and sent, how spelling is checked, and much more. The following steps show you some of the more useful settings you can change in Outlook Express.

Begin

1 Open the Options Dialog Box

In Outlook Express, open the **Tools** menu and choose the **Options** command to open the **Options** dialog box.

Click

2 Set General Options

Use the **General** tab to set some basic options about how Outlook Express behaves. You can have Outlook Express open the **Inbox** as soon as you start the program, play a sound when messages arrive, and change the time interval for checking for new messages.

3 Set Read Options

Click the **Read** tab to configure settings pertaining to incoming messages. For example, Outlook Express marks a message as read 5 seconds after you select and view it in the preview pane. You can increase this value or change the option altogether. You can also set how many news articles are downloaded when you update a newsgroup.

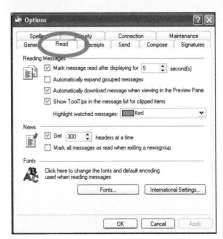

4 Set Send Options

Click the **Send** tab to change settings regarding how Outlook Express sends messages. You can specify such things as whether copies of outgoing messages should be saved in the **Sent Items** folder, whether the contents of original messages should be included in replies, and the format of outgoing messages. Note that HTML formatting lets you apply formats to the characters in your text (bold, italic, font size, and so on), but may not be readable by people using older e-mail programs.

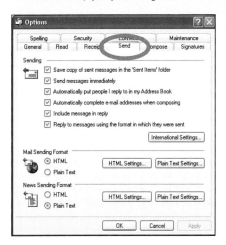

5 Create a Signature

A *signature* is text that is automatically included at the end of outgoing messages. Click the **Signatures** tab to set up a signature. You can even set up multiple signatures and then select which one to attach to a message.

6 Set Spelling Options

If you have Microsoft Office installed on your computer, Outlook Express can take advantage of its spell-checking features. Click the **Spelling** tab to change how Outlook Express spell-checks outgoing messages. You can specify that messages are checked automatically and can specify several options for what kinds of words are checked. If you don't have Office installed, you will not see the **Spelling** tab.

7 Set Connection Options

If you connect to the Internet using a modem, click the **Connection** tab to change how Outlook Express manages the connection. You can have Outlook Express check with you before dialing a connection and have it hang up automatically after sending and receiving messages.

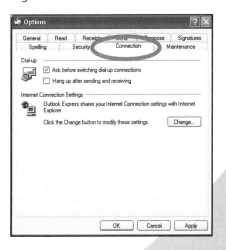

End

How to Receive an Attached File

One of the greatest uses of e-mail is your ability to attach files to a message and send them to others. Sending an e-mail attachment sure beats copying the file to a floppy disk and carrying or mailing it. In the steps that follow, you'll see how to open a file that is attached to a message you have received.

Begin

1 Start Outlook Express

Click the **Outlook Express** shortcut on the **Quick Launch** bar.

Click

2 Select a Message with an Attachment

A message with an attachment shows up in your message list with a paper clip icon in the attachment column. When you select the message by clicking it once, the paper clip icon also appears in the header of the message in the preview pane.

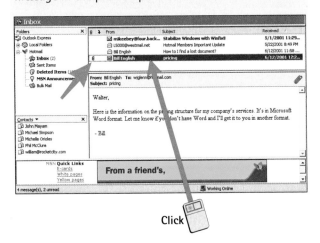

Click

3 Open the Attached File

Click the paper clip icon in the header of the message in the preview pane to open a drop-down list that shows the files attached to the message. In the list, click the attachment you want to open. If Windows knows what program is associated with the file (Microsoft Word for a **.doc** file, for example), the file opens in that application. Otherwise, Windows prompts you to save the file.

Click

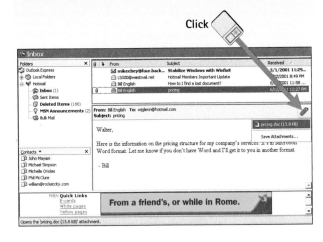

4 Save the Attachments

Choose **Save Attachments** from the paper clip's drop-down list to save all attached files to a specific location.

Click

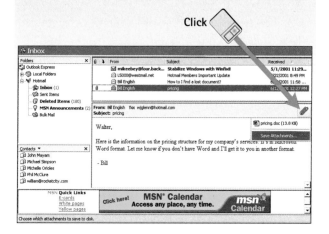

5 Choose a Save Location

In the **Save Attachments** dialog box, select the attachments to be saved and enter a location in the **Save To** box. You can also click the **Browse** button to find a location instead of typing it in. Click the **Save** button to save the selected attachments to the specified location.

Click

How-To Hints

File Associations

Windows knows what files go with what programs because of file *associations*. All files have a three-letter extension (the three characters after the dot in the filename) that tells Windows what program the files should open with. For more on associations, see Part 2, "Working with Files and Folders."

End

TASK 6

How to Send an Attached File

Outlook Express allows you to send messages with files attached. The first step to sending a file attachment is to create a new message (see Task 1). You can attach more than one file to a single e-mail message by repeating Steps 3 and 4 before you click **Send** in Step 5.

1 Start a New Message

Click the **Create Mail** button on the Outlook Express toolbar to start a new message.

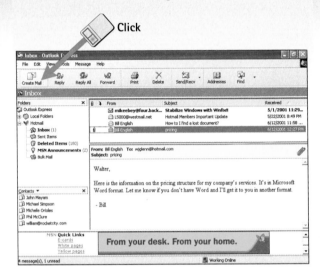

Click

2 Write Your Message

Address and write your message the same way that you normally would.

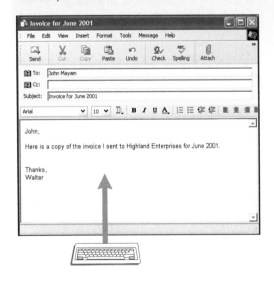

3 Insert a File Attachment

When your message is ready to send, choose **Insert, File Attachment** from the menu bar. You also can click the **Attach** button on the Outlook Express toolbar. The **Insert Attachment** dialog box opens.

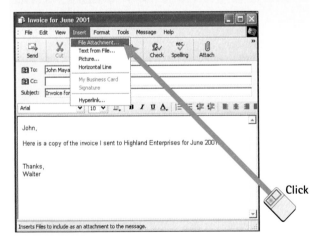

Click

4 Select the File

Locate the file you want to send by browsing through the folders in the normal manner. Select the file by clicking it once and then click the **Attach** button.

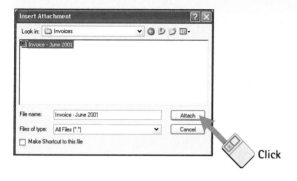

Click

5 Send the Message

Files attached to the current e-mail message are listed in the **Attach** box under the **Subject** box. When you're ready to send the message and its attachments, click the **Send** button on the toolbar.

Click

How-To Hints

Sending a File from Windows

You can send a file using e-mail right from Windows. In either **Windows Explorer** or the **My Documents** window, right-click the file and choose **Send To Mail Recipient** from the short-cut menu. This command starts a new Outlook Express message with the file already attached.

Attachment Etiquette

Even modest documents can make for pretty large files. Many people use modems to access the Internet, and large files can take some time to download. If you plan to send someone a large file attachment, it is best to send them a brief message ahead of time warning them that you will send the file and perhaps asking them for the best time at which you should send it.

End

How to Subscribe to a Newsgroup

A news server often hosts as many as thirty or forty thousand newsgroups. To make it easier to sift through these newsgroups, most newsreaders, including Outlook Express, let you subscribe to particular groups. Subscribing does not mean that you have to pay anybody to use the group. It's just a way of telling Outlook Express which groups to show you in your program window—sort of a favorites list for newsgroups. Your Internet service provider will give you instructions on how to set up Outlook Express to use its news server. You will have to provide Outlook Express with the name of the server and possibly your username and password, as well.

Begin

1 Switch to Your News Server

News servers to which you have access show up in your Outlook Express window under your mailbox folders. Clicking a server once selects that server and lists in the right window the newsgroups you are subscribed to. Here you see only the one news server, cleverly called **News Server**, in the **Folders** list; click it to start exploring newsgroups.

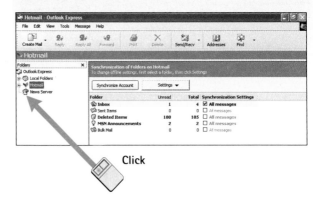

Click

2 Open the Newsgroups List

To see what newsgroups the server you specified in Step 1 carries, click the **Newsgroups** button. The **Newsgroup Subscriptions** dialog box opens.

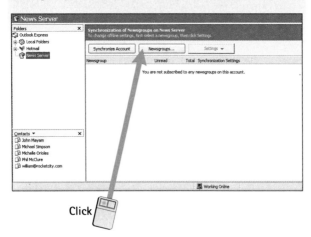

Click

3 Browse for a Newsgroup

All newsgroups available on the selected news server are displayed in this window. You can browse for newsgroups by scrolling through the list. However, with many thousands of groups available, this approach could take a while.

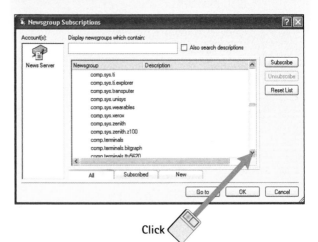

Click

4 Search for a Newsgroup

Fortunately, Outlook Express offers a convenient way to search for newsgroups. Enter any text in the **Display newsgroups which contain** box to show only those newsgroups that have that text in their titles. Most newsgroup titles have something to do with their topic.

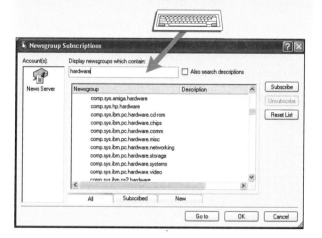

5 Go to a Newsgroup

When you find a newsgroup you'd like to investigate, you can go to it to check it out (that is, to browse the messages and see whether the newsgroup is worthwhile) by clicking the group once to select it and then clicking the **Go to** button. Task 8, "How to Read a Newsgroup Posting," explains how to investigate a newsgroup.

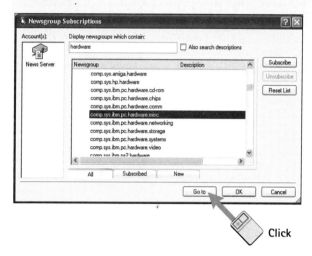

Click

6 Subscribe to a Newsgroup

If you find a newsgroup that you want to read often, it's easiest to subscribe to it so that it shows up in your **Outlook Express** window. Go back to the newsgroups list (refer to Step 2 for instructions); select the group you want to subscribe to and click the **Subscribe** button.

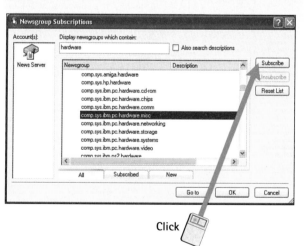

Click

7 View Subscribed Newsgroups

Newsgroups to which you have subscribed show up in the newsgroup list with a subscription icon next to them. You can also view a list of only those newsgroups to which you have subscribed by clicking the **Subscribed** tab at the bottom of the newsgroup list.

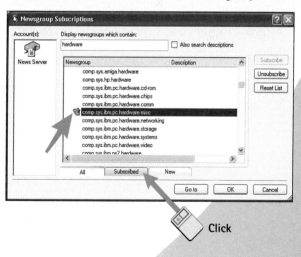

Click

End

How to Read a Newsgroup Posting

Reading newsgroup postings is a lot like reading e-mail messages. Just keep in mind that the postings are available to the general public and that any message can be part of a *thread* (which is an original message, a reply to that original message, or a reply to those replies).

Begin

1 Open a Newsgroup

First, open a newsgroup by clicking one of the groups listed under your news server. The newsgroup opens, and new *headers* (the part of the message that lets you know the message subject and who the message is from) are downloaded from the server. This process sometimes takes a minute or so.

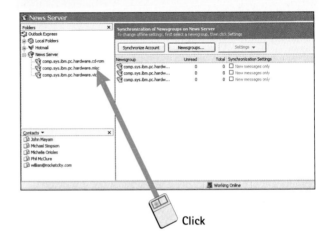

Click

2 Select a Message

After the message headers are downloaded, the messages are displayed to the right, much like e-mail messages are listed. Click any message to download the message body from the server and display it in the preview pane at the bottom of the screen.

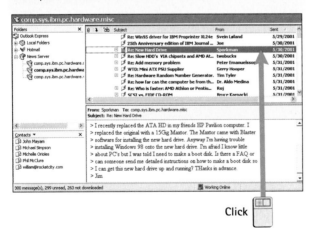

Click

3 Expand a Thread

Messages with a plus sign next to them are part of a thread and have replies. Click the plus sign to expand the thread and see the other messages. Replies are indented from the original message.

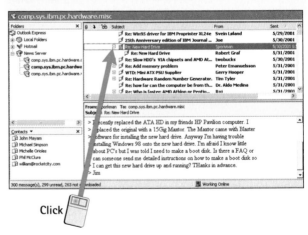

Click

4 Post a Reply to the Group

If you want to post a reply to a message for the whole newsgroup to read, select the message by clicking it once and then click the **Reply Group** button on the toolbar. A window opens that lets you type and send your reply. Your message is sent to the news server, where it will appear within about ten minutes as a thread underneath the original message to which you replied.

Click

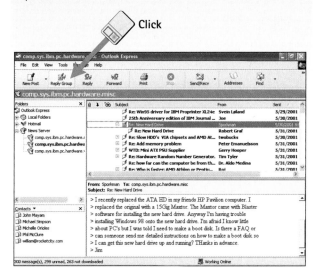

5 Send a Reply to the Poster

You can also reply to the poster of a message privately by e-mail. To do this, select a message and click the **Reply** button on the toolbar. A standard new e-mail message window opens with the address already filled in. The message you send is not posted to the newsgroup; it is sent only to the person who originally wrote the current message.

Click

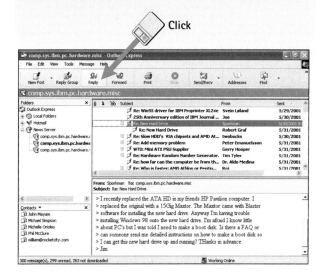

How-To Hints

Questionable Content

Many Internet newsgroups host content that you might find very offensive. These groups are usually easily identified by the name of the newsgroup itself and can thus be avoided. Nonetheless, Outlook Express contains no safeguards to make these groups off-limits. For this reason, many companies do not permit the use of newsgroups at all. Don't let the possibility of objectionable content scare you away from using them, however. Newsgroups can also be a very valuable resource.

Privacy

When you post a message to a newsgroup, the e-mail address configured in your newsreader program (Outlook Express, for example) is posted along with that message. Many collectors of e-mail addresses collect names from newsgroup postings. Collections are then sold to those people who send you all that unsolicited e-mail. If privacy is a major concern of yours, you may want to avoid posting to newsgroups, or you can change the e-mail address configured in your newsreader program to a fake address such as **see_my_signature_file@fakeISP.com**.

How to Post to a Newsgroup

You've seen how to subscribe to a newsgroup and how to browse the messages inside a particular newsgroup. You've also seen how to reply to existing messages you find. Posting a new message of your own is a very easy task, much like sending an e-mail message.

Begin

1 Open a Newsgroup

Open the newsgroup to which you want to post a message by clicking it once in the **Folders** list, under the name of the news server.

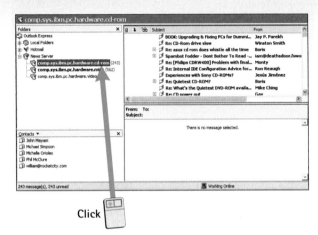

Click

2 Start a Message

After you are connected to a newsgroup, start a new posting by clicking the **New Post** button on the Outlook Express toolbar. A new, blank message window opens with the newsgroup's address filled in for you.

Click

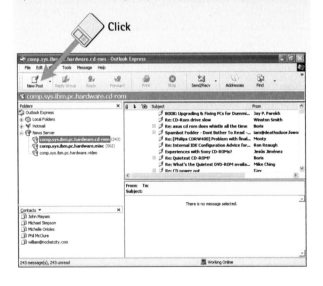

3 Enter a Subject

In the new message window, type the subject for your message in the **Subject** box. Try to keep it fairly short (so that others can see it all in their Inbox windows), but also be as specific as possible. The title bar of the message window changes to reflect the text of the subject you enter.

4 Write a Message

Type your message into the main window.

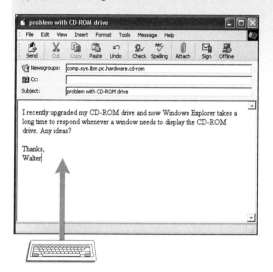

5 Post the Message

After you have typed your message, click the **Send** button on the toolbar to post your message. Check back with the newsgroup occasionally to see whether anyone has responded.

Click

How-To Hints

Newsgroup Etiquette

There is a certain etiquette expected of people who post to newsgroups, and other users are very likely to let you know if you ignore that etiquette. First, don't type your message all in capital letters, even if you think it looks more urgent that way. Capitals are used to indicate shouting and anger. If you have a helpful reply to someone's question, post it publicly so that everyone can read it instead of replying privately. When you reply to a message, try not to include the entire original message in the post unless the original text is very brief. Instead, trim the message so that only the pertinent parts are reposted. Finally, don't post advertisements for products or services in any newsgroups that don't specifically allow it. This kind of post is known as *spam* and is considered poor form. You should also avoid posting entire messages only to make replies such as "thank you" or "I agree" that don't add value to the conversation.

End

Task

1 How to Set Up a Small Network   **124**

2 How to Set Up Additional User Accounts   **128**

3 How to Share an Internet Connection   **130**

4 How to Use My Network Places   **132**

5 How to Add a Network Place   **134**

6 How to Find a Computer on the Network   **136**

7 How to Find a File on the Network   **138**

8 How to Share a File or Folder with Others   **140**

9 How to Map a Network Drive   **142**

Working on a Network

*I*f you use Windows XP in a corporate environment, chances are that your computer is already on a network. If you have more than one computer at home or in a small office, you might be surprised to learn how easy it is to network those computers together yourself.

A *network* is really just a bunch of computers (and sometimes other devices) that are connected together—a setup often referred to as a local area network, or LAN. Sometimes these LANs are connected together over different types of telephone lines to form one large network—often called a wide area network, or WAN. The first task in this part gives you an overview of setting up a network. By referring to that task, to the tasks in the Appendix, "Installing Windows XP," and to the setup instructions that come with whatever networking hardware (networking cards, hubs, and so on) you decide on, you should have no problem setting up a small network.

When your computer is part of a network, you can share files, folders, and printers on one computer with other computers on the network. On a Windows network, computers and users are grouped together in one of two ways: *domains* or *workgroups*. Domains are fairly complicated networks, often used by large companies. Powerful computers called *servers* provide security, Internet access, file storage, and much more to less powerful computers called *workstations*. Workgroups are used on smaller networks and are usually groups of workstations networked together with no servers. Each of the workstations takes an equal part in the network and are often called peers. If you are setting up your own network, you'll almost certainly use a workgroup.

When you allow other people to access resources on your computer, you must think about security. There might be some resources that you want everyone on the network to be able to access. There are other resources that you want only certain people to be able to use. Windows XP lets you arrange this with *permissions*. For each resource you share with the network, permissions allow you to specify who can access that resource and exactly what he or she can do with it. You'll learn more about permissions and what you can do with them in Part 9.

Don't worry if all of this sounds complicated. Windows XP does a pretty good job of hiding the complexities of networking. ●

How to Set Up a Small Network

Windows XP makes it easy to configure a small network after all the networking hardware is in place and the computers are physically connected. The installation instructions that come with the hardware you're using to create the network will help you physically connect your computers. Windows XP is all you need to handle the communications between the connected devices. This task provides an overview of setting up your network.

2 Install Network Adapter Cards

A network adapter card must be installed into each computer that will be on the network. The card translates information back and forth between your computer and the network cable attached to the card. Follow the instructions that come with your network card to install it in your computer. When possible, try to use the same brand and model card in all the computers in the network; this will make troubleshooting and replacing cards much easier later.

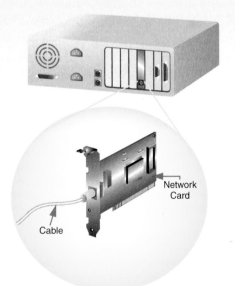

Network Card

Cable

Begin

1 Buy Your Networking Hardware

The majority of networks installed today (and usually the only type of cards, hubs, and other hardware available in stores these days) use a type of cable called *twisted pair*. Twisted pair cable looks like a thick phone cable with jacks on the ends that are slightly wider than normal phone jacks. Cables and hardware are rated based on industry standards. As of the publication of this book, the highest standard officially available is Category 5e, although standards for Category 6 are in the works. Make sure that all the hardware and cables you use are rated at least Category 5e.

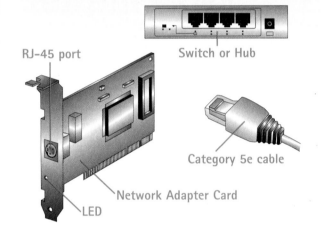

RJ-45 port

Switch or Hub

Category 5e cable

Network Adapter Card

LED

3 Set Up a Hub or Switch

If you have only two computers to network, you can connect them directly together using a *crossover cable* (a cable in which some of the wires are switched). Connect one end of the cable to each computer and that's it. If you have more than two computers, each computer must be connected to a central hub or switch with a normal cable (that is, not a crossover cable). Switches offer some advantages over hubs (including speed and ease of configuration), and are only about 15–20% more expensive. Use a switch when possible.

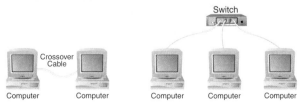

Switch

Crossover Cable

Computer   Computer   Computer   Computer   Computer

4 Set Up a Router

If you have a broadband Internet connection, such as a cable modem or DSL line, routers are available that can connect directly to your cable or DSL modem and then share your Internet connection automatically with the rest of your network. Many of these routers contain a built-in switch so that you can simply connect your computers right to it without using a separate hub or switch. Some routers even contain built-in firewalls that protect your computers from the Internet. If you don't want to use a router, you can still share an Internet connection with other computers on the network using Windows XP.

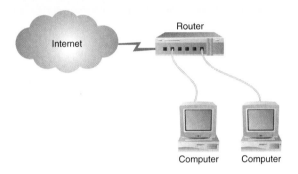

Internet — Router — Computer Computer

6 Connect Cables

After you've decided where the computers (and other network hardware) will be located, it's time to hook up the cables. Just plug one end of a cable into each computer and plug the other end into one of the jacks on your switch or hub. When the cables are connected, the physical part of setting up the network is finished. Next, you'll be working with Windows.

Switch

5 Set Up Other Networking Devices

Devices such as printers and fax machines can connect directly to the network cable in the same way that a computer with a network card does. These devices can then be shared by all computers on the network. On a small network, you probably won't use such devices. Instead, you might want to share the printer (or other device) attached to one of your computers with the rest of the network. For now, just make sure that the device is hooked up to the computer in the location you desire. You'll configure it later.

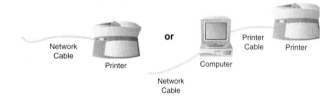

Network Cable — Printer — **or** — Computer — Printer Cable — Printer — Network Cable

7 Install Windows XP

You'll have to install Windows XP on each of the computers on the network. It doesn't matter which edition of Windows XP you use—Home Edition or Professional. You can even use one edition on some computers and the other edition on other computers. In fact, you can even use previous versions of Windows on some of the computers (although you might have to do a little more configuring than with Windows XP). All editions and versions of Windows will talk to one another on the network. For details on installing Windows XP, see the Appendix.

Continues

8 Name the Computers

During the installation of Windows XP, you will be asked to provide a name for your computer. The setup program suggests one for you, but it is usually a somewhat convoluted name with lots of numbers in it. The name of the computer distinguishes it from the other computers on the network. For this reason, it is best to use simple names that help you identify each computer. For example, you might want to name the computers after the people who use them (**John**, **Mary**, and **Simon**, for example) or after the rooms where the computers are located (**Den**, **Kitchen**, and **Bedroom**, for example).

9 Join the Same Workgroup

During the installation of Windows XP, you will be asked to make the computer a member of either a domain or workgroup. For a small network, you will want to choose the **Workgroup** option and type in the name of the workgroup. It doesn't really matter what workgroup name you use, as long as all the computers on the network use the same workgroup name. You could use your own last name or anything else you like. You can read more about this step (and the rest of the Windows XP installation) in the Appendix.

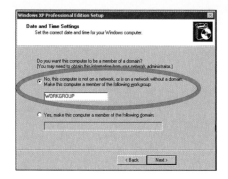

10 Set Up Network Adapter Cards

After you have installed Windows on each computer, turn on the computers. It is likely that Windows XP figured out what type of network adapter card you are using and configured it for you during installation. If Windows could not determine the network card, you will be asked the first time you start Windows after the installation to insert the disk that came with your network adapter card. Windows then finishes configuring your card (you might be prompted to restart the computer).

11 Make Sure the Network Works

When all the computers are turned on and Windows has started, you'll want to determine whether the network is actually working. Double-click the **My Network Places** icon on your desktop and then click the **View workgroup computers** link on the left side of the window. The resulting window should show a list of computers on the network. If no computers are shown, try another computer on the network. If none of the computers show any other computers, something is probably wrong with your switch or hub. If some computers show up and some don't, something is probably wrong with those computers. Double-check your installation.

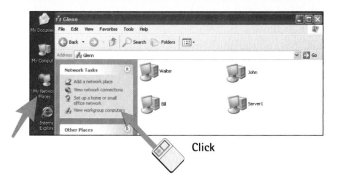

Click

12 Share Folders and Files

When you know that the network is working, it's time to set up a few things. The first thing you'll want to do is go to each computer and share the folders and files you want other computers to be able to access. You learn how to do this in Task 8, "How to Share a File or Folder with Others."

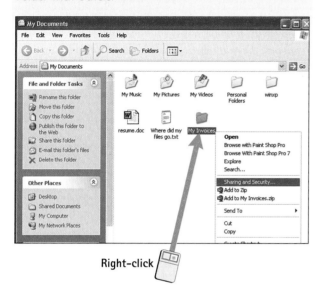

Right-click

13 Share Printers

You'll also want to share any printers that you want other computers to use. This process is covered in Part 3, "Printing."

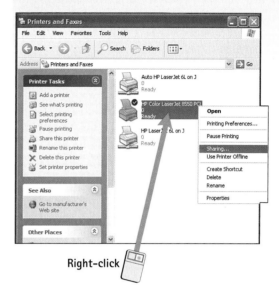

Right-click

14 Share an Internet Connection

If one of your computers has an Internet connection (whether it be a dial-up modem connection or a broadband connection such as cable or DSL), you can share the connection with all the computers on the network. Sharing an Internet connection is covered in Task 3, "How to Share an Internet Connection."

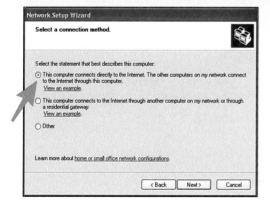

15 Get to Work

Your network should now be ready to use. Remember to check the rest of this part and the other parts of this book (particularly Part 5, "Using Internet E-Mail and Newsgroups," and Part 9, "Protecting Your Files") for more on using your network.

End

How to Set Up Additional User Accounts

User accounts provide an easy and secure way to share a single computer with more than one person. Although you could let different people share the same user account, creating different accounts has some advantages. For example, if each person using the computer has an individual user account, each person can have his or her own desktop settings (background, icons, sounds, and so on), **Favorites** folder in Internet Explorer, and set of folders in Outlook Express. When you first install Windows, two accounts are created. One is named by whatever name you provide to Windows during installation (usually your name). The other is called a **Guest** account and has very limited capabilities. This task shows you how to set up additional user accounts.

Begin

1 Open User Accounts

Click the **Start** button and choose **Control Panel** to open the **Control Panel** window. Double-click the **User Accounts** icon to open the **User Accounts** window. It's possible that your **Control Panel** window will open in category view, which groups the various icons in the **Control Panel** according to their use and even hides some of the more useful ones. If your **Control Panel** is in category view (you'll know because it will look different from the figure here), click the **Switch to Classic View** link on the left side of the window to enter the more useful classic view.

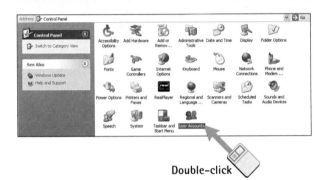

Double-click

2 Create a New Account

The **User Accounts** window shows the accounts currently configured on the computer. Click **Create a new account**.

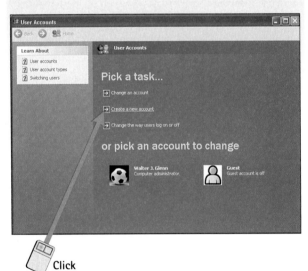

Click

3 Name the New Account

Type a name for the new account. With a small number of users, it is usually best to use the first name of the person for whom you are creating the account. If two people have the same first name, you might want to use a last initial or some other variation of the name.

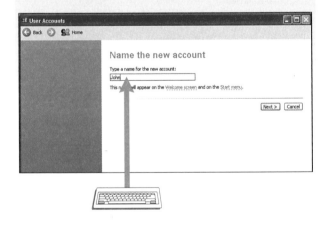

4 Choose the Type of Account to Create

Each user account you create can be one of two types. A person with a **Computer Administrator** account can add, change, and delete other user accounts. That user can also install and remove software and make changes (usually done through the **Control Panel**) that affect all users of the computer. A person with a **Limited** account can change their own password, work with programs already installed by a **Computer Administrator**, and make limited configuration changes (such as to desktop backgrounds). After you choose the type of account you want to create, click **Create Account**.

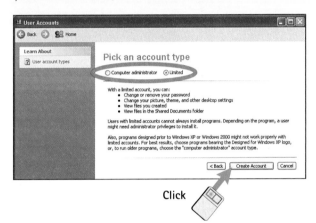

Click

5 Change an Account

From the main **User Accounts** window, you can also change existing user accounts if you are allowed to do so (you must be using an account of the **Computer Administrator** type to make these kinds of changes). Click the **Change an account** link.

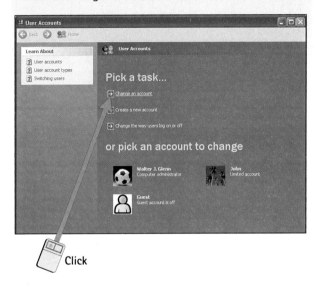

Click

6 Choose an Account to Change

Click the account to which you want to make changes.

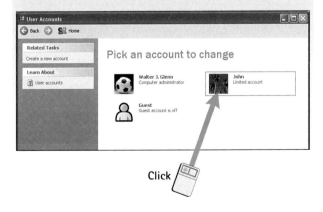

Click

7 Select Changes to Make

Click the link for the change you want to make. You can change the name of the account, the picture that appears beside it, the type of account, and the password. You can also delete the account altogether.

Click

End

TASK 3

How to Share an Internet Connection

One of the biggest advantages of a home network (aside from playing games together and transferring large files easily) is the ability to share a single Internet connection among several computers. This task explains how to set up the computer that has the Internet connection so that the connection is shared with the other computers on the home network.

1 Start the Home Networking Wizard

These steps should be performed on the computer that has the Internet connection. Refer to the How-To Hints at the end of this task for instructions on setting up the other computers in your network. Click **Start** and choose **All Programs, Accessories, Communications, Network Setup Wizard**.

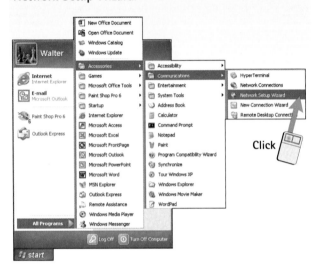

Click

2 Click Next Twice

Click **Next** to go past the **Welcome** page of the wizard. Click **Next** again to go past the page that tells you that your computers must be connected together before starting the wizard.

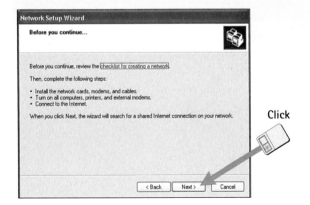

Click

3 Select the Connection Method

Select the first listed option—**This computer connects directly to the Internet**. When you set up the other computers on your home network (as explained in the How-To Hints at the end of this task), you'll select one of the other options in this list. Click **Next** to go on.

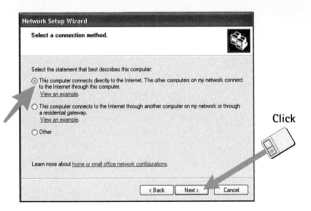

Click

4 Choose the Internet Connection

Choose the specific connection that your computer uses to connect to the Internet. This connection could be a modem or it might be a networking card if you are directly connected. Click **Next** to continue.

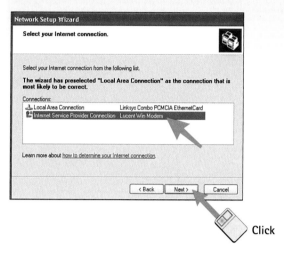

Click

5 Enter a Description for the Computer

Optionally, you can type a description for the computer that makes it easier for others on the network to identify it as the computer sharing an Internet connection. Click **Next** to go on.

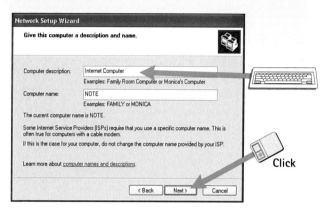

Click

6 Apply Network Settings

The wizard presents a summary of the settings you have chosen. When you have reviewed them and are sure that you want to apply them, click **Next**. When you are done, the wizard will let you know that the process has been successful; click **Finish** to exit the wizard.

Click

How-To Hints

Setting Up Other Computers on the Network

After you have set up the computer with the Internet connection, run the **Home Networking Wizard** from each of the other computers on the network. On those computers, select the **This computer connects to the Internet through another computer on my network** option when asked for a connection method in Step 3.

Configuring a Firewall

When you set up a network connection that Windows recognizes as an Internet connection Windows automatically configures firewall software on the connection. For the most part, this software requires no configuration on your part. If you suspect that the firewall is not active for a connection, click the **Start** button and choose **Network Connections**. Right-click the connection that is used for the Internet, choose **Properties**, and select the **Advanced** tab. You can enable or disable the firewall for the connection on this tab.

End

TASK 4

How to Use My Network Places

Most of what you do on the network is done using the **My Network Places** icon on your desktop. If you do not see the **My Network Places** icon on your desktop, you can find it on your **Start** menu or add it to your desktop using the procedure described in Part 1. With it, you can access all the shared resources your network has to offer, add new network places of your own, and even search for computers and documents on the network.

Begin

1 Open My Network Places

Double-click the **My Network Places** icon on your desktop to open the **My Network Places** window.

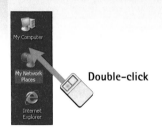

Double-click

2 View Workgroup Computers

The **My Network Places** window shows a list of all the shared folders on the local network. You can double-click any of them to open the folder and look for files. If you are in a workgroup, you'll also see a **View workgroup computers** link in the left column; if you are in a domain, you'll see an **Entire Network** link. Both links work the same way and let you further browse the resources on a network. Click the appropriate link or icon to begin browsing.

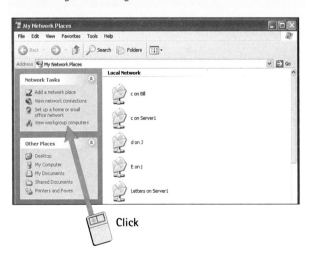

Click

3 Open a Computer

The workgroup window shows all the other computers in your workgroup. Double-click a computer to open its window.

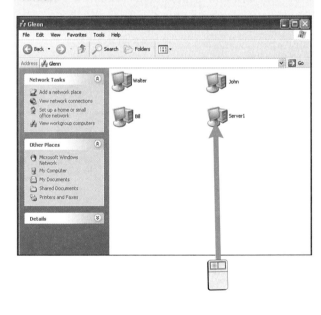

Click

4 Open a Shared Folder

When you open a particular computer, all the resources shared on that computer are listed in this window. The computer's "resources" include shared folders, files, and printers. Double-click any shared object to open it.

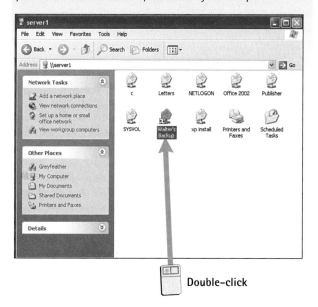

Double-click

5 Open a File

You can use items in a shared folder just as you use items on your own computer. Double-click a file to open it.

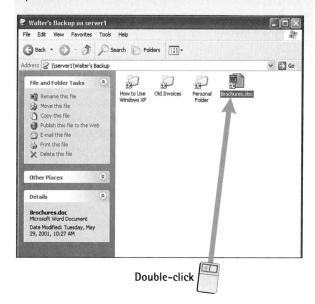

Double-click

6 Copy a File to Your Computer

Instead of just opening and modifying a file on someone else's computer, you might want to copy it to your computer. To do that, just drag the file directly onto your desktop or into any open folder on your desktop.

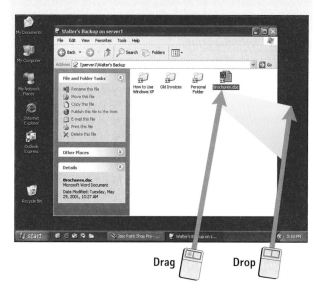

Drag   Drop

How-To Hints

Using Files and Folders

For more information on using files and folders, see Part 2, "Working with Files and Folders."

End

How to Add a Network Place

Although you can use **My Network Places** to browse the network looking for the right folder, you might want to add frequently used shared folders on your network, Web sites, or even FTP sites directly to the **My Network Places** window. Doing so lets you quickly get to files you use often.

Begin

1 Add a Network Place

In the **My Network Places** window, click the **Add a network place** link to launch the **Add Network Place Wizard**. On the welcome page of the wizard, click **Next** to continue.

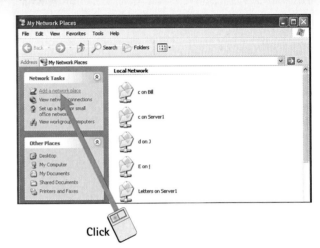

Click

2 Select Other Network Location

You can configure a remote storage location on the Microsoft Network if you have an account there, or you can configure a shortcut to a place on your local network. In this example, you'll create a shortcut to a place on your local network: Select **Other Network Location** and click Next.

Click

3 Browse for a Computer

If you know the exact path to the network resource you want, enter it in the text box. Don't be concerned that the text asks for the "name of a server." Type the path of any resource for which you are creating a network place. If you don't know the exact path, click the **Browse** button.

Click

4 Select the Network Resource You Want

The **Browse** window lists all the computers in your domain or workgroup. Select the computer that contains the shared resource you want from the list, select the folder in that computer, and click **OK**. Note that you can select an entire computer if you want to make a network shortcut.

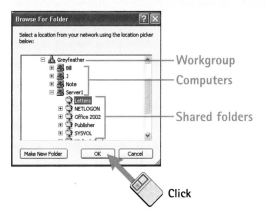

Workgroup
Computers
Shared folders

Click

5 Click Next

The path for the resource you've chosen appears in the **Type the location** text box on the wizard page. Click **Next** to go on.

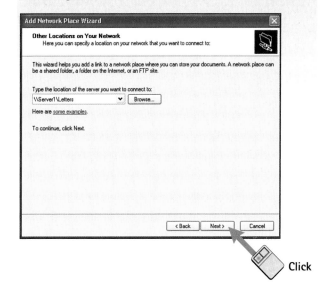

Click

6 Enter a Name for the Network Place

A name for the new shortcut is suggested for you. If you want to name it something different, type the new name in the **Enter a name for this network place** box and click **Next**.

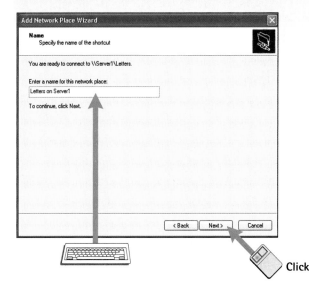

Click

7 Finish

Click **Finish**. When you are done, the new shortcut is available in the **My Network Places** window.

Click

End

TASK 6

How to Find a Computer on the Network

Using the **My Network Places** window to browse your network and locate a computer works fine if there are not a lot of computers on your network. Sometimes, however, the list of computers can be so long that scrolling around looking for a particular computer can be quite time consuming. Fortunately, Windows lets you quickly find a computer on the network, even if you know only part of its name.

Begin

1 Open My Network Places

Double-click the **My Network Places** icon on your desktop to open the **My Network Places** window.

Double-click

2 Open the Search Pane

Click the **Search** button on the toolbar to open the **Search Companion** pane on the left side of the **My Network Places** window.

Click

3 Enter a Computer Name

Type the name of the computer you are looking for in the **Computer name** text box. You can type just part of a name if you don't remember the whole thing.

4 Search for the Computer

Click the **Search** button to begin the search. Results of your search are displayed in the right pane of the **My Network Places** window.

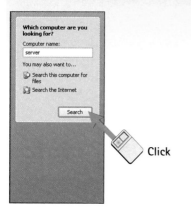

Click

5 Open the Computer

You can open any computer displayed in the search results list simply by double-clicking it. In this example, my search for a computer with the partial name **server** turned up only one match: **Server1**.

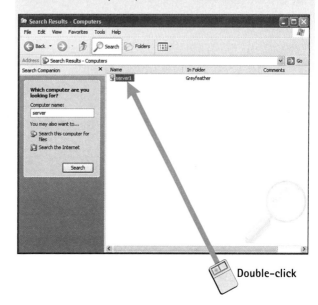

Double-click

6 Close the Search Pane

Click the **Search** button on the toolbar again to close the **Search Companion** pane and get back to work.

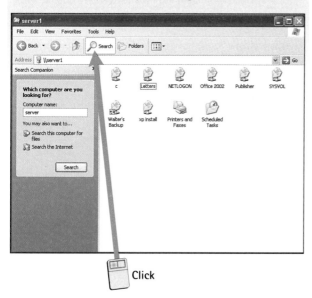

Click

How-To Hints

Auto-filling

As it does in many other places throughout the system, Windows remembers searches you have performed in the past. As you type your search term, Windows will try to fill in the rest of the search term for you based on what it remembers.

End

How to Find a File on the Network

Windows does not really have the built-in capability to search an entire network full of computers for a particular file. However, it is easy enough to perform a regular search on a shared folder. This, at least, saves you from having to rummage through the shared folder and its subfolders yourself. The trick is to know at least the names of the computer and shared folder holding the document for which you are looking.

Begin

1 Open Computers Near Me

In the **My Network Places** window, click the **View workgroup computers** link to open the workgroup window. If you are on a domain, click the **Entire Network** link instead. Both links work the same way.

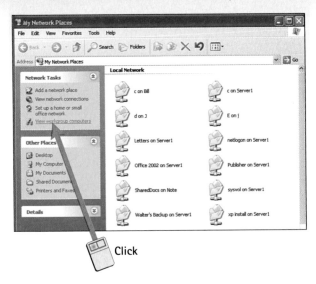

Click

2 Open a Computer

Double-click the computer on which you want to search for a file.

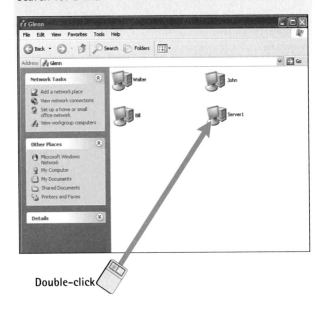

Double-click

3 Search a Shared Folder

Find the shared folder in which you want to search for a file. Right-click the folder and choose **Search** from the shortcut menu that appears. The **Search Results** window opens with the **Search Companion** pane on the left.

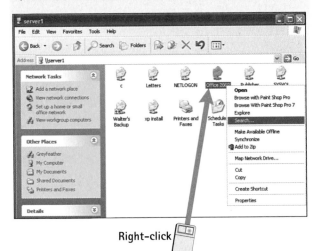

Right-click

4 Enter the Name of a File

Type the name of a file for which you want to search in the text box. You can also enter part of a name if you don't remember the whole thing.

5 Search for the File

Click the **Search** button to begin the search. Results are displayed in the right pane of the **Search Results** window.

Click

6 Open the File

After you find the file for which you are looking, double-click it to open it, or drag it to your desktop to copy it from the shared folder to your computer.

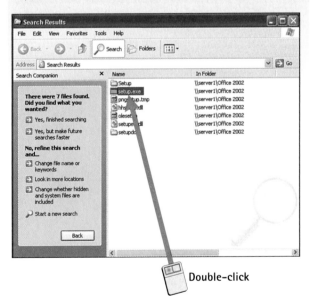

Double-click

How-To Hints

Searching from the Start Menu

You can also get to the **Search Results** window by choosing **Search** from the **Start** menu. When the **Search Results** window appears, select the type of file for which you want to search. Next, enter the filename and use the **Look In** drop-down list to browse to the shared folder you want to search. Learn more about the Windows search feature in Part 2, "Working with Files and Folders."

End

How to Share a File or Folder with Others

In addition to giving you access to other user's files, folders, and printers, networks allow you to share your resources with other users. To share resources, your computer must be on a network and your network administrator must have already set up your computer so that you can share items with others.

Begin

1 Open the Sharing Dialog Box

Using the **My Computer** or **My Documents** window, find the folder or file you want to share. Right-click it and choose **Sharing and Security** from the shortcut menu to open the **Sharing** tab of the item's **Properties** dialog box. This task focuses on sharing a folder, but the process of sharing a file is the same.

2 Share the Folder

Click the **Share this folder on the network** option to enable sharing of the folder.

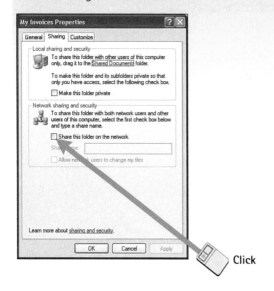

3 Change the Share Name

Windows names the shared folder the same as the original name of the folder. If you want, type a new share name in the text box for the folder you are sharing.

4 Allow Network Users to Change Files

When you share the file, Windows automatically turns on the **Allow network users to change my files** option. If you would rather other people be able to view your files, but not change them, disable this option.

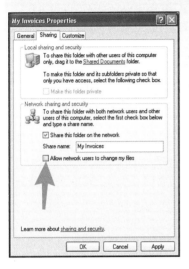

5 Learn More

The Windows XP Help system contains a large amount of useful information on sharing files. To access this information quickly, click the **sharing and security** link at the bottom of the tab.

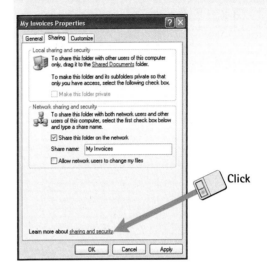

Click

6 Close the Properties Dialog Box

Click **OK** to close the **Properties** dialog box. Users can now access the folder you just shared.

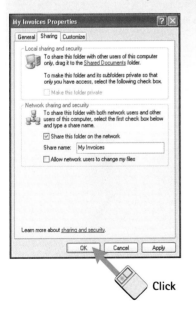

Click

How-To Hints

How Do You Know It's Shared?

A shared file or folder shows up on your computer as a standard icon with a hand underneath the icon.

Setting Permissions

By using the procedure outlined in this task, you are sharing a resource with everyone on a network. See Part 9, "Protecting Your Files," for more on sharing with selected users.

End

How to Map a Network Drive

Earlier in this part, you learned how to add a new Network Place so that you could access frequently used shared folders more easily. Before there was such a thing as the **My Network Places** window, you created shortcuts to other locations on the network by mapping a network drive. When you *map* a network drive, you essentially tell your computer to treat a shared resource as a drive on your computer—the resource even gets its own drive letter and shows up in the **My Computer** window. Older programs sometimes don't know how to use Network Places and can only open files on real disk drives. By mapping a network drive, you can fool these programs into thinking that a shared folder is a real disk drive.

Begin

1 Open Computers Near Me

In the **My Network Places** window, click the **View workgroup computers** link. If you are on a domain, click the **Entire Network** link instead. Both links work the same way.

Click

2 Open a Computer

Find the computer that contains the shared folder you want to map as a network drive and double-click it.

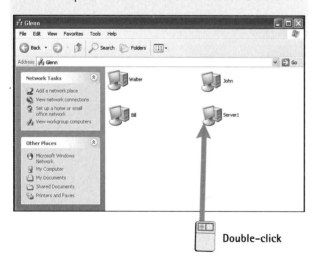

Double-click

3 Select a Shared Folder

Find the shared folder you want to map and select it by clicking it once.

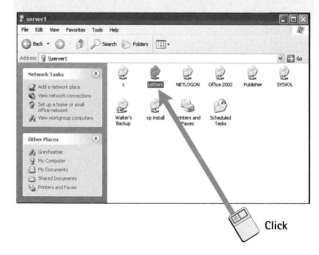

Click

4 Choose Map Network Drive

From the **File** menu, choose the **Map Network Drive** command. The **Map Network Drive** dialog box opens.

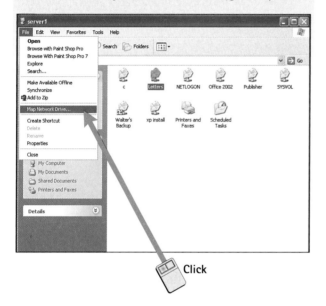

Click

5 Select a Drive Letter

Select a drive letter using the **Drive** drop-down menu. Only letters that are not already used on your computer are listed here, so you don't have to worry about conflicts.

Click

6 Reconnect at Logon

If you want the network drive to be remapped to the same drive letter each time you log on to your computer, click the **Reconnect at logon** option. When you're done, click **Finish**.

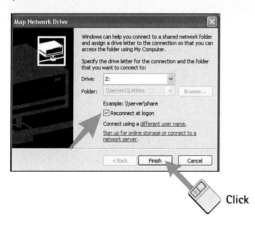

Click

7 View the New Drive

In the **My Computer** window, the new network drive appears using the drive letter you assigned it in Step 5. Network drives look like a regular disk drive with a network cable attached.

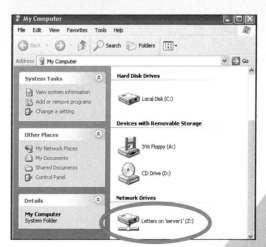

End

Task

1   How to Create and Fill a Briefcase   **146**

2   How to Take a Briefcase with You   **148**

3   How to Update Files in a Briefcase   **150**

4   How to Make Items Available Offline   **152**

5   How to Use Offline Items   **154**

6   How to Synchronize Offline Items   **156**

7   How to Change Offline Settings   **158**

PART 7

Working Away from the Network

*M*any people work when they're away from their network or computer. Some connect over a modem, some take work to another computer on disk, and some actually take their computers on the road with them. Windows XP offers two distinct ways to work when you are away from your usual setup. The first way is with a utility named the **Windows Briefcase**. The second way is to use offline folders.

The *briefcase* is a special folder designed primarily for users who want to take work to another computer using a floppy, Zip, or other type of removable disk. All you have to do is copy files from your main computer into the briefcase, move the briefcase to a disk, and carry the disk with you. Offline folders are available only in Windows XP Professional, not in the Home Edition. You can work on and save the files right in the briefcase. When you return, carry the disk back, move the briefcase back onto your main computer, and synchronize the updated files in the briefcase with the originals on your hard disk. When you *synchronize* a briefcase, any files with a later modification date replace those of the same names with an earlier modification date. This means that the files you changed while you were away replace those on your main computer.

Offline folders are designed for those who actually take their computers away from a network, as do users of notebook computers or those who dial into the network periodically with a modem. Offline folders are available only in Windows XP Professional, not in the Home Edition. You can mark any shared folder available on the network to be available offline. The contents of these folders are copied to the hard drive on your computer. When you are disconnected from the network, you can work on any of the files in the shared folders. When you reconnect to the network, the files are synchronized with the originals. Some people also use offline folders while they are still connected to the network. This allows them to work on copies of the original files instead of on the originals themselves. ●

How to Create and Fill a Briefcase

Creating a briefcase in Windows is pretty easy. After it is created, you can move files into and out of it the same way you move other folders on your computer. You can create a briefcase directly on the desktop or in any folder using the method described in this task.

Begin

1 Create the New Briefcase

Right-click any empty space on your desktop, point to **New** on the shortcut menu, and then choose **Briefcase**. A new icon with the label **New Briefcase** appears on the desktop.

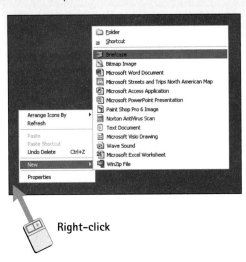

Right-click

2 Open the New Briefcase

Double-click the **New Briefcase** icon to open it. The first time you open any new briefcase, you are shown a welcome screen that gives you a brief introduction to using it.

Double-click

3 Open My Documents

To place objects in the briefcase, you must first locate those objects. Double-click the **My Documents** icon on the desktop to open the **My Documents** window.

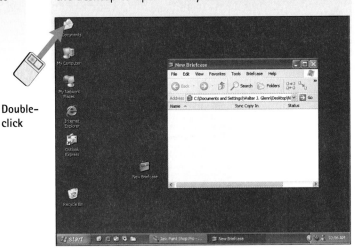

Double-click

4 Tile Windows Vertically

Right-click a blank space on the taskbar and choose **Tile Windows Vertically** so that you can see both the **My Documents** and the **New Briefcase** windows side by side.

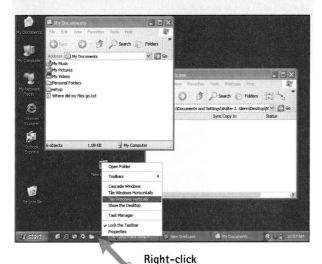

Right-click

5 Drag a File to the Briefcase

Copy any file or folder to your briefcase by simply dragging it to the **New Briefcase** window. You can copy as many files and folders as you want to the briefcase.

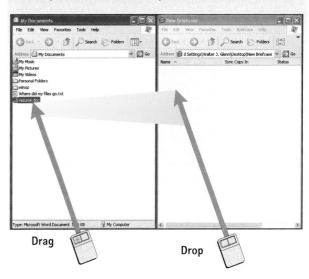

Drag

Drop

How-To Hints

Watch Your Disk Space

If you are using a floppy disk to carry your briefcase, do not copy more files to your briefcase than the disk can hold. Find out how big a briefcase is by right-clicking it and choosing **Properties** from the shortcut menu. If you routinely place more files in the briefcase than will fit on a typical 1.44Mb floppy disk, consider investing in a Zip disk drive. Zip disks hold 100MB or 250MB of data (depending on which drive you buy). You'll need a Zip drive at home and at work.

Renaming Your Briefcase

Rename your briefcase the same way you do any folder. Right-click its icon and choose **Rename** from the shortcut menu. See Part 2, "Working with Files and Folders," for more on renaming folders.

End

How to Take a Briefcase with You

Taking a briefcase with you is as simple as copying it to a floppy disk (or other removable disk). Any computer running Windows 95/98/Me, Windows NT 4.0, Windows 2000, or Windows XP will recognize the briefcase for what it is.

Begin

1 Open My Computer

Double-click the **My Computer** icon on your desktop to open the **My Computer** window.

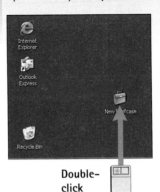

Double-click

2 Move the Briefcase to Your Floppy Drive

Move the mouse pointer over the briefcase icon. Click and hold the left mouse button, then drag the briefcase over the floppy drive icon in the **My Computer** window. Release the mouse button to move the briefcase. You can also right-click the briefcase and choose the **Send To, 3½" floppy A:** command from the shortcut menu.

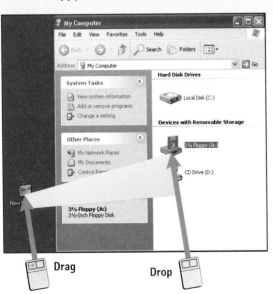

Drag   Drop

3 Open the Briefcase on Your Home Computer

When you're at the computer away from the network, pop the floppy disk into the computer. Open the **My Computer** window, open the floppy drive, and double-click the **New Briefcase** icon to open the briefcase.

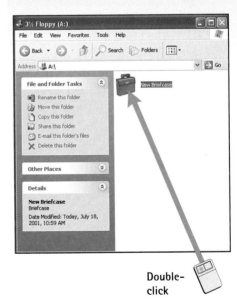

Double-click

4 Open a File from the Briefcase

In the briefcase, find the file you want to work on and double-click to open it.

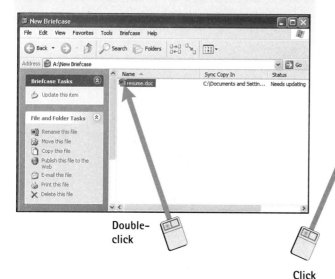

Double-click

Click

5 Save the File

The file opens in whatever application was used to create it. To open a Word file from the briefcase, for example, you must have Microsoft Word installed on your home computer. When you're done working, save the file in the normal manner. The file is updated in the briefcase on the floppy disk.

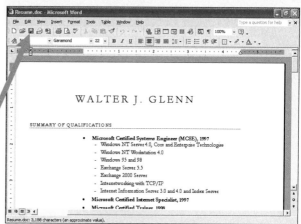

6 Move the Briefcase to Your Work Computer

When you get back to your main computer, insert the floppy disk in the drive, open the **My Computer** window, open the floppy drive, and drag the briefcase onto your desktop. In Task 3, you'll see how to update the files on your main computer with the files in the briefcase.

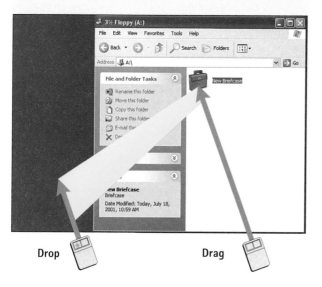

Drop

Drag

How-To Hints

Speeding Up Access

Working from a floppy disk can significantly increase the time required to open and save files. You can move the briefcase to your computer's hard disk (just open the **My Computer** window, double-click the floppy disk drive, and drag the briefcase icon to your desktop) to speed things up. When you're done, drag the briefcase icon back off your desktop onto the floppy disk icon in the **My Computer** window.

Using the Internet

If you have Internet access both at home and at work (or whatever two locations you work from), you can transfer the briefcase between computers over the Internet. E-mail works great for this. Send the briefcase as an attachment to an e-mail message. For more information on sending attachments, see Task 6, "How to Send an Attached File," in Part 5, "Using Internet E-Mail and Newsgroups."

End

How to Update Files in a Briefcase

Now that you are back at work, you have files in your briefcase that have changed from the originals that are still on your work computer. The next step is to update the original files. You do this from within your briefcase.

Begin

1 Open Your Briefcase

Double-click the **New Briefcase** icon to open the **New Briefcase** window. If the briefcase is still on a floppy disk, you should move it back to your desktop first for quicker access.

Double-click

2 Note the Status of Files

In the **New Briefcase** window, choose **View, Details** from the menu bar to switch to **Details** view. The **Status** column tells you which files on your work computer's hard disk need to be updated.

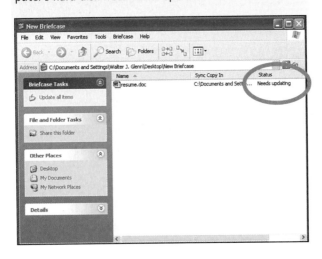

3 Select a File to Update

Select any file you want to update by clicking it once. You can select additional files by holding down the **Ctrl** key while you click other files.

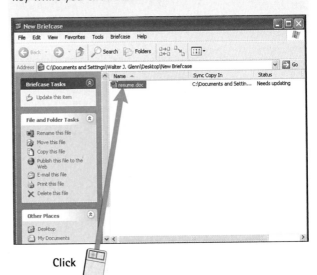

Click

4 Update Selection

From the **Briefcase Tasks** list on the left side of the window, choose the **Update this item** link to update the selected files.

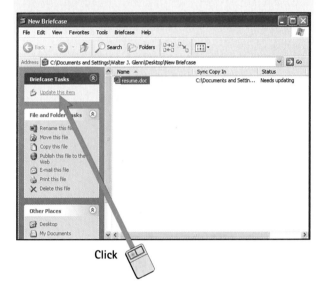

Click

5 Review the Update

After you choose the **Update this item** link, you are given the chance to review the updates in the **Update** window. The version of the file in the briefcase is shown on the left. The original file on your hard disk is shown on the right. The arrow in between indicates which version should be updated.

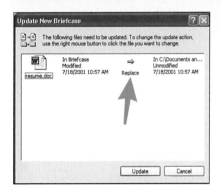

6 Update the File

When you are ready to begin the update, just click the **Update** button. Windows replaces the file on the hard disk with the file in the briefcase. Now both files are identical.

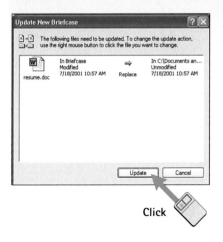

Click

How-To Hints

Updating All

Use the **Update All** button on the toolbar in the **New Briefcase** window to update all the files in the briefcase that need to be updated. A link of the same name is available on the left side of the window if no files are selected.

Resolving Conflicts

If the **Update** window shows a red arrow pointing down between the two versions of a file, it means that both versions have been updated since the original was copied to the briefcase. When this happens, you should open both versions of the file and figure out for yourself which is the most recent.

End

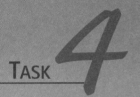

How to Make Items Available Offline

If you are running Windows XP Professional, you can make any shared folder on the network available as an offline folder so that you can use the files inside that folder when you disconnect from the network. Windows does this by copying the files in the shared folder to a temporary location on your computer's hard disk. When you are connected to the network, you can work on the original files. When you disconnect from the network, you work on the temporary copies. When you connect again, any temporary files you worked on are copied back to the original location and replace the older originals. The first time you set up offline access for an item, a wizard helps you. After that, you'll do it manually, as described in these steps.

Begin

1 Open My Network Places

While still connected to the network (either through a direct cable connection or remotely with a dial-up connection), double-click the My Network Places icon to open the My Network Places window.

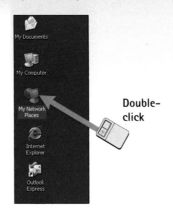

Double-click

2 Open Computers Near Me

Browse for a shared folder on the network using the techniques in Part 6, "Working on a Network." If you don't see the shared folder that contains the files you want make available offline in the My Network Places window, click the View workgroup computers link to browse all the computers on your network for the shared folder. If you are in a domain instead of a workgroup (such as on a large corporate network), you'll see a link named Entire Network instead of View workgroup computers. Both links work the same way.

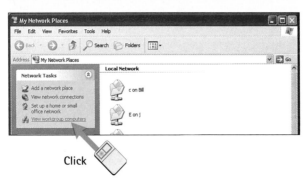

Click

3 Open a Computer

When you find the computer on the network that holds the shared folder you want to change into an offline folder, double-click to open its window.

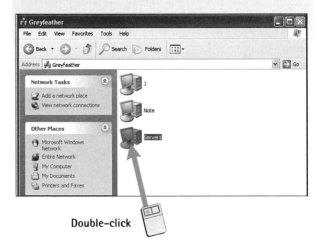

Double-click

4 Locate a Shared Folder

Scroll through the computer window to find the shared folder you want to make available offline. Click once to select it.

Click

5 Make It Available Offline

Right-click the folder you want to make available offline and choose **Make Available Offline** from the shortcut menu.

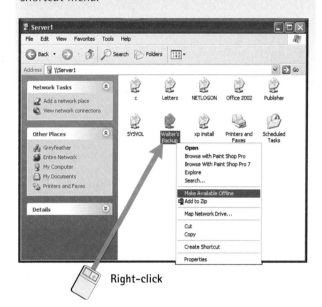

Right-click

6 Make Subfolders Available

You can decide whether to make just the folder you selected available offline or all of its subfolders available, as well. Choose the appropriate radio button and click **OK**. Files from the network folder are copied as temporary files to your computer's hard disk. Should you disconnect from the network, you can work on these temporary files until you reconnect. To use the folder offline, refer to the next task.

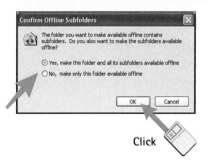

Click

How-To Hints

Making an Item Unavailable

After you make a folder available offline, you can make it unavailable again by right-clicking the folder and choosing the **Make Available Offline** command from the shortcut menu. The temporary files are removed from your hard drive. When you no longer need offline access to a folder, you should make the folder unavailable to reclaim the disk space taken up by the temporary files.

End

How to Use Offline Items

After you set up a folder to be available offline, that folder is surprisingly easy to use. All you have to do is open **My Network Places** and browse to the folder the same way you do when you are connected to the network. When you are offline, only the folders configured for offline use are visible.

Begin

1 Open My Network Places

On the computer that you have taken off the network (your laptop or the remote computer that is no longer connected to the workplace through a telephone connection), double-click the **My Network Places** icon to open the **My Network Places** window. Note that you cannot access items offline unless you have first made those items available as described in the preceding task.

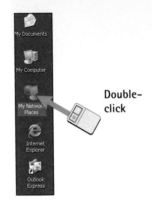

Double-click

2 Open Computers Near Me

Click the **View workgroup computers** or **Entire Network** link (depending on the type of network you're on) to browse for the computer that contains the offline folders you want to access.

Click

3 Open a Computer

When you are disconnected from the network, only computers that have shared folders configured for offline use are visible in the window. Double-click the computer's icon to open it.

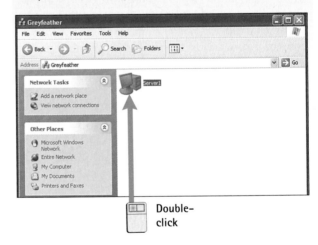

Double-click

4 Open an Offline Folder

When you open a computer, only the shared folders configured for offline use show up in the computer's window—these folders are called, appropriately enough, *offline folders*. Double-click any offline folder to open it.

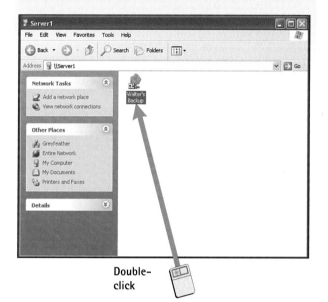

Double-click

5 Open a File

Folders and files in an offline folder have two small arrows at the bottom left of their icons to show that they are offline copies of original files on the network. Double-click any file or folder to open it, just as you would with any regular file or folder.

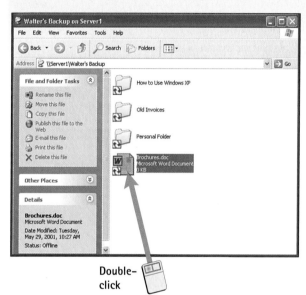

Double-click

How-To Hints

Offline Permissions

When you are using offline folders and files, the same permissions (such as only being able to read and not change a file) apply to you that would apply if you were using the actual shared folders or files on the network. So don't think that you can bypass security just by using offline folders. For more information on permissions, see Part 9, "Protecting Your Files."

Your Network Places

If you have added any of your own Network Places that point to a shared folder (see Part 6, "Working on a Network," for more on this), you might notice that there is no **Make Available Offline** command on the Network Places shortcut menu. To make that shared folder available offline, you actually have to browse to the real shared folder the Network Place represents.

End

How to Synchronize Offline Items

When you have been working on files offline, all you have to do is log back on to the network to automatically synchronize all the files you worked on while you were disconnected. For notebook users, this means hooking your computer back up to the network and logging on. For remote users, this means dialing in and logging on. If you are working with offline folders while you are still connected to the network, you have to synchronize files manually. In this task, you learn to synchronize files manually.

Begin

1 Synchronize a Specific Folder

Use the **My Network Places** icon on your desktop to browse to the offline folder or file you want to synchronize. Right-click the folder or file and choose **Synchronize** from the shortcut menu. The item is automatically synchronized with the original shared item on the network.

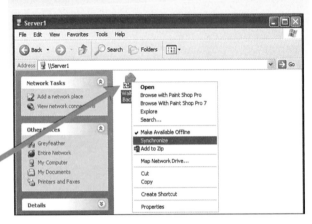

Right-click

2 Synchronize Multiple Folders

You can also synchronize multiple folders and files at once. To do this, open the **Tools** menu of any open folder on your computer and choose **Synchronize**. This method also gives you more control over synchronization by opening an **Items to Synchronize** dialog box.

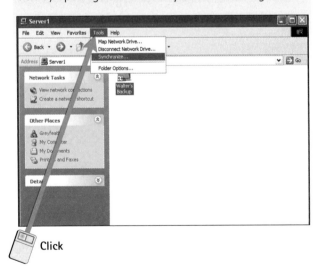

Click

3 Choose Items to Synchronize

The **Items to Synchronize** dialog box shows a list of offline items you can synchronize with their online versions. Select the items you want to synchronize and click **Synchronize**. Remember, when you synchronize an offline item, newer versions of files replace older versions of files. If you worked on files when you were offline, those new versions replace the older versions of the files that were left on the network.

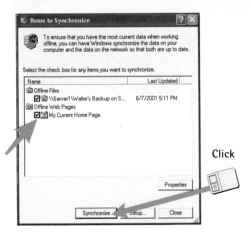

Click

4 Set Up Automatic Synchronization

There are a few ways in which you can configure the automatic synchronization of your files. In the **Items to Synchronize** dialog box, click the **Setup** button to open the **Synchronization Settings** dialog box.

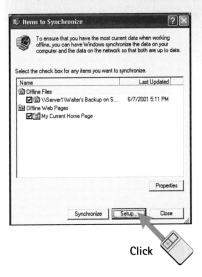

Click

5 Set Up Logon/Logoff Synchronization

From the list, select the items you want to be automatically synchronized when you log on or log off the network. Then choose whether you want the selected items to synchronize during logon, logoff, or both. You can also have Windows ask you before synchronizing any items.

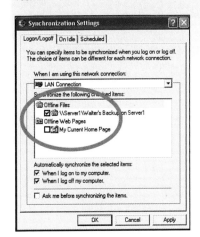

6 Switch to On Idle Tab

In the **Synchronization Settings** dialog box, click the **On Idle** tab to configure your computer to synchronize offline files during idle time—when your computer is connected to the network but is not being used.

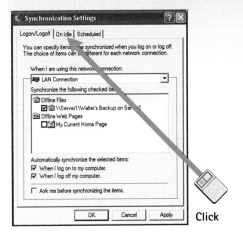

Click

7 Set Up Idle Synchronization

Choose the folders you want to be synchronized during idle time from the list and enable the **Synchronize while my computer is idle** option. You can also click the **Advanced** button to specify how many minutes should pass before your computer is considered idle.

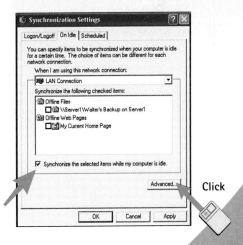

Click

End

How to Change Offline Settings

For the most part, the default settings for offline folders should work pretty well. However, there are a few settings that might be useful to you. For example, you can change when files are synchronized, how much disk space offline files can use, and whether Windows continuously reminds you when you are using offline instead of online files.

Begin

1 Open the Control Panel

Click the **Start** button and then click **Control Panel**. The **Control Panel** window opens.

Click

2 Open Folder Options

Double-click the **Folder Options** icon to open the **Folder Options** dialog box. For more on using the **Control Panel**, see Part 10, "Changing Windows XP Settings." You can also open the **Folder Options** dialog box from the **View** menu of any open folder.

Double-click

3 Open Offline Files Tab

In the **Folder Options** dialog box, click the **Offline Files** tab.

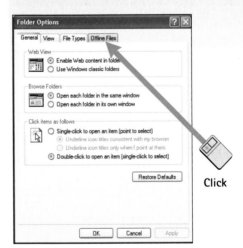

Click

4 Synchronize at Log Off/On

By default, the **Synchronize all offline files when logging on** and **Synchronize all offline files when logging off** options are enabled. If you prefer not to wait through this process each time you log off and on, disable these options. If you disable these options, remember to synchronize your files for offline use (as explained in Task 4, "How to Make Items Available Offline," before disconnecting from the network.

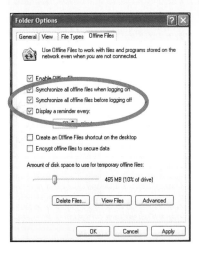

5 Enable Reminders

When the **Display a Reminder every** option is enabled, a small icon appears in the system tray next to your clock to indicate that offline files are being used. In addition, a text bubble appears once in a while as yet another reminder. You can specify the interval at which this reminder appears.

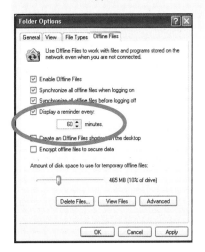

6 Place a Shortcut on the Desktop

When you enable the **Create an Offline File shortcut on the desktop** option, a shortcut named **Shortcut to Offline Files** appears on the desktop. Double-clicking this shortcut opens a window that displays all the files you have configured for offline use.

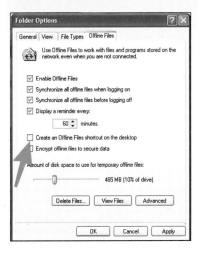

7 Choose Amount of Disk Space to Use

By default, offline folders are allowed to use 10% of the space on your hard drive. You can change this to any amount you like by simply dragging the slider to adjust the percentage. When you're done changing the settings for the offline folder, click **OK** to close the dialog box.

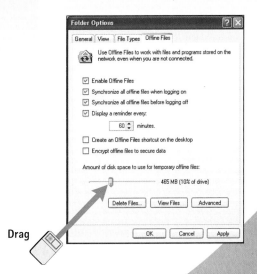

Drag

End

Task

1 How to Play Music and Movies   162

2 How to Record Music   164

3 How to Find Music Online   166

4 How to Make Movies   168

5 How to Work with Pictures   172

6 How to Play Games   174

PART 8

Having Fun with Windows XP

You can't work all the time, and when you want to have some fun with your computer, Windows XP is ready for you with several built-in "fun" programs.

Windows Media Player can play audio CDs, MP3 music files, and movies in a variety of formats. You can use Windows Media Player to search for music on the Internet and even record your own CDs.

With **Windows Movie Maker**, you can take still pictures, movie files, home movies, and even music and put them all together to create your own movie. You can edit and play that movie at any time and even send it to friends.

Windows also includes a number of great games, from the classic **Solitaire** and **Hearts** to fast-action **Pinball**. With the variety of Internet games that are available at sites all over the world, you'll never be without a gaming partner again.

How to Play Music and Movies

Unless you have set up a different player program as your default player, Windows plays music and video files using the Windows Media Player. When you insert an audio CD, video CD, or DVD into your disc drive or double-click a music or movie file stored on your computer, Windows Media Player opens automatically and begins playing. To start this task, use **Windows Explorer** or the **My Documents** window to browse to a music file (a file with the extension **.mp3**, **.wav**, and so on) or a video file (a file with the extension **.mpg**, **.avi**, **.asf**, and so on); double-click it to launch the Windows Media Player.

Begin

1 Pause

You can pause the playback of the audio or video file at any time by clicking the **Pause** button once. While playback is paused, the **Pause** button changes to a **Play** button; click the **Play** button to start playback where you left off.

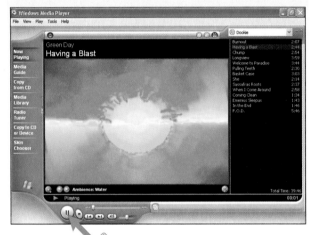

Click

2 Stop

You can stop playback by clicking the **Stop** button. When playback is stopped, the **Pause** button turns into a **Play** button.

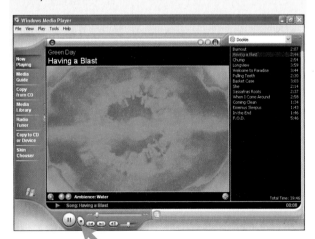

Click

3 Play

When no music or movie is being played or when the movie or audio file is paused, a **Play** button appears. Click it once to start playback.

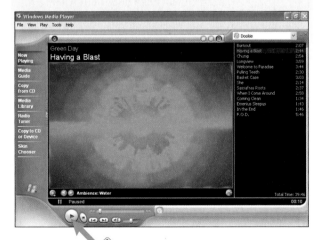

Click

4 Change Volume

Change the volume for the music or video being played by dragging the **Volume** slider to the right (for louder) or to the left (for softer).

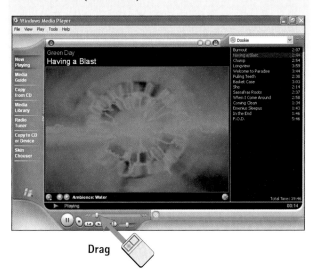

Drag

5 Go Backward and Forward

During playback, you can skip to the previous or next tracks by clicking the single arrows with lines next to them. During playback of some sorts of media (such as movies), you might also see rewind and fast-forward buttons which are small left and right-facing double arrows.

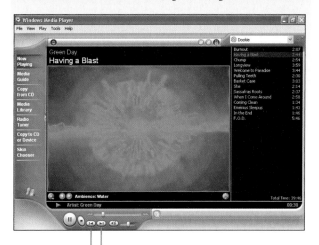

Back One Track ⌐ └ Forward One Track

6 Pick a Track

If you are playing a CD or DVD with multiple tracks, each track is shown in the playlist on the right side of the player screen. Click any track to begin playing it.

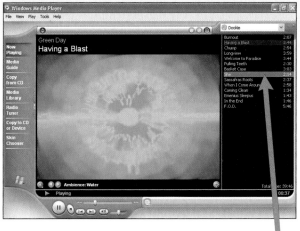

Click

7 Select a Visualization

Visualizations are graphics that move along with the music file as it plays. Windows Media Player includes a number of interesting visualizations. Click the left and right arrows under the visualization window to browse through the available visualizations one at a time; alternatively, click the button with an asterisk to choose a particular visualization from a drop-down list.

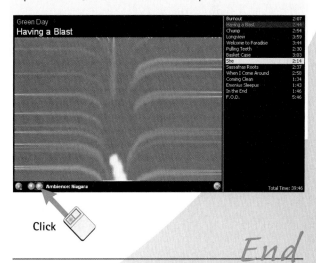

Click

End

How to Record Music

Windows Media Player makes copying tracks from audio CDs easy. You can record songs from an existing audio CD to a file on your hard disk or to another CD if you have a recordable CD drive. You can also convert songs to the popular MP3 format. You can even listen to songs as they're being copied. Copying music for anything other than strictly personal use is a violation of copyright laws. If you want to copy a song to a CD that you can play in your car, you're probably okay. If you want to use a song in a presentation at the office, you're on shaky legal ground.

Begin

1 Start Windows Media Player

Click **Start**, point to **All Programs**, point to **Accessories**, point to **Entertainment**, and then click **Windows Media Player**.

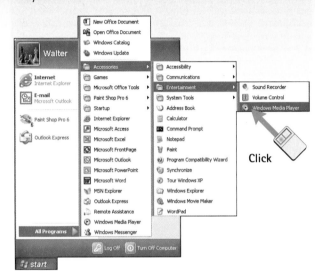

Click

2 Switch to Copy from CD

Click the **Copy from CD** button. If your music CD is not already in the computer's CD-ROM drive, insert it now. If the music begins playing, click the **Stop** button to stop playback.

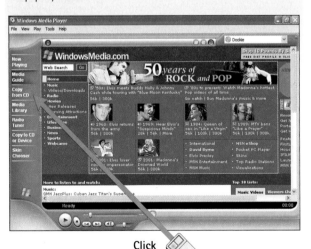

Click

3 Find Album Information

If **Windows Media Player** does not display the album and track information for your CD, click the **Get Names** button at the top of the list. A wizard opens, asks you a few questions, and helps you search the Internet for album information (here you see only generic album information, such as track length).

Click

4 Select Tracks to Copy

By default, all the tracks on the CD are selected to be copied. Deselect a track by clearing the check from the box next to the track (click the box once). Only tracks with check marks will be copied.

Click

5 Open the Options Dialog Box

By default, tracks are copied to the **My Music** folder inside your **My Documents** folder. You can change this location and specify some additional settings from the **Options** dialog box. Open it by choosing **Tools, Options**.

Click

6 Set Options

On the **Copy Music** tab, you can change where the tracks are copied, the file format (such as MP3 and several others) in which the tracks are copied, whether content copy protection is enabled (which basically means that the recording you make can't be further copied and shared), and the quality of the recording (higher quality takes up more disk space). When you've made your selections, click **OK**.

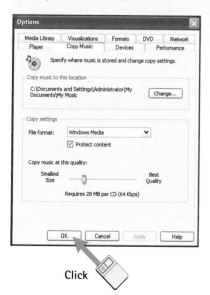

Click

7 Copy the Music

Click the **Copy Music** button to begin copying the selected tracks to the location specified in the **Options** dialog box, with the selected options.

Click

End

How to Find Music Online

Windows Media Player provides two ways to find music on the Internet. The **Media Guide** feature lets you browse for downloadable music and video files. The **Radio Tuner** lets you tune in to streaming Internet audio in dozens of different formats.

Begin

1 Start Windows Media Player

Click **Start**, point to **All Programs**, point to **Accessories**, point to **Entertainment**, and then click **Windows Media Player**.

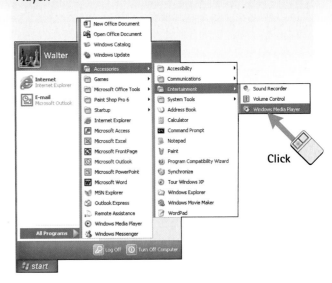

Click

2 Switch to Media Guide

Click the **Media Guide** button to open an Internet connection and jump to the WindowsMedia.com Web site.

Click

3 Browse the Web Site

Use the WindowsMedia.com Web site to browse for all kinds of files you can play in Windows Media Player. The kinds of files available to you on this site include music, videos, news and sports broadcasts, and much more.

4 Switch to Radio Tuner

If you want to listen to a radio station across town or across the globe, switch to the **Radio Tuner** feature. Many radio stations around the world (but not all) broadcast over the Internet. Click the **Radio Tuner** button.

Click

5 Start a Preset List

Just as you can with the radio in your car, Windows Media Player lets you create preset lists of stations. Unlike your car radio (which has a limited number of preset buttons), you can create any number of lists and fill each list with as many stations as you want. A list named **My Stations** is created for you. Switch to it by clicking its link.

Click

6 Find a Station

To find stations to add to your list, use the list of categories on the right side of the window to browse for stations. You can also search for stations by keyword or click the **Find More Stations** link to browse a complete list of radio stations available on the Web.

7 Listen

After you have displayed a list of stations, select a station and then click the **Play** link to begin listening. Click the **Add to My Stations** link to add the selected station to your list.

Click

End

How to Make Movies

Windows XP includes a program named **Windows Movie Maker** that lets you import pictures and movies, edit them, and put them together as a movie. Movie Maker is complex enough that an entire book could be written about it, but this task should give you an idea of what it can do.

Begin

1 Start Movie Maker

Click **Start**, point to **All Programs**, point to **Accessories**, and then click **Windows Movie Maker** to launch the program.

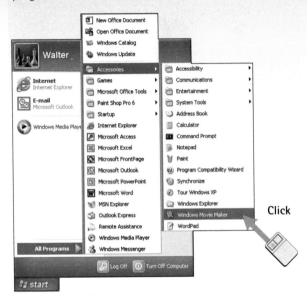

Click

2 Import Files

To import picture or movie files already on your computer into Movie Maker, select **File, Import** from the menu bar.

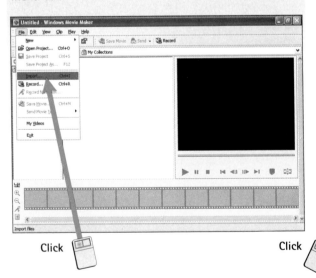

Click

3 Record Video

To record video from a VCR or camcorder, select the **Record** command from the **File** menu. To use this feature, you must have a video card that supports recording from an external device, and the device must be hooked up correctly to this video card.

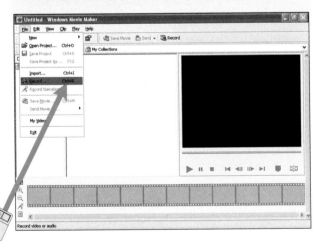

Click

4 View a Collection

When you import pictures or record video into Movie Maker, the files are displayed as part of a collection. By default, the media files are placed into a collection named **My Collection**. When you select a collection from the **Collections** list on the left side of the screen, the files in that collection are displayed as thumbnails on the right side of the screen.

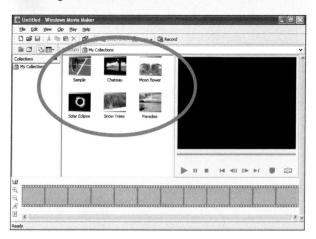

5 Create a New Collection

To organize the files you access in Movie Maker, you can create new collections. Right-click anywhere in the **Collections** list and choose **New Collection** from the shortcut menu.

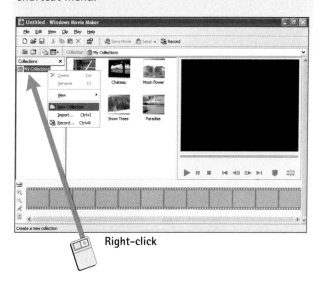

Right-click

6 Name the New Collection

As soon as you create a new collection, you are given the chance to rename it. Type a name for the new collection.

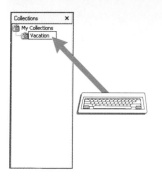

7 Move Files to the New Collection

To move files between collections, select the thumbnails of the files you want to move (the same way you do in Windows), drag them to the new collection in the **Collections** list, and drop the files.

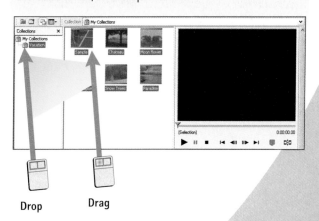

Drop   Drag

Continues

8 Move Pictures to the Storyboard

The *storyboard* is the filmstrip at the bottom of the Movie Maker window. It represents the movie you are currently creating. Each frame of the filmstrip is a picture in the movie. Drag each picture individually to a frame on the storyboard. This task shows the steps to make a slideshow movie out of still pictures.

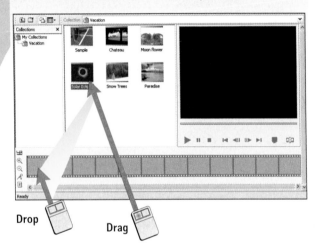

Drop

Drag

9 Show the Timeline

After you have moved all the pictures to the storyboard, you can display the timeline for the movie. The timeline helps you adjust the length of each frame (just slide the divider between frames to adjust the size) and position an audio soundtrack should you decide to include one.

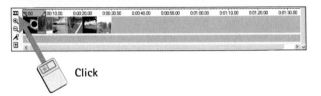

Click

10 Select All Clips on Storyboard

After you have adjusted the lengths of your frames and are ready to make your movie, select all the clips on the storyboard (hold down the **Ctrl** key and click each of the clips in turn).

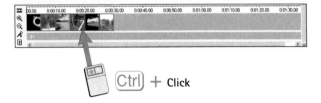

Ctrl + Click

11 Combine the Clips

Combining the clips tells Movie Maker that you want each picture to play in succession when you play the movie. With all clips selected, choose **Clip, Combine** from the menu bar.

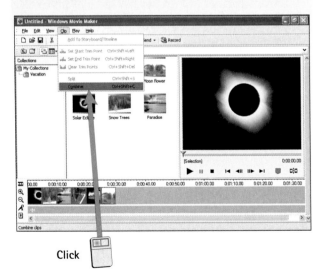

Click

12 Play the Movie

To see what your movie looks like at any time, click the **Play** button. All the frames shown in the storyboard play in sequence. You can assess the flow of the scenes and adjust the duration of the frames in the storyboard.

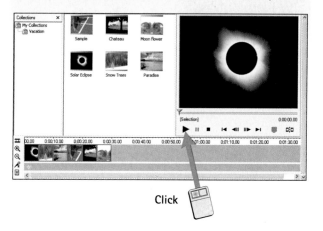

Click

13 Save the Movie

When you are satisfied with your movie, choose **File, Save Movie** from the menu bar. This command opens the **Save Movie** dialog box.

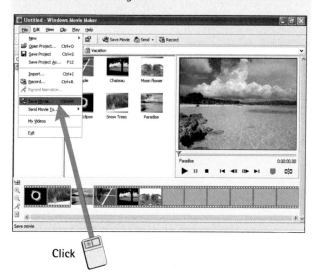

Click

14 Click OK

Use the **Save Movie** dialog box to adjust the quality of the saved movie. Higher-quality movies take up more disk space. When you have made your selection from the **Setting** drop-down list and provided any labeling information, click **OK** to save the movie. Movie Maker converts all the clips and individual pictures files in the storyboard into a single movie file. After the movie is saved, you are given the chance to watch it in Windows Media Player.

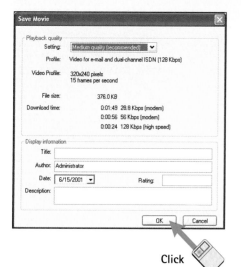

Click

How-To Hints

Recording Audio

You can record your own narration or even include a music soundtrack for your movie. To record narration, just click the button that looks like a microphone to open the **Record Narration Track** dialog box. Click the **Record** button and speak into your computer's microphone to narrate your movie. To add music, click the **Change** button on the **Record Narration Track** and choose a source for the audio. You can record audio from a music CD or another audio device (such as digital tape) that you have hooked up to your computer's sound card.

End

How to Work with Pictures

Most Windows applications store picture files in a folder named **My Pictures**, which you'll find inside the **My Documents** folder. This folder was created to include tools that are specific to working with picture files.

Begin

1 Open My Documents

Double-click the **My Documents** icon on your desktop to open the **My Documents** window. If you don't see the **My Documents** icon on your desktop, you can find it on your **Start** menu, and you can add it to your desktop using the procedure covered in Part1.

Double-click

2 Open My Pictures

Double-click the **My Pictures** icon to open the **My Pictures** folder.

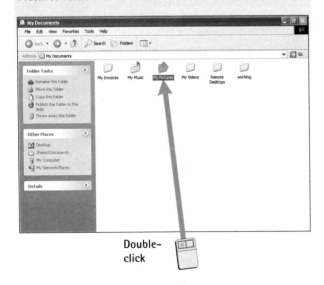

Double-click

3 Select a Picture

Select any picture in the **My Pictures** folder by clicking it once.

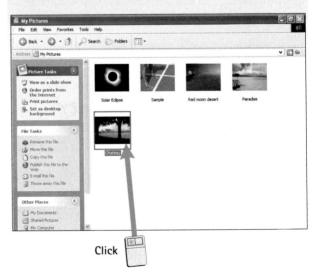

Click

4 Print Pictures

To print the selected picture or pictures, click the **Print Pictures** link in the **Picture Tasks** list on the left side of the window.

Click

5 View as Slideshow

If no pictures are selected or if multiple pictures are selected, click the **View as a slide show** link in the **Picture Tasks** list. Windows shows the selected pictures one by one in full-screen mode. You are given controls to advance, rewind, and stop the slide show.

Click

6 View as Filmstrip

Select the **Filmstrip** command from the **View** menu.

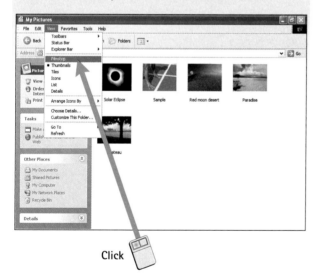

Click

7 Work with the Picture

In filmstrip view, the selected picture is shown enlarged. Use the tools under the enlarged picture to zoom in and out on, size, and rotate the picture. These adjustments affect only the display of the picture and not the picture file itself. In filmstrip view, you can use the **Next** and **Previous** buttons to move through the slides one at a time.

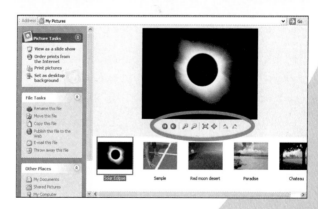

End

TASK 6

How to Play Games

Windows XP includes a number of games that you can play when you get tired of working. Some games you can play by yourself (such as the classic Solitaire); other games require you to sign on to the Internet to find other online gamers you can challenge to rounds of checkers, spades, and backgammon.

1 Start Solitaire

Click **Start**, point to **All Programs**, point to **Games**, and click **Solitaire**. The game opens in a new window.

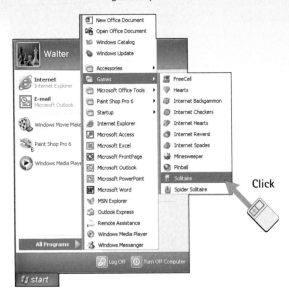

Click

2 Move Cards

To move a card, click it with the left mouse button and drag it to its new location on the seven row stacks. Double-click a card to move it directly to one of the four suit stacks in the top-right corner of the board.

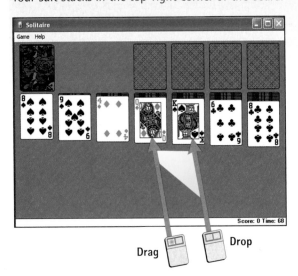

Drag   Drop

3 Get Help

Most Windows games have help systems that explain the rules of the game. To learn about the rules of the game and how to play the game, choose **Help**, **Contents** from the menu bar.

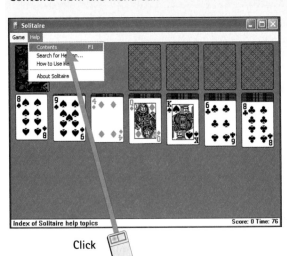

Click

4 Start an Internet Game

Several Internet games are included with Windows. Start one the same way you would a game that can be played from your computer's hard disk: Click **Start** and choose **All Programs, Games**; then choose the name of the Internet game you want to play.

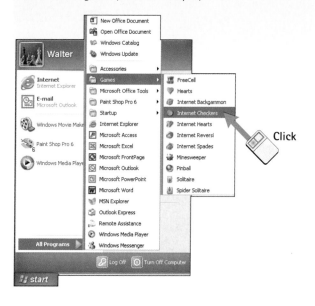

Click

5 Enter Zone.com

To play on the Internet, you must connect to Microsoft's **Zone.com** Web site by clicking **Play**. You do not have to register or give any personal information. An opponent of your skill level will be selected for you, and the game will begin immediately. Set your skill level using the **File** menu of any open game.

Click

6 Play

Play the game the way you would play a normal "non-computer" game. In checkers, for example, just drag a checker where you want it to go.

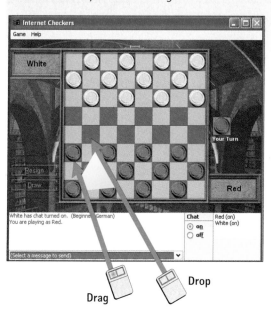

Drag   Drop

7 Send a Message

During play, you can send any of a number of preset messages to your opponent. Select one from the drop-down list at the bottom of the screen. Unfortunately, you cannot type your own messages.

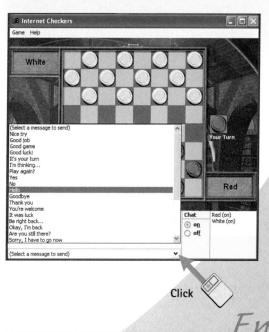

Click

End

Task

1 How to Set Local Permissions on a
Domain-Based Network **178**

2 How to Set Shared Permissions on a
Domain-Based Network **180**

3 How to Encrypt a File or Folder **182**

4 How to Lock Your Workstation **184**

5 How to Assign a Screen Saver
Password **186**

6 How to Change Your Logon Password **188**

9

Protecting Your Files

*P*art of Windows XP's claim to fame is that it is built on Windows NT technology, which is a more secure operating system than most. Security is most important when your computer is part of a networking environment (including the Internet) where it is possible that other users can access your system. Windows XP security is a complicated topic. Fortunately, there are only a few things with which you really have to be concerned. If you're using a computer at home, the default security settings are probably fine; changing them is fairly simple.

In the tasks in this part, you will learn about a few basic aspects of Windows XP security. First, you will learn to set *permissions* on your files. Permissions are given to particular users so that they can access files. You use permissions only if your computer is a member of a *domain* (such as on a large corporate network). If you have a home or small office network (called a *workgroup*), you can skip the first two tasks of this part. There are two types of permissions: local and shared. Local permissions apply to the files as they exist on your hard drive. People who log on to your computer must have the correct permissions assigned to their usernames to get to your files. Shared permissions apply to files that you make available to other users on the network (users who don't have to log directly on to your computer). Sharing files is discussed in Part 6, "Working on a Network." Local and shared permissions interact, as well. Think of it this way: All users must have appropriate local permissions. Users accessing your computer from the network must also have shared permissions. A user who is given shared access but denied local access, for example, cannot access the file at all.

The remaining tasks in this part apply whether you are in a workgroup or a domain. You will learn how to encrypt folders and files, making the files completely unreadable by other people who use your computer by logging on as a different user. You'll learn how to lock your workstation while you are away from your computer, which saves you from having to log off and back on when you aren't gone for long. You'll also learn to set a password on your screen saver—which helps when you forget to lock your workstation. Finally, you'll learn how to change your logon password. ●

How to Set Local Permissions on a Domain-Based Network

For each person in the domain who might use your computer, you can assign a specific set of permissions to use an object. Permissions you assign to files and folders differ slightly, but each allows you to assign a certain level of control to the object. You can choose to give a person full control, permission to modify things but not delete them, permission only to read files and run programs, or permission to create new items. To assign permissions to a folder or file, you must be the creator of the file, have administrative permissions on the computer (as the special **Administrator** user account does), or have been given special permission to change permissions.

1 Open a Folder's Properties

Find the folder for which you want to assign permissions. Right-click it and choose **Properties** from the shortcut menu.

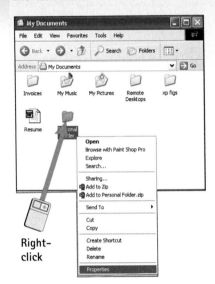

Right-click

2 Switch to the Security Tab

Switch to the **Security** tab of the **Properties** dialog box by clicking it once.

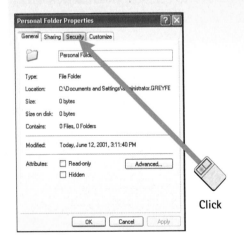

Click

3 Select a User or Group

From the list of users who have access to the folder, select a user or group by clicking the entry once. If you don't see the person on the list, you can add users by clicking the **Add** button and choosing from a list of available users.

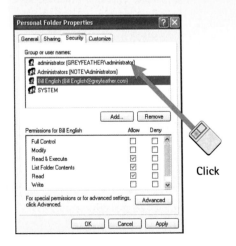

Click

4 Set Permissions

After you have selected a user or group account, set permissions by clicking the check boxes. Sometimes, objects inherit permissions from the folder they are in; when that happens, the permissions check boxes are shaded. Select the opposite permission (**Allow** or **Deny**) to override the permission. If a box is clear (unchecked), it means that no permissions have been inherited or explicitly assigned to the object, and permissions could be inherited in the future should the permissions for a parent folder change.

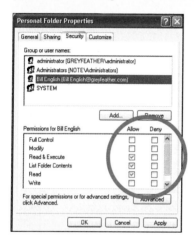

5 Configure Advanced Settings

Click the **Advanced** button to set other security options, such as whether files and folders inside the current folder will inherit the permissions set for the folder.

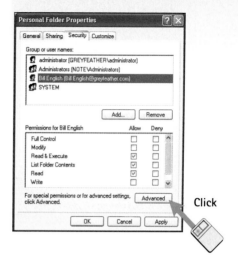

Click

How-To Hints

NTFS

The use of local file permissions requires that your disk be formatted using the NTFS file system, which is Windows XP's native file system. Unless you are on a computer that also runs a previous version of Windows such as Windows 98 or Me, the chances are that your disk uses the NTFS system. If you don't see any of the dialog boxes mentioned in the previous steps on your computer, you probably don't use NTFS. Check the instructions in your Windows documentation for steps on how to convert an existing drive to NTFS. Check the Appendix for instructions on how to set up a computer to use NTFS during Windows installation.

Windows Help

If you want to know more about Windows security, including what each of the permissions means and how they interact with one another, consult the Windows Help system (as discussed in Part 1, "Using the Windows XP Desktop").

End

How to Set Shared Permissions on a Domain-Based Network

Permissions are also set on folders you share over the network in a domain. The actual process for sharing a folder is discussed in Part 6, "Working on a Network." The following steps show you how to change permissions on a folder that is already shared.

Begin

1 Open the Sharing Dialog Box

You can identify shared folders on your computer by the small picture of a hand that looks like it's holding the folder. Right-click a shared folder and choose the **Sharing and Security** command from the shortcut menu.

Right-click

2 Open the Permissions Dialog Box

In the folder's **Properties** dialog box, click the **Permissions** button to open the **Permissions** dialog box for the folder.

Click

3 Remove the Everyone Group

By default, a special group named **Everyone** is given the **Full Control** permission over a shared folder. It is best to remove this group altogether. Just select it and click the **Remove** button.

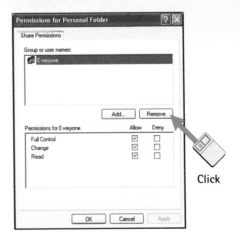

Click

4 Add a New User

Click the **Add** button on the **Permissions** dialog box to open a dialog box that helps you find users in the domain. Type the name of a user (or group) in the **Enter the object names to select** box or click the **Advanced** button to browse for certain types of user. Click **OK** when you're done.

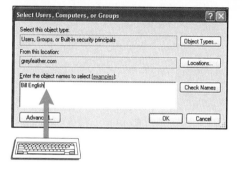

5 Set Permissions

New users and groups you add are given only **Read** permission by default, meaning that these people can open files in the folder, but cannot change or delete them. You can allow or deny other actions by enabling the check boxes.

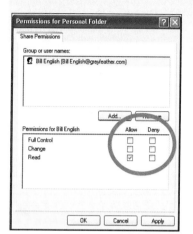

How-To Hints

Standalone Computers

If your computer is not on a network and part of a **Windows** domain, you probably will not see the **Sharing** command on the shortcut menu, or be able to assign shared permissions. Of course, if you're not part of a network, why would you want to share folders?

End

How to Encrypt a File or Folder

Windows XP allows you to *encrypt* files or folders so that other people who use your computer cannot make sense of the files even if they manage to bypass permissions and gain access to them. The whole process of encryption is pretty transparent on your end. After you encrypt a file or folder, you can continue to use it normally. You only need to decrypt it if you want to share it with others or if you want to take it to another computer to use yourself.

Begin

1 Open a File's Properties

Right-click the file or folder you want to encrypt and choose the **Properties** command from the shortcut menu. The **Properties** dialog box opens.

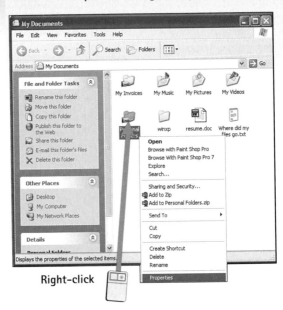

Right-click

2 Open Advanced Options

On the **General** tab of the **Properties** dialog box, click the **Advanced** button to open the **Advanced Attributes** dialog box.

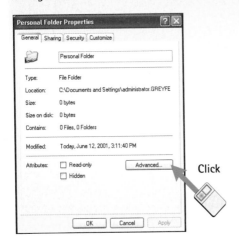

Click

3 Encrypt the Folder

Enable the **Encrypt contents to secure data** check box. Note that there is also an option here that lets you compress files and folders to save disk space. You cannot use both encryption and compression on an object at the same time.

Click

4 Close the Dialog Boxes

Click the **OK** button to close the **Advanced Attributes** dialog box; click the **OK** button on the **General** tab of the folder's **Properties** dialog box to close it.

Click

5 Encrypt Files and Subfolders

A dialog box appears that lets you choose whether to encrypt only the selected folder or also to encrypt the subfolders within that folder. Whether or not you encrypt the subfolders, the files directly inside the selected folder are encrypted. Choose the option you want and click the **OK** button.

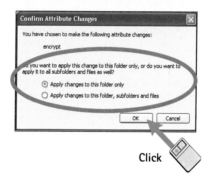

Click

How-To Hints

Decrypting a Folder

To decrypt a folder, simply follow the preceding steps and disable the **Encrypt contents to secure data check box** on the **Advanced Attributes** dialog box in Step 3.

When It Doesn't Work

As is true with local file permissions, encryption is available only if you are using the NTFS file system. Also note that Windows XP system files cannot be encrypted. Finally, note that encrypted files become unencrypted if you copy or move the file to another computer or to a removable disk (such as a floppy disk).

No Visual Indicator

When you encrypt a file or folder, Windows XP gives no visual indicator that encryption is enabled. To see whether an object is encrypted, you must open its **Properties** dialog box and see whether the **Encrypt contents to secure data** check box is enabled.

End

How to Lock Your Workstation

When you leave your desk for any period of time, it is best to log off of Windows XP using the procedure described in Part 1, Task 10, "How to Log Off Windows XP." Sometimes, however, you might want to prevent even other authorized users from gaining access to your computer (which they can do if you have logged off). Windows XP Professional lets you lock your workstation. When your workstation is locked, only you or a system administrator can unlock the computer. Windows XP Home Edition does not allow you to lock your computer.

Begin

1 Press Ctrl+Alt+Delete

Press the **Ctrl**, **Alt**, and **Delete** keys all at once. You can perform this action no matter where you are in the system, even if you have programs running.

Ctrl + Alt + Del

2 Lock Your Computer

From the **Windows Security** dialog box, click the **Lock Computer** button. The **Computer Locked** window appears. Now, no one but you (and the network's system administrator) can unlock the computer to use it.

Click

3 Unlock Your Computer

When your computer is locked, you unlock it in much the same way that you log on to Windows. First, press the **Ctrl**, **Alt**, and **Delete** keys all at once. The **Unlock Computer** dialog box opens.

Ctrl + Alt + Del

4 Enter Your Password

Type your logon password in the **Password** box and then click the **OK** button.

5 Return to Work

After you unlock your workstation, you'll find it in exactly the same state in which you left it—running programs and all.

How-To Hints

Locking Is Quicker

Many people find that locking their computers when leaving their desks is quicker than logging off, mainly because logging off requires that you save your work, stop and shut down programs, and then log on and relaunch programs again when you get back. This is normally fine, especially if you won't be away for long, but your network administrator might prefer that you log off when you leave for long periods, such as overnight or over weekends.

End

How to Assign a Screen Saver Password

Often, people forget to log off or lock their workstations every time they leave their desks, especially if they're late for a meeting or it's 4:57 on a Friday afternoon. One way to create a kind of security safety net is to use a screen saver that is password protected. With such a system in place, once the screen saver activates, you or someone using an account with administrator permissions (such as the special **Administrator** account) must enter your password to get back into the computer. If you are the administrator of your own computer (as is the case on a home network), there is no real way to recover from a forgotten password.

Begin

1 Open the Control Panel

Click **Start** and then click **Control Panel** to open the Windows **Control Panel** window.

Click

2 Open the Display Applet

The **Control Panel** features a number of applets that let you change various settings for your computer. The screen saver options are controlled by the **Display** applet. Double-click the **Display** applet to open the **Display Properties** dialog box.

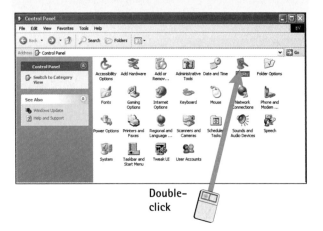

Double-click

3 Switch to the Screen Saver Tab

Switch to the **Screen Saver** tab by clicking it once.

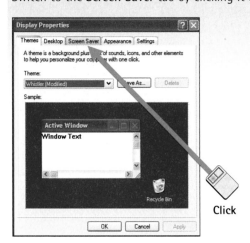

Click

4 Choose the Password Protected Option

Click the **Password protected** option to require that a password be entered when returning to the desktop from a screen saver. If no screen saver is selected, this option is not available. For more on how to set up a screen saver, see Part 10, "Changing Windows XP Settings." When password protection is enabled and you come back to your computer from the screen saver (by moving the mouse or touching a key), you must enter the same username and password you use to log on to Windows.

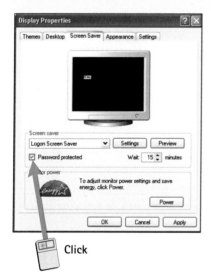

Click

How-To Hints

Remembering to Log Off

Although a screen saver password can help you protect your system, it is not a good substitute for logging off or locking your workstation. Even though the screen saver is up, you are still logged on to Windows, and any programs you left open are still running. Both situations can present security problems. In fact, many network administrators don't allow users to use screen saver passwords at all for fear that they will grow reliant on them.

End

How to Change Your Logon Password

It is a good idea to change your logon password periodically in case someone has gained access to it. On more secure networks, it is often company policy that users must change their passwords every month or two. On some even more secure networks, administrators change and distribute new passwords and do not allow users to select passwords themselves. Check with your network administrator to find out the policy for your network. If you're on a home network, it's up to you how often your passwords change.

Begin

1 Open the User Accounts Window

Open the **Control Panel** window and double-click the **User Accounts** icon to open the **User Accounts** window.

Double-click

2 Choose an Account to Change

Click the account for which you want to change the password.

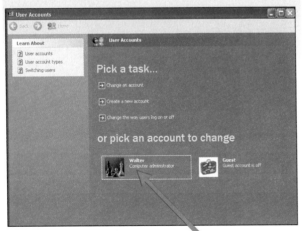

Click

3 Click Change My Password

On the list of options for managing the selected user account, click the **Change my password** link.

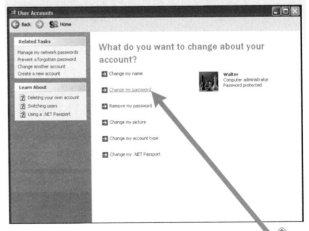

Click

4 Type Your Current Password

You must enter your current password to ensure that you have the right to change the password. Type the current password into the **Type your current password** text box.

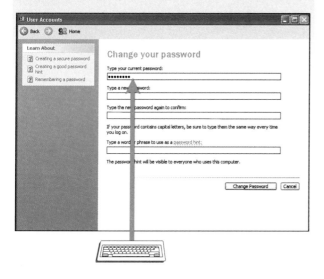

5 Type and Confirm the New Password

Type your new password in the **Type a new password** box and then type it again in the **Type the new password again to confirm** box. Click the **Change Password** button to change to the new password. You are returned to the screen that lists the maintenance choices for the account (shown in Step 3).

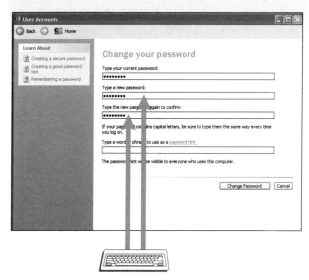

How-To Hints

Password Security

For the best possible security, don't write your password down anywhere and never tell it to anyone. You should change your password every so often just in case it has been discovered. If your administrator supplies you with a password, memorize it and destroy the paper it came on.

Password Hints

Never create passwords with names, dates, or words that might appear in the dictionary. If you find it hard to remember cryptic passwords full of uppercase and lowercase characters and numbers, you can create a password that is both secure and easy to remember. One way is to think of two four-letter words and join them with a two-digit number. For example, **lion72dunk** is pretty easy to remember and almost impossible to guess. You can also think of an easy-to-remember seven- or eight-letter word. Then, instead of typing the word itself, type the characters that are to the upper-left of the real characters on the keyboard. This way, an easy-to-guess word such as **astronomy** becomes **qw549h9j6**. Remember to check with your administrator about the password policies used on your network.

End

Task

1 How to Change the Volume **192**

2 How to Set Up a Screen Saver **194**

3 How to Change Your Desktop Theme **196**

4 How to Change Your Wallpaper **198**

5 How to Change Desktop Appearance **200**

6 How to Change Display Settings **202**

7 How to Change Mouse Settings **204**

8 How to Change Keyboard Settings **206**

9 How to Customize the Taskbar **208**

10 How to Change Folder Options **210**

11 How to Change Power Options **212**

12 How to Change System Sounds **214**

13 How to Add an Item to the Start Menu **216**

14 How to Add an Item to the Quick Launch Bar **218**

15 How to Start a Program When Windows Starts **220**

16 How to Set Accessibility Options **222**

PART 10

Changing Windows XP Settings

*A*fter you have worked with Windows XP for a while and gotten used to the way things work, you might find that there are changes you would like to make. Windows XP is wonderfully customizable and provides many options for changing its interface to suit the way you work.

Most of the changes you will make take place using the Windows **Control Panel**, which is a special folder that contains many small programs called *applets*. Each applet is designed to let you adjust settings for a particular part of your system. For example, the **Display** applet lets you change display settings such as background color, window colors, screen saver, and screen size. You can access the **Control Panel** through either the **Start** menu or the **My Computer** window, as you will see in the tasks in this part.

You'll also find that many of the **Control Panel** applets are also directly available from the shortcut menu of various desktop items. For example, right-clicking the desktop and choosing **Properties** from the shortcut menu that opens is exactly the same as opening the **Display** applet from the **Control Panel**. You'll see several such ways for accessing common controls in the following tasks. ●

How to Change the Volume

If you have speakers hooked up to your computer, you've probably noticed that some programs and certain things that Windows does (called *events*) make sounds. Many speakers have physical volume control knobs on them, but there is also a convenient way to change the volume from within Windows itself.

Begin

1 Click the Volume Icon

A small volume icon that looks like a speaker appears in the system tray next to your clock to indicate that sound is configured on your computer. Click the icon once with your left mouse button to open the **Volume** dialog box.

Click

2 Change the Volume Setting

Click and drag the slider with your left mouse button to adjust the volume. Your computer beeps when you release the slider to give you an idea of the volume you've set.

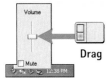

Drag

3 Mute Your Speakers

Click the **Mute** option to silence your speakers. While your speakers are muted, the volume icon is overlaid with a red circle and slash. When you want the speakers to play again, open the **Volume** dialog box again and deselect the **Mute** option.

Click

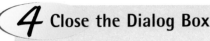 **Close the Dialog Box**

Click anywhere out on your desktop once to close the
Volume dialog box.

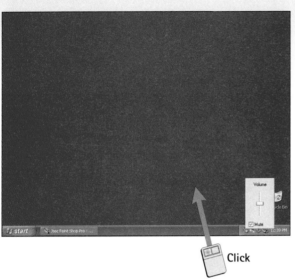

Click

How-To Hints

Double-Clicking

The main volume control adjusts the volume for all the sounds on your computer, no
matter where that sound comes from. Double-click the **Volume** dialog box to open a more
sophisticated volume control that lets you adjust the volume for each audio device configured
on your system. For example, you might want to lower the volume for CD-ROMs but leave the
volume for **Wave** files (which are used for Windows system events) alone.

Where's My Volume Icon?

On some computers, the volume icon on the system tray may be disabled. If you don't see one,
but would like to, first open the **Start** menu and click **Control Panel**. In the **Control Panel**
window, double-click the **Sounds and Audio Devices** icon. On the **Volume** tab of the **Sounds
and Audio Devices Properties** dialog box that opens, select the **Place Volume icon in the
taskbar** option.

End

How to Set Up a Screen Saver

On older monitors (those more than ten years old), screen savers help prevent a phenomenon called burn-in, where items on your display can actually be permanently burned in to your monitor if left for a long time. Newer monitors don't really have a problem with this, but screen savers are still kind of fun and do help prevent passers-by from seeing what's on your computer when you're away. Windows XP provides a number of built-in screen savers.

Begin

1 Open the Display Properties

Right-click any open space on your desktop and choose the **Properties** command from the shortcut menu. The **Display Properties** dialog box opens.

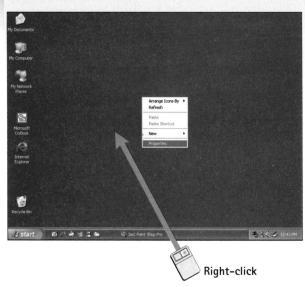

Right-click

2 Switch to the Screen Saver Tab

Switch to the **Screen Saver** tab by clicking it once.

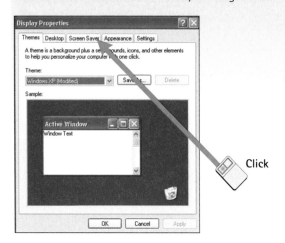

Click

3 Choose a Screen Saver

By default, Windows comes with no screen saver active. Click the arrow next to the **Screen saver** drop-down list to choose from a number of available screen savers.

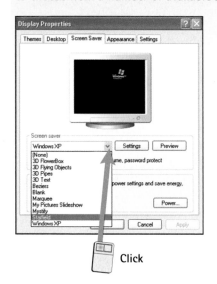

Click

4 Preview the Screen Saver

When you choose a screen saver, Windows displays a small preview of it right on the picture of a monitor in the dialog box. To see how the screen saver will look when it's actually working, click the **Preview** button. Move the mouse or press a key during the preview to get back to the dialog box.

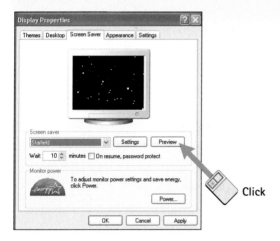

Click

5 Adjust Settings

Each screen saver has its own specific settings so that you can change how the screen saver behaves. Settings for the **Starfield** screen saver, for example, let you control how many stars are displayed and how fast they move. Click the **Settings** button to experiment with options for any screen saver.

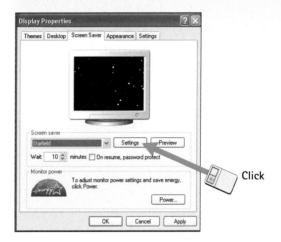

Click

6 Adjust Wait Time

The **Wait** field specifies how long your computer must be idle before the screen saver kicks in. By default, this value is 15 minutes, but you can change it to whatever you want by using the scroll buttons. You can make a screen saver password protected by clicking the **password protect** option on the **Screen Saver** tab. See Part 9, "Protecting Your Files," for more information. Click **OK** when you're done setting up the screen saver.

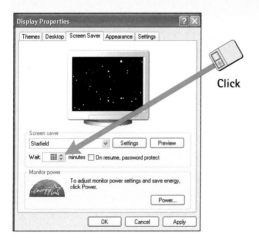

Click

How-To Hints

Getting Back to Work

After the screen saver kicks in, you won't be able to see the work that was on your screen because the screen saver "takes over." To get back to work, banish the screen saver simply by moving the mouse or pressing any key on the keyboard. The screen saver will come back on after the next lull in your activity.

Getting New Screen Savers

New screen savers are available for purchase at most software stores; many are available for free on the Internet. When you download a screen saver, it usually appears as a file with the extension **.scr**. Just copy the file to the **System32** folder inside your **Windows** folder to have it show up on the list in Step 3.

End

How to Change Your Desktop Theme

A *desktop theme* determines the overall look and feel of your desktop. A theme includes a background picture, a set of desktop icons, a color scheme for window elements, a predetermined set of sounds for Windows events, and a set of display fonts. All these aspects of the theme are customizable.

Begin

1 Open Display Properties

Right-click any open space on your desktop and choose the **Properties** command from the shortcut menu. The **Display Properties** dialog box opens.

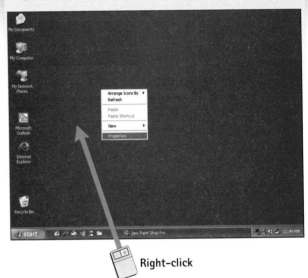

Right-click

2 View the Current Theme

On the **Themes** tab of the dialog box, the name of the current theme is displayed along with a sample of what the theme looks like on your desktop.

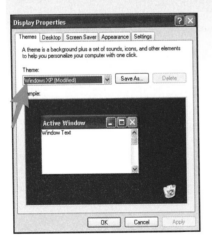

3 Select a Theme

Click the arrow next to the **Theme** drop-down list and choose a different theme.

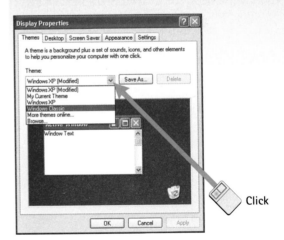

Click

4 Sample the New Theme

A sample of the selected theme is displayed in the **Sample** window so that you can see what the theme will look like before actually applying it to your desktop.

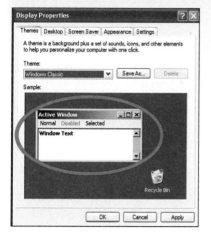

5 Set the New Theme

To apply the new theme to your desktop and close the **Display Properties** window, click **OK**. To apply the theme and keep the dialog box open, click **Apply**.

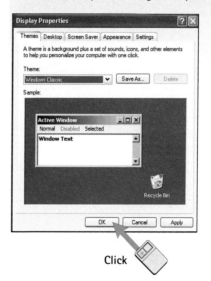

Click

How-To Hints

Finding More Themes

Use the **More themes online** selection from the **Theme** drop-down list to go to the Windows Media Web site. There, you'll find a number of desktop themes you can download. After you download them, they will appear in your **Theme** list.

Browsing for Themes

If you downloaded a theme from a Web site other than the Windows Media site, it may be saved somewhere on your hard disk and not show up in your **Theme** list. Select the **Browse** option from the **Theme** drop-down list to open a standard dialog box that lets you find the theme on your hard disk. Theme files have a **.theme** extension.

End

How to Change Your Wallpaper

Wallpaper is a pattern or picture that is displayed on your desktop just to make things a bit more fun. By default, Windows uses no wallpaper; you see only the standard blue desktop color. Windows XP includes a number of interesting wallpapers you can use to spruce up your display.

Begin

1 Open Display Properties

Right-click any open space on your desktop and choose the **Properties** command from the shortcut menu. The **Display Properties** dialog box opens.

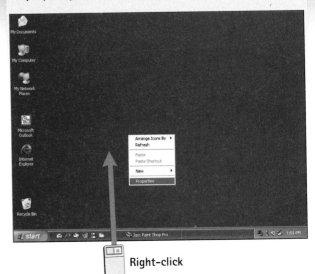

Right-click

2 Switch to the Desktop Tab

Click the **Desktop** tab once to bring that page to the front.

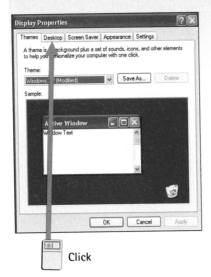

Click

3 Choose a Wallpaper from the List

Choose any wallpaper from the **Background** list by clicking it once. Some wallpapers listed are pictures, and some are patterns that can be tiled to create effects on your desktop. Whatever wallpaper you choose is displayed in the picture of a monitor in the dialog box.

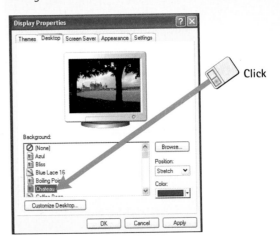

Click

4 Use Your Own Picture

If you have a picture file on your computer that you want to use as wallpaper, click the **Browse** button to open a dialog box that lets you locate the file. Background pictures can have the following extensions: **.bmp**, **.gif**, **.jpg**, **.dib**, and **.htm**.

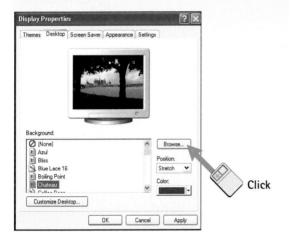
Click

5 Adjust the Picture Display

You can display background pictures in one of three ways. You can **Center** a picture on the screen, **Stretch** a picture so that it fills the screen, or **Tile** a small picture so that it appears multiple times to fill the screen. Click the **Position** drop-down list to experiment with these options.

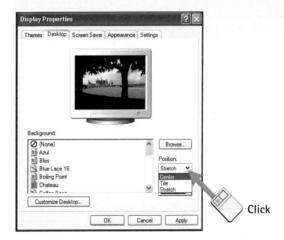
Click

6 Set a Color

If you would rather not use a picture, but are tired of staring at a blue desktop, try setting a different color. Click the down-arrow next to the current color to open a palette for choosing a new color.

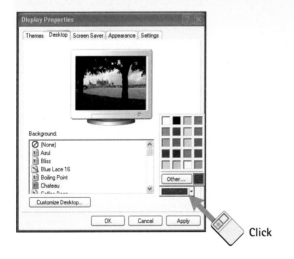
Click

7 Apply the Settings

Click the **Apply** button to apply any new wallpaper to your desktop and keep the **Display Properties** dialog box open so that you can more easily experiment with backgrounds. After you find a background you like, click the **OK** button to get back to work.

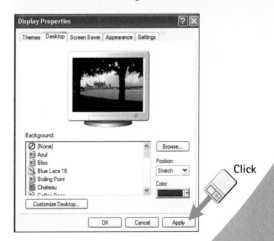
Click

End

How to Change Desktop Appearance

Changing your desktop appearance can really affect how you work. Windows lets you change the colors used on your desktop background, parts of windows, and even menus. For example, if you find yourself squinting at the text on the monitor, you can adjust the point size of the display font. If you don't like blue title bars on dialog boxes, you can change the color of that element, too.

Begin

1 Open Display Properties

Right-click any open space on your desktop and choose the **Properties** command from the shortcut menu. The **Display Properties** dialog box opens.

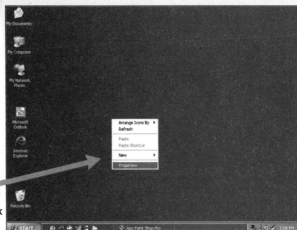

Right-click

2 Switch to the Appearance Tab

Switch to the **Appearance** tab by clicking it once.

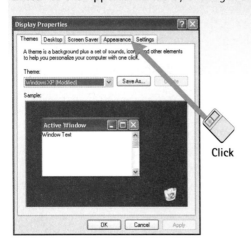

Click

3 Choose a Window and Button Style

Windows has two styles for windows and buttons. **Windows XP** style uses the new rounded windows and stylized buttons. **Windows Classic** style uses windows and buttons that look like previous versions of Windows. If you are using the **Windows Classic** style, the **Advanced** button lets you set colors for the different window elements. If you are using the **Windows XP** style, the **Advanced** button is not available.

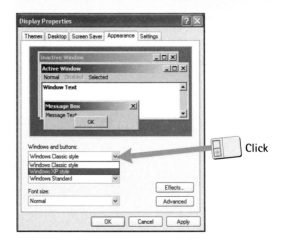

Click

4 Choose a New Color Scheme

If you're using the **Windows XP** style, you have only a few choices for the color scheme, including blue (the default), olive, and silver. If you're using the **Windows Classic** style, you can choose from many predefined color schemes. Choose a scheme using the **Color scheme** drop-down list. The sample window in the dialog box changes to show you what a color scheme will look like.

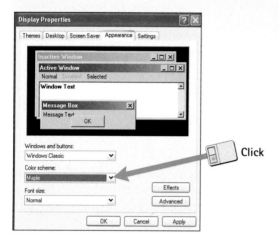

Click

5 Adjust Font Size

Some of the color schemes allow for more than one font size to be used when displaying menus, window text, and dialog boxes. Use the **Font size** drop-down list to choose a **Normal**, **Large**, or **Extra Large** display font.

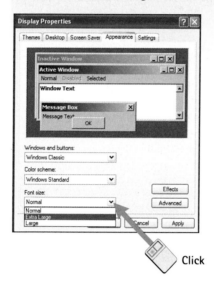

Click

6 Open the Effects Dialog Box

Click the **Effects** button to open a separate dialog box for adjusting special desktop settings.

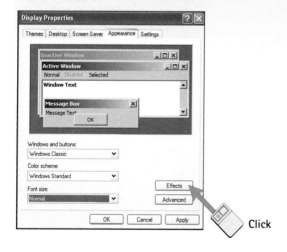

Click

7 Adjust Effects

Many of the effects you can choose in this dialog box affect the speed with which windows are displayed on your computer. Using transition effects for menus, showing window contents while dragging the windows, and showing shadows under menus all make displaying windows on the desktop take just a little longer. Consider turning them off if you have a slower computer. Click **OK** twice to close both dialog boxes and apply the settings.

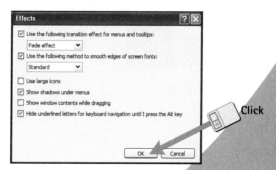

Click

End

How to Change Display Settings

Display settings control various aspects of your video adapter and monitor. You can change the display settings to control the screen resolution (how many pixels are shown on your screen) and the color quality (how many colors are available for the display to use). Using a higher resolution lets you fit more on your desktop. Using better color quality makes things look better. However, both options depend on the quality of your video card and monitor, and using higher settings can slow down your system a bit.

Begin

1 Open Display Properties

Right-click any open space on your desktop and choose the **Properties** command from the shortcut menu. The **Display Properties** dialog box opens.

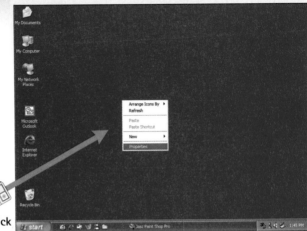

Right-click

2 Switch to the Settings Tab

Switch to the **Settings** tab by clicking it once.

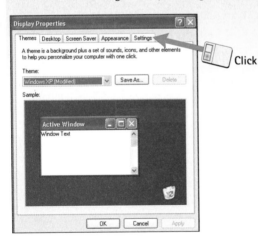

Click

3 Choose a New Color Depth

Color depth refers to the number of colors your screen can display. The default setting depends on the video card and monitor you use. Click the **Color quality** drop-down list to choose a new color setting. Keep in mind that the settings available to you depend on the hardware you use. And although using the highest available color quality is usually the better choice, it can slow down your system just a bit. You'll have to play with the settings to find what you like best.

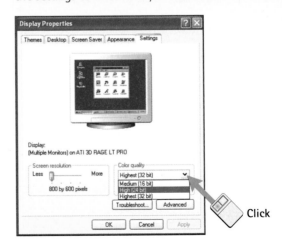

Click

4 Choose a New Screen Resolution

Screen resolution refers to the size of items displayed on your screen. Increasing the area means that you can see more items on your screen at once, but also means that those items will appear smaller. Adjust the screen area by dragging the **Screen resolution** slider.

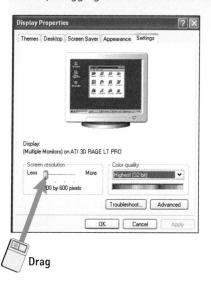

Drag

5 Start the Display Troubleshooter

If you are having display problems, click the **Troubleshoot** button to open the Windows Help system and go directly to the display troubleshooter.

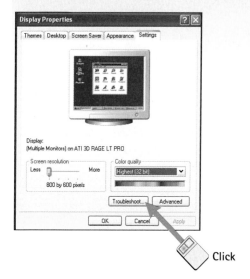

Click

6 Open Advanced Properties

Click the **Advanced** button to open a separate dialog box with controls for changing the video adapter and monitor drivers your computer is using, along with other advanced display settings.

Click

How-To Hints

Using Advanced Settings

Be careful when changing the advanced display settings. Although these settings can be useful, they can also cause problems. Incorrectly changing the drivers for your adapter or monitor can cause your display to stop working. Changing the refresh rate on your monitor can result in a more stable image, but changing it to a rate your monitor doesn't support can damage the monitor. In general, you should probably leave these settings alone if your display is working fine.

End

How to Change Mouse Settings

Because the mouse will likely be your main tool for getting around in Windows, it should come as no surprise that Windows allows you to change the way your mouse works. Among other things, you can change the clicking speed that makes for a successful double-click and the speed at which the pointer moves across the screen.

Begin

1 Open the Control Panel

Click **Start** and then select **Control Panel** to open the **Control Panel** window.

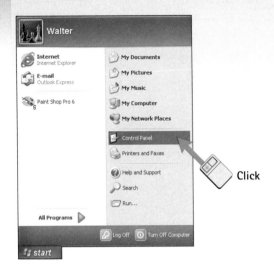

Click

2 Open the Mouse Icon

Double-click the **Mouse** icon to open the **Mouse Properties** dialog box.

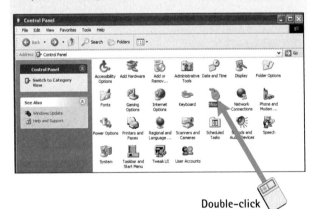

Double-click

3 Change Button Configuration

Choose the **Switch primary and secondary buttons** option to swap the functions of the left and right buttons. This option is useful if you use your mouse with your left hand.

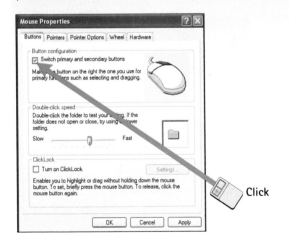

Click

_4_ Adjust Double-Click Speed

The **Double-click speed** option refers to how close together two clicks of the mouse button must be for Windows to consider them a double-click rather than two single clicks. Drag the slider with your left mouse button to adjust the speed and then test it by double-clicking the folder icon in the test area.

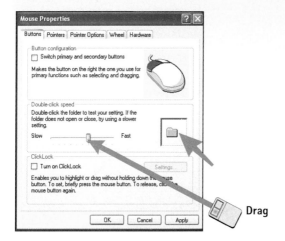

Drag

_5_ Adjust the Pointer Speed

Click the **Pointer Options** tab to switch to that page. Here you can set several options relating to how the mouse pointer moves. Drag the **Motion** slider to set how fast the pointer moves across the screen when you move the mouse. Click the **Apply** button to experiment with any settings you make while keeping the **Mouse Properties** dialog box open.

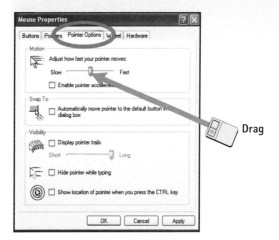

Drag

_6_ Enable Acceleration

Acceleration refers to whether the movement of your pointer accelerates if you begin moving your mouse more quickly. Without this option, the pointer keeps moving at a single speed no matter how quickly you move your mouse. Usually, you want this option enabled so that the speed you move the mouse on the table top is mimicked in the speed at which the mouse pointer moves onscreen. However, you sometimes may find that the mouse pointer moves too quickly or acts erratically with this option enabled.

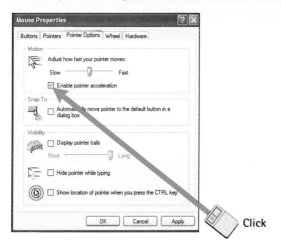

Click

_7_ Snap to Default

Normally, when a new dialog box opens, the mouse pointer stays right where it is; you must move it to the buttons on the dialog box to do anything. With the **Snap To** option enabled, the mouse pointer automatically jumps to whatever the default button is (usually **Yes**, **No**, **OK**, or **Cancel**).

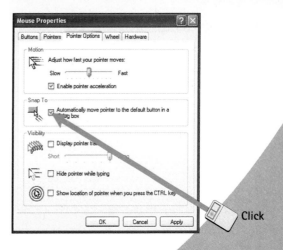

Click

End

How to Change Keyboard Settings

Windows allows you to change a number of settings related to how your keyboard works. You can change the delay that occurs between when you press a key and when the key starts to repeat from holding it down. You can also change the rate at which the key repeats. Finally, you can change the blink rate for your cursor (the little vertical line that blinks where you are about to type something).

Begin

1 Open the Control Panel

Click **Start** and then choose **Control Panel** to open the **Control Panel** window.

Click

2 Open the Keyboard Icon

Double-click the **Keyboard** icon to open the **Keyboard Properties** dialog box.

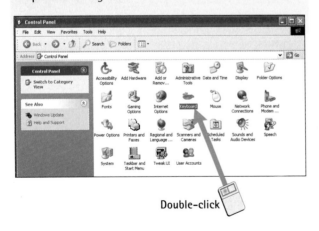

Double-click

3 Change the Repeat Delay

The **Repeat delay** option specifies the delay that occurs between when you press a key and when the key starts to repeat from holding it down. Drag the slider to change the rate.

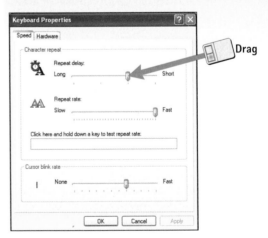

Drag

4 Change the Repeat Rate

When you hold a key down longer than the repeat delay you specified in the previous step, the key begins to repeat. Drag the **Repeat rate** slider to change the repeat rate.

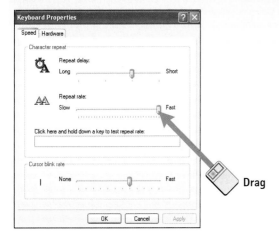

Drag

5 Test Your Settings

Click in the test box and then press and hold any key to test your repeat delay and repeat rate settings.

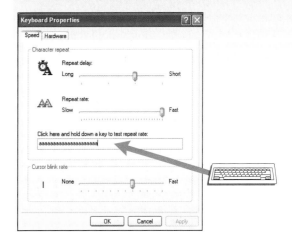

6 Change the Cursor Blink Rate

Whenever you click in a text box to type a value or to type a document, a little vertical line called a *cursor* blinks to let you know where the characters you type will appear. The cursor is sometimes also called the insertion point. Drag the **Cursor blink rate** slider to change the rate at which the cursor blinks. A sample cursor to the left of the slider blinks according to your settings.

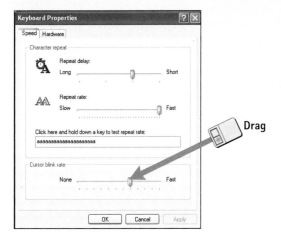

Drag

End

How to Customize the Taskbar

The taskbar is one of the more important tools you use when working in Windows XP. There are several ways you can customize its use, as you will see in the following steps.

1 Open Taskbar Properties

Right-click anywhere on the taskbar and click **Properties**. The **Taskbar and Start Menu Properties** dialog box opens.

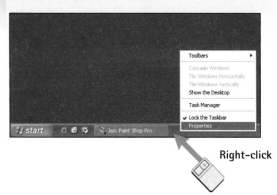

Right-click

2 Lock the Taskbar

By default, you can drag the taskbar to other edges of the screen, resize the taskbar, and adjust the size of the system tray and Quick Launch portions of the taskbar. Enable the **Lock the taskbar** option to prevent this from happening.

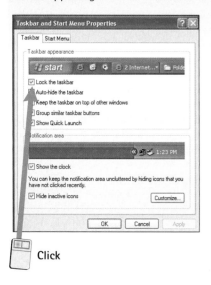

Click

3 Make the Taskbar Autohide

Enable the **Auto hide the taskbar** option to have the taskbar automatically scroll off the edge of the screen when it's not in use. Move your pointer to the edge of the screen to make the taskbar scroll back into view. Note that this option cannot be used when the taskbar is locked.

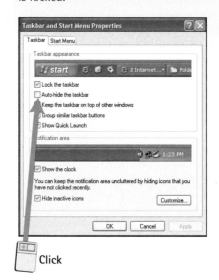

Click

4 Keep the Taskbar on Top

By default, the taskbar is always on the top of your display. Thus, when you move a window into the same space occupied by the taskbar, the taskbar still appears in front of the window. Disable the **Keep the taskbar on top of other windows** option so that other items can appear in front of the taskbar.

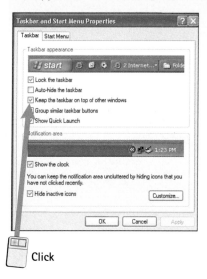

Click

5 Group Similar Buttons

When you start a program (such as Internet Explorer) more than once, a separate button appears on the taskbar for each instance of the program. When you enable the **Group similar taskbar buttons**, only one button appears for each program and a number to the side indicates how many documents for that program are open.

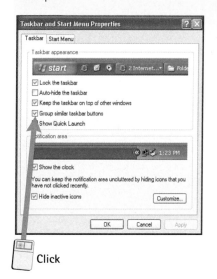

Click

6 Show the Clock

The **Show the clock** option causes Windows to display the clock in the system tray at the far right of your taskbar. Disable this option to hide the clock. Double-click the clock to open a dialog box that lets you set the time and date.

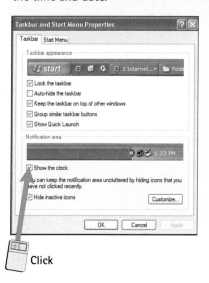

Click

7 Hide Inactive Icons

By default, the system tray is collapsed so that only the most frequently used icons are shown. If you don't like this space-saving feature, turn it off by disabling the **Hide inactive icons** check box.

Click

End

How to Change Folder Options

Windows XP handles folders in much the same way as previous versions of Windows. You have the option of viewing a folder as a Web page, in which a pane on the left side of the folder view gives you information about any selected item. You also have the option of having Windows open a new window for each folder you want to open. The following steps explain how to access these options using the **Control Panel**. You can also access the **Folder Options** dialog box from the **View** menu at the top of any open folder.

Begin

1 Open the Control Panel

Click the **Start** button and then choose **Control Panel**. The **Control Panel** window opens.

Click

2 Open the Folder Options Icon

Double-click the **Folder Options** icon to open the **Folder Options** dialog box.

Double-click

3 Use Web View

Web View is an option that shows Web content in folders. Normally, this just means that a pane at the left of a folder window shows information about selected item(s) in that folder. Some folders, however, might have more specialized content. Enable the **Use Windows classic folders** option to disable this feature.

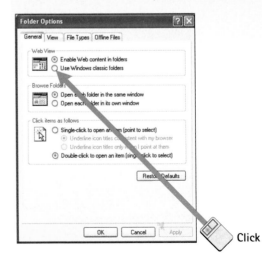

Click

4 Change Folder Browsing

Normally when you open a folder, that folder opens in whatever window you are using at the time. If you would rather Windows open a whole new window for each folder you open, select the **Open each folder in its own window** option here.

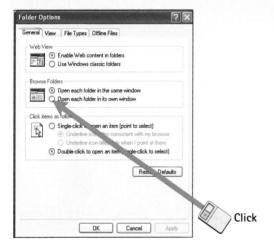

Click

5 Change Click Settings

By default, you single-click items to select them and double-click items to open them. If you prefer, enable the **Single-click to open an item (point to select)** option so that you only have to single-click items to open them, much like you do in Internet Explorer. With this option enabled, holding the mouse pointer over an item for a second selects the item.

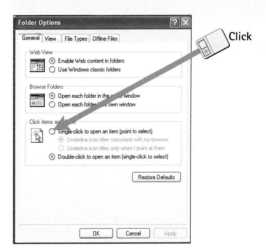

Click

6 Restore Defaults

If you find that you don't like the folder settings you have already made, click the **Restore Defaults** button to change the settings back to their original configuration.

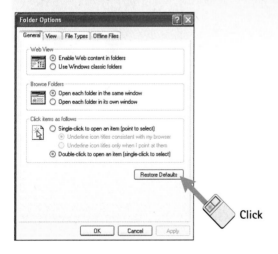

Click

How-To Hints

Advanced Options

The **View** tab of the **Folder Options** dialog box features a long list of specific settings relating to how folders work, such as whether hidden system files should be displayed, whether file extensions should be displayed or hidden, and whether Windows should remember the view for each folder you open. After you are familiar with using Windows, you may want to check the options on this list and see whether any appeal to you.

End

How to Change Power Options

You might find it useful to adjust the way Windows handles your power settings. To save energy, Windows can automatically turn off parts of your computer, such as the hard drive and monitor, after a certain amount of time. The next time you try to access these devices, the power is immediately restored and you can proceed with your tasks without delay.

Begin

1 Open Control Panel

Click **Start** and then choose **Control Panel**. The **Control Panel** window opens.

Click

2 Open the Power Options Icon

Double-click the **Power Options** icon to open the **Power Options Properties** dialog box.

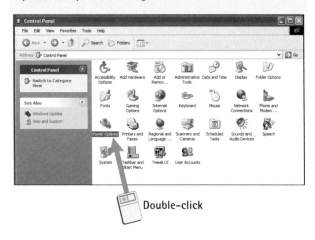

Double-click

3 Choose a Power Scheme

The easiest way to configure power settings is to choose a custom scheme designed to fit the way you use your computer. Click the **Power schemes** drop-down list to choose from a number of schemes.

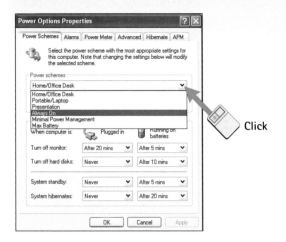

Click

4 Turn Off Monitor

If you want to customize power settings beyond just choosing a scheme, you can choose how long the computer should be idle before certain devices are turned off. Click the **Turn off monitor** drop-down menu to specify how long the computer should be idle before your monitor is turned off. Note that you can specify a different delay time if your computer is running on batteries.

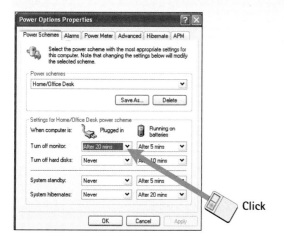

Click

5 Turn Off Hard Disks

Click the **Turn off hard disks** drop-down menu to specify how long the computer should be idle before your hard drive is turned off. Note that you can specify a different delay time if your computer is running on batteries.

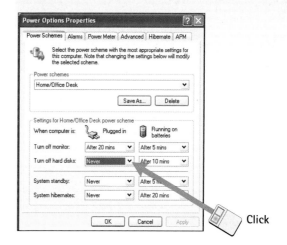

Click

6 Send System to Standby

Some computers have the capability to go into *standby*, where only a trickle of power is used to keep track of what's in your computer's memory. When you come back from standby, everything should be as you left it. Use the drop-down menu to specify how long the computer should be idle before it goes into standby. Note that you can specify a different delay time if your computer is running on batteries.

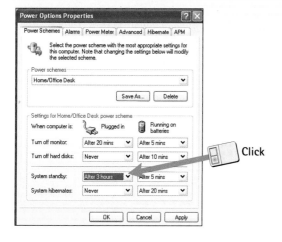

Click

How-To Hints

Where Are All Those Options?

Depending on the type of computer and type of hardware installed, the **Power Options Properties** dialog box you see may be different than the one shown in this task. Notebook computers, for example, have settings both for when the computer is plugged in and when it is running on batteries. Notebooks also boast several more tabs on the dialog box to configure such things as advanced standby and hibernation modes. The best place to find out information about these advanced options is in the documentation for the computer itself.

End

How to Change System Sounds

If you have speakers on your computer, you might have noticed that certain things you do in Windows (such as emptying the Recycle Bin, starting Windows, and logging off) make certain sounds. These things are called *events*. Windows events also include things you don't do yourself, such as when an error dialog box is displayed or when e-mail is received. You can easily change the sounds associated with Windows events by using the following steps.

Begin

1 Open the Control Panel

Click **Start** and then choose **Control Panel**. The **Control Panel** window opens.

Click

2 Open the Sounds and Audio Devices Icon

Double-click the **Sounds and Audio Devices** icon to open the **Sounds and Audio Devices Properties** dialog box.

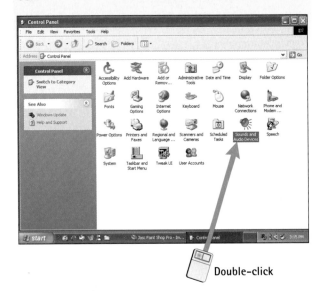

Double-click

3 Switch to the Sounds Tab

Click the **Sounds** tab to bring it to the front.

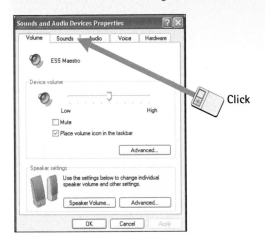

Click

4 Choose an Event

From the **Program events** list, select any system event, such as **Default Beep**.

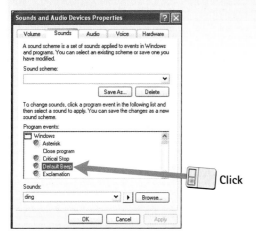

Click

5 Choose a Sound File

Click the arrow next to the **Sounds** drop-down list to select a sound to associate with the selected event. You can also use your own sound file (any **.wav** file) by clicking the **Browse** button.

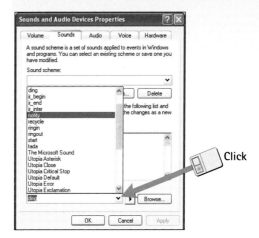

Click

6 Play the Sound

Click the **Play** button to hear the selected sound.

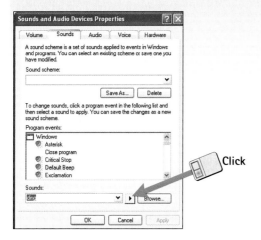

Click

7 Choose a Sound Scheme

Windows comes with a couple of different sound schemes, which are sets of sounds similar in effect that are applied to all the major system events at once. Use the **Sound Scheme** drop-down list to choose a scheme.

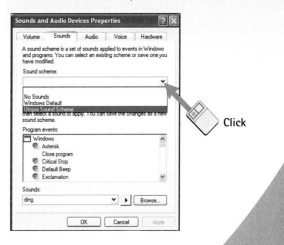

Click

End

How to Add an Item to the Start Menu

The Start menu is loaded with shortcuts to various programs and folders on your computer. Whenever you install a new program, that program usually adds a shortcut of its own to the Start menu automatically. You can also add items of your own. You can add shortcuts to programs, documents, or even folders.

Begin

1 Find the Item You Want to Add

Use the My Computer or My Documents window to find the item you want to add to the Start menu. This item can be a document, a program, or even a folder.

2 Drag the Item over the Start Menu

Using the left mouse button, click and drag the item over the Start button, but *do not* release the mouse button yet.

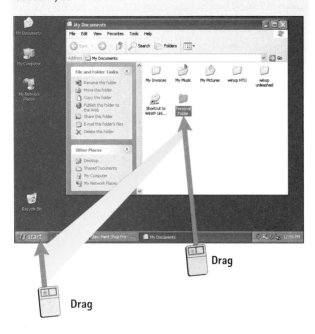

Drag

Drag

3 Place the Item in the More Programs Folder

After holding the item over the Start button for about two seconds, the Start menu opens. Continue dragging the item over the All Programs folder and then onto the All Programs menu that appears. When you find where you want to place the item (a horizontal line appears to guide placement), let go of the mouse button. After you have placed the shortcut, just click it to launch the original program.

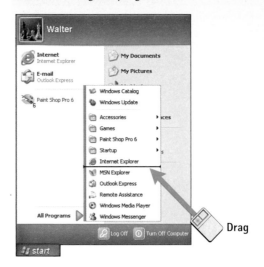

Drag

4 Rename the Shortcut

Right-click the new shortcut and choose **Rename** from the shortcut menu to give the shortcut a new name. This name appears in a pop-up window when you hold your pointer over the shortcut for a second.

Right-click

5 Delete the Shortcut

Right-click the shortcut in the **Start** menu and choose **Delete** from the shortcut menu to remove the shortcut from the **Start** menu.

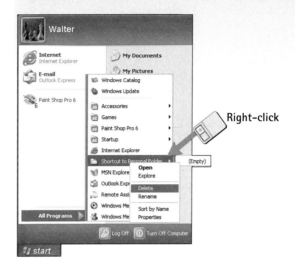

Right-click

How-To Hints

Adding Shortcuts

Unfortunately, you can only add shortcuts to the **All Programs** menu and not to the main **Start** menu itself, as you could in previous versions of Windows. Still, this does provide an easier way to open programs, folders, and files than by browsing for them on your hard drive.

End

How to Add an Item to the Quick Launch Bar

The **Quick Launch** bar is handy feature located in the task bar next to the **Start** button. You can use it to open certain programs with a single click. Only three shortcuts appear by default on the **Quick Launch** bar: one to launch Internet Explorer, one to launch Outlook Express, and one to show your desktop when there are windows in the way. Fortunately, it's pretty easy to add new shortcuts for programs, documents, and folders. In fact, many programs (such as Microsoft Outlook) add their own shortcuts during installation.

Begin

1 Find the Item You Want to Add

Use the **My Computer** or **My Documents** window to find the item to which you want to make a Quick Launch shortcut.

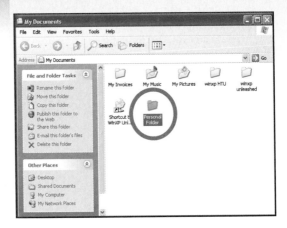

2 Drag the Item to the Quick Launch Bar

Click the item with your left mouse button and, while holding the button down, drag the item into a blank space on the **Quick Launch** bar. You can even drag the item between two existing shortcuts to put it exactly where you want.

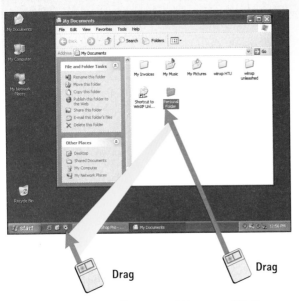

Drag Drag

3 Rename the Shortcut

Right-click the new shortcut and choose **Rename** from the shortcut menu to give the shortcut a new name. This name appears in a pop-up window when you hold the mouse pointer over the shortcut icon for a second.

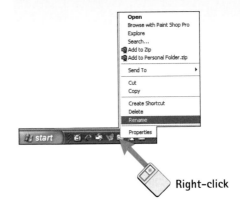

Right-click

4 Delete the Shortcut

Right-click the shortcut and choose **Delete** from the shortcut menu to remove the shortcut from the **Quick Launch** bar and place it in the **Recycle Bin**. Hold the **Shift** key down when selecting **Delete** to permanently delete the shortcut without sending it to the Recycle Bin.

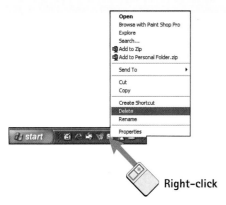

Right-click

How-To Hints

Rearranging Shortcuts

You can rearrange existing shortcuts in the **Quick Launch** bar by simply dragging them to new locations on the **Quick Launch** bar.

Moving the Quick Launch Bar

You can move the **Quick Launch** bar separately from the taskbar by clicking at the leftmost edge of the **Quick Launch** bar (marked by two rows of small, dimpled dots) and dragging it. You can move the bar to one of the other edges of your display or into the center of the window.

Don't See a Quick Launch Bar?

On some computers, the **Quick Launch** bar may be disabled. If you don't see the **Quick Launch** bar and want to add it, right-click anywhere on your taskbar and choose **Properties**. On the **Taskbar** tab of the **Taskbar and Start Menu Properties** dialog box that opens, choose the **Show Quick Launch** option.

End

How to Start a Program When Windows Starts

Windows maintains a special folder named **Startup** that lets you specify programs, folders, and even documents that open every time Windows starts. You can see the **Startup** folder and what's in it by selecting **Start, All Programs**, and **Startup**. The following steps show you how to add shortcuts to that folder.

Begin

1 Find the Item You Want to Add

Use the **My Computer** or **My Documents** window to find the item you want to add to the **Startup** folder menu. This item can be a document, program, or even a folder.

2 Drag the Item over the Start Menu

Using the left mouse button, click and drag the item over the **Start** button, but *do not* release the mouse button yet.

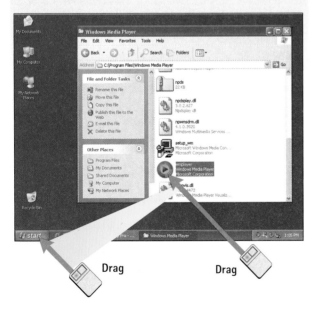

Drag   Drag

3 Drag the Item over the All Programs Folder

Continue dragging the item and hold it over the **All Programs** option on the **Start** menu. Do not release the mouse button yet.

Drag

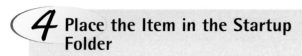

4 Place the Item in the Startup Folder

When the **All Programs** folder opens, drag the item to the **Startup** folder and drop it there.

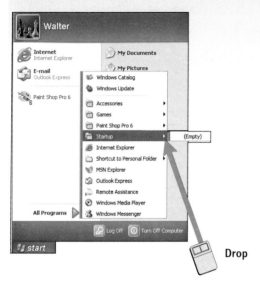

Drop

How-To Hints

Removing Startup Programs

Many of the programs you install (and even Windows itself) have small associated programs that are configured to start when your computer starts. For example, Windows Messenger starts automatically and so does the AOL Instant Messenger when you install AOL. You can usually tell these programs have started because you can see icons representing them in the system tray at the right side of the taskbar. If you have programs starting automatically that you would rather did not, try checking the **Startup** folder first. If there is a shortcut in there for the program, you can delete it and the program will not start automatically anymore. If you're not sure whether it's necessary that the program start when Windows starts, try moving the shortcut to your desktop and restarting Windows to see what happens. You can always move the shortcut back into the **Startup** folder if you decide you need it. If a program is starting and you don't see a shortcut for it in the **Startup** folder, try clicking or right-clicking the icon in the system tray. Sometimes you will find an option to exit the program or even prevent it from starting with Windows.

End

16

How to Set Accessibility Options

Windows includes a number of accessibility options intended for people with disabilities (some people without disabilities find these settings useful, as well). These options include a small window that magnifies whatever part of the screen your mouse pointer is on and the ability to make Windows flash the display instead of making sounds. All these options are available through the Windows **Control Panel**.

Begin

1 Open the Control Panel

Click the **Start button** and then choose **Control Panel**. The **Control Panel** window opens.

Click

2 Open Accessibility Options

Double-click the **Accessibility Options** icon. The **Accessibility Options** dialog box opens.

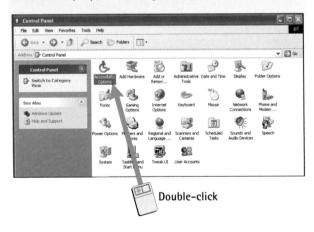

Double-click

3 Set Keyboard Options

Switch to the **Keyboard** tab to set various accessibility options for working with the keyboard. The **StickyKeys** option lets you press one key at a time (**Ctrl** and then **Shift**, for example) instead of having to press them simultaneously. The **FilterKeys** option tells Windows to ignore brief or quickly repeated keystrokes that may be caused by unsteady hands on the keyboard. The **ToggleKeys** option plays sounds to indicate when the **Caps Lock**, **Num Lock**, and **Scroll Lock** keys are turned on or off.

_4_ Set Sound Options

Switch to the **Sound** tab to set options for using sound in addition to the visual feedback your computer gives you in certain circumstances. The **SoundSentry** option generates visual warnings (such as flashes) when your system would otherwise just play a sound. The **ShowSounds** option generates captions for the speech and sounds made by certain programs.

_5_ Set Display Options

Switch to the **Display** tab to find settings that make it easier to read the screen. The **High Contrast** option causes Windows to display the desktop using colors and fonts that are easier to read. The **Cursor Options** adjust the size and blink rate of the cursor that appears where text is about to be typed.

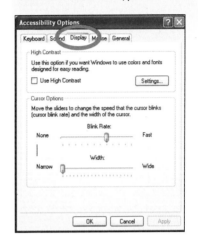

_6_ Set Mouse Options

Switch to the **Mouse** tab to enable **MouseKeys**, a feature that lets you use your keyboard's number pad to control the mouse pointer. Click the **Settings** button to open a dialog box that lets you control the pointer speed and turn on and off the **MouseKeys** feature using the **Num Lock** key on your keyboard.

_7_ Set General Options

Switch to the **General** tab to set options that pertain to all accessibility features, such as when they are used and whether they are automatically turned off after a period of time. When you have specified all the options you want, click **OK** to apply the settings and close the dialog box.

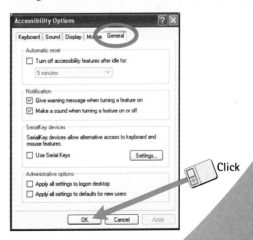

Click

End

Task

1 How to Back Up Your Files   226

2 How to Restore Files from a Backup   228

3 How to Use Automated System Recovery   230

4 How to Free Up Space on Your Hard Disk   232

5 How to Defragment Your Hard Disk   234

6 How to Schedule a Task to Occur Automatically   236

7 How to Use the Windows Troubleshooters   238

8 How to Get System Information   240

9 How to Use System Restore   242

10 How to Compress Files and Folders   244

PART 11

Using the System Tools

*C*omputers are pretty complicated. A lot of things can happen during the course of normal use that can slow a computer down or keep certain things from working as they should. If you are connected to a network, the chances are that you have a network administrator to rely on for fixing problems when they occur. If you don't have an administrator, you'll have to take things into your own hands. There are a few things you can do to help make sure that your computer is performing well and your work is not lost if something does go wrong. Windows XP provides a number of important system tools to help you protect your files and maintain your computer.

In this part, you learn how to back up your files and how to restore files from a backup. You also learn to create an Emergency Repair Disk, which holds critical information for restoring your system should something go wrong. You learn to use the Disk Cleanup tool to remove unnecessary files from your computer to help free up disk space. You also learn to use the Disk Defragmenter, a tool that helps organize the files on your disk so everything moves a bit faster. You learn to use the built-in automatic troubleshooters and information tools that Windows provides for determining why a component is not working the way it should and what you can do to fix it. Finally, you'll learn how to use the System Restore tool and how to compress folders and drives.

How to Back Up Your Files

Any experienced computer professional will tell you that the single most important thing you can do to prevent loss of work should your computer fail is to back up your files. Many companies have automated routines for backing up users' files, and you should check with your administrator to see what the policy is at your company. Windows XP comes with a program named **Backup**, which lets you back up files on your computer to floppy disks, a Zip drive, a recordable CD-ROM drive, or even another computer on your network. Even if your network has backup routines in place, you might also want to use the Backup program on your more important files.

Begin

1 Start Backup

Click the **Start** button and select **All Programs, Accessories, System Tools,** and **Backup.**

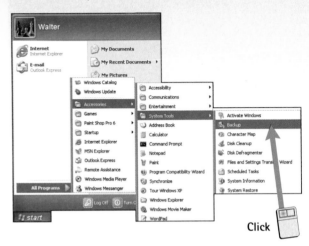

Click

2 Start the Backup Wizard

Click the **Backup Wizard** button to start the **Backup Wizard.** The first page of the wizard is a welcome page. Just click the **Next** button when you see the welcome page.

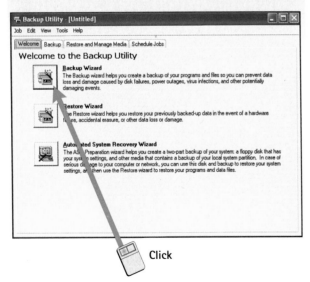

Click

3 Choose What to Back Up

Choose what you want to back up on your computer. Unless your backup media (floppy, tape drive, and so on) is very fast, it is usually best to back up only selected files.

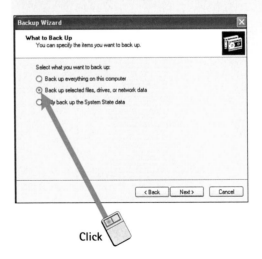

Click

4 Choose the Files to Back Up

This page of the **Backup Wizard** works just like Windows Explorer. In the left pane, select a folder you want to browse. Files in that folder appear in the right pane. Click the boxes next to the files to indicate that you want to include those files in the backup. You can also select whole folders. When you have selected all the files you want to back up, click the **Next** button to go on.

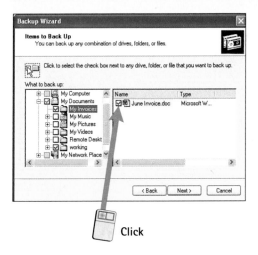

Click

5 Choose Where to Back It Up

No matter how many files you back up, the whole backup is saved as a single file with a **.bkf** extension. Type the path for the drive and folder where you want to save the backup. If you don't know the exact path, click the **Browse** button to locate it. Using the **Browse** button also lets you locate drives on other computers on the network. Click the **Next** button to go on.

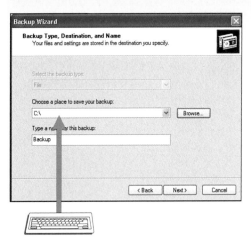

6 Finish

The last page of the **Backup Wizard** gives you a second look at all the settings you've made. Click the **Back** button to go back and change settings. Make sure that your backup media (floppy disk, CD-ROM, tape, Zip disk, and so on) are inserted in the appropriate drive. Click the **Finish** button to go on with the backup.

Click

7 View the Report

While the backup is in progress, a dialog box appears that shows you how things are going. When the backup is finished, Windows lets you know that it was completed successfully. Click the **Report** button to view a detailed report on the backup. Click **Close** to finish up.

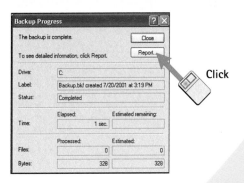

Click

End

How to Restore Files from a Backup

Whether you are restoring files from a backup following a computer failure or you just want to dig up an old file you deleted, Windows makes the process pretty easy. Before you get started, make sure that the disk you backed up to (Zip disk, CD-ROM, or whatever) is inserted in your drive.

Begin

1 Start Backup

Click the **Start** button and choose **All Programs, Accessories, System Tools**, and **Backup**.

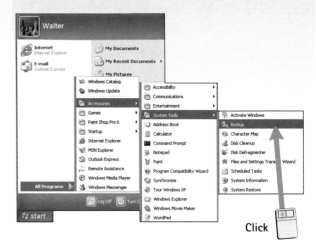

Click

2 Start the Restore Wizard

Click the **Restore Wizard** button to start the **Restore Wizard**. The first page of the wizard is a welcome page. To continue, just click the **Next** button when you see the welcome page.

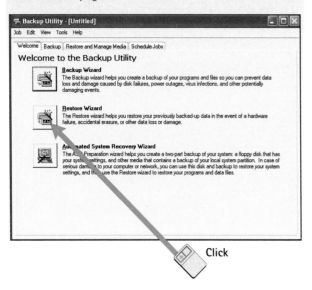

Click

3 Choose What to Restore

A list of backup sessions on your backup media is displayed. Choose the backup session you want to restore by clicking the check box next to it. Sessions are listed by date. If you want to know exactly what is in a session, right-click it and choose **Catalog** from the shortcut menu. When you're done, click the **Next** button.

Click

4 Finish

The last page of the **Restore Wizard** gives you a second look at all the selections you've made. Click the **Back** button to go back and change settings. Click the **Finish** button to go on with the restore process.

Click

5 Enter the Backup Filename

Type the path and name of the backup file you want to restore from. If you don't know the exact path or name, click the **Browse** button to locate the file. When you're ready to start, click the **OK** button.

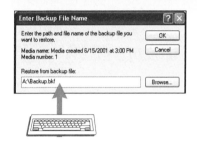

6 View the Report

While the restore is in progress, a dialog box appears that shows you how things are going. When the restore is finished, Windows lets you know that it was completed successfully. Click the **Report** button to view a detailed report on the backup. Click **Close** to finish up.

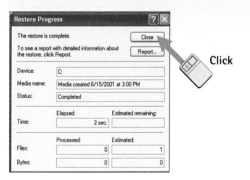

Click

How-To Hints

Choosing a Backup Session

If you are using a large backup media, such as CD-ROM, you may have a number of backup sessions available from which to restore. Sessions are listed by date and by the name you gave them during the backup. This is why it is important to give your backup sessions names that mean something to you. You can also right-click any session and choose **Catalog** from the shortcut menu to browse the actual files contained in the backup.

End

How to Use Automated System Recovery

Automated System Recovery is a two-part backup process. First, a snapshot of your vital system settings and files is taken and backed up to the backup media of your choice. Second, an Emergency Recovery Disk is created that you can use to boot your system and recover the saved system settings in the event of failure.

Begin

1 Start Backup

Click the **Start** button and choose **All Programs, Accessories, System Tools,** and **Backup.**

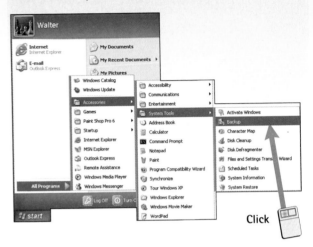

Click

2 Start the Automated System Recovery Wizard

Click the **Automated System Recovery Wizard** button to start the **Automated System Recovery Wizard.** On the welcome page of the wizard that opens, click **Next** to go on.

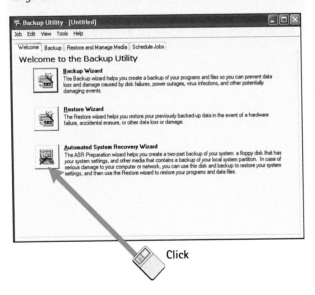

Click

3 Enter a Backup Destination

Type the path for the location where selected files should be backed up. The files will probably consume a good amount of disk space, so you will need to select a location on your hard disk or use a large backup medium, such as a tape, a Zip drive, or a CD-RW. Click **Next** to go on.

Click

4 Click Finish

Click the **Finish** button to begin the backup.

Click

5 Insert a Disk

After Windows backs up certain vital system information to the location you specified, it will prompt you to insert a floppy disk in the A: drive. This floppy disk will become your Automated System Recovery disk (also known as the Emergency Repair Disk). Insert a blank, formatted floppy disk into your A: drive and click the **OK** button.

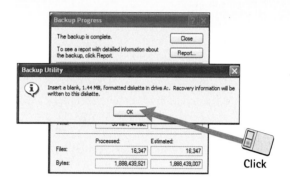

Click

6 Finish and Label the Disk

When the Automated System Recovery disk has been created, a dialog box lets you know the process was successful. Click the **OK** button to finish. Be sure to label the disk and keep it in a safe place.

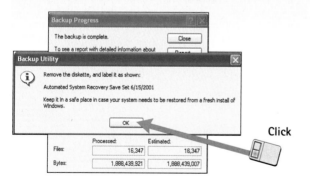

Click

How-To Hints

Using the ASR Disk

If your computer experiences a major system failure (for example, it cannot finish booting), you will have to repair the operating system. If you suffer a hardware failure (such as a crashed hard disk), you can run this process after repairing the hardware to restore your system. To start the emergency repair process, start your computer using the original Windows XP setup disks or CD-ROM. During setup process, you are given the option of performing setup or performing a repair. Choose to repair the system; the setup program prompts you to insert the ASR disk.

End

TASK 4

How to Free Up Space on Your Hard Disk

Even with the size of today's large hard drives, you might still find conservation of disk space an issue. During normal operation, Windows and the programs you run on it create temporary and backup files. Unfortunately, these programs (Windows included) are sometimes not very good at cleaning up after themselves. Windows includes a tool named **Disk Cleanup** that you can use to search for and delete unnecessary files.

Begin

1 Run Disk Cleanup

Click the **Start** button and choose **All Programs, Accessories, System Tools,** and **Disk Cleanup.**

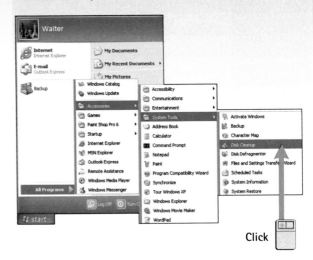

Click

2 Select the Drive to Clean Up

Use the drop-down list to select the hard drive on which you want to free up space. Click the **OK** button after you have chosen your drive. Disk Cleanup scans the specified drive for files. This process might take a few minutes.

Click

3 Select the Items to Remove

After Disk Cleanup has finished scanning your drive, it presents a list of categories for files it has found. Next to each category, Windows shows how much drive space all the files in that category take up. You can mark categories for deletion by clicking the check boxes next to them.

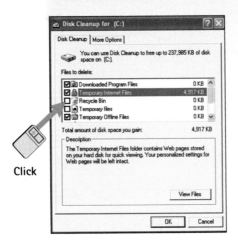

Click

4 View Files

Categories that are already checked, such as **Downloaded Program Files**, are always safe to delete. Other categories might contain important files, and it is up to you to decide whether they should be deleted. Select a category by clicking its name once and click the **View Files** button to see what's contained in that category.

Click

5 Click OK

When you have selected all the categories for files you want to delete, click the **OK** button to proceed. Windows asks whether you are sure you want to delete the files. If you are, click the **Yes** button.

Click

How-To Hints

Taking Out the Trash

One way to keep space free on your hard drive is to regularly empty your **Recycle Bin**. Right-click the bin and choose **Empty Recycle Bin** from the shortcut menu to delete all the files it holds. You can also double-click the **Recycle Bin** to display a list of the files it contains and then delete individual files.

Deleting Only Certain Files

When you click the **View Files** button (as described in Step 4), a standard window opens showing the files in that location. If you want to delete only some of the files, select them in this window and delete them by pressing the **Delete** key. Make sure that you deselect the folder when you return to the **Disk Cleanup Wizard** or you'll end up deleting all the files anyway. Also, when you delete selected files using the **View Files** method, the files are moved to the **Recycle Bin**. You must empty the **Recycle Bin** to finish freeing the disk space. When you remove files using the **Disk Cleanup Wizard**, the files are permanently deleted.

End

How to Defragment Your Hard Disk

When you delete a file on your computer, Windows doesn't really remove it. It just marks that space as available for new information to be written. When a new file is written to disk, part of the file might be written to one available section of disk space, part might be written to another, and part to yet another space. This process fitting files in pieces on the disk is called *fragmentation*. It is a normal process, and Windows keeps track of files just fine. The problem is that when a drive has a lot of fragmentation, it can take Windows longer to find the information it is looking for. You can speed up drive access significantly by periodically defragmenting your drive.

Begin

1 Run Disk Defragmenter

Click the **Start** button and choose **All Programs, Accessories, System Tools,** and **Disk Defragmenter.**

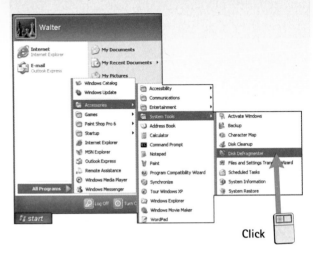

Click

2 Choose a Drive

The window at the top of the screen lists all the hard drives on your computer. Select the drive you want to defragment by clicking it once.

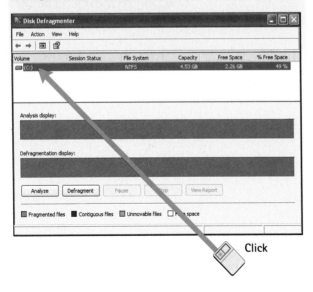

Click

3 Analyze Drive

Click the **Analyze** button to have **Disk Defragmenter** analyze the selected drive for the amount of fragmentation on it. This process might take a few minutes, and the process is depicted graphically for you while you wait.

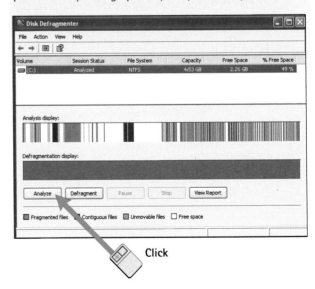

Click

4 View Report

When the analysis is done, a dialog box appears that lets you view a report or go ahead with defragmentation. You can also perform these actions from the main program window itself. Click the **View Report** button to view a detailed report of the fragmented files that the analysis has discovered.

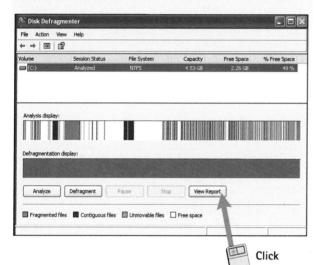

Click

5 Defragment Drive

Should the analysis and report prove that your drive needs to be defragmented, you can start the procedure by clicking the **Defragment** button. This process can take a while—even an hour or so—depending on the size of your hard drive and how fragmented it is.

Click

How-To Hints

Some Helpful Tips

Make sure that you close all programs before beginning the defragmentation process. Also make sure that all documents are finished printing, scanning, downloading, and so on. In other words, your computer should not be busy doing anything else. During the defragmentation process, you will not be able to run any other programs. Unless you enjoy watching the defragmentation process, take a coffee break.

End

How to Schedule a Task to Occur Automatically

Windows XP includes a task scheduler that lets you schedule certain programs to run automatically. This can be particularly useful with programs such as **Disk Cleanup** and **Disk Defragmenter**, although you can schedule virtually any program. You might, for example, schedule **Disk Cleanup** to run automatically every Friday night after work and **Disk Defragmenter** to run once a month or so, saving you the time of running these programs when you have better things to do.

Begin

1 Start Scheduled Tasks

Click the **Start** button and choose **All Programs, Accessories, System Tools,** and **Scheduled Tasks.**

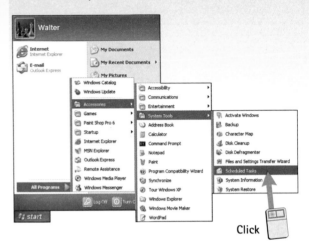

Click

2 Add a Scheduled Task

Double-click the **Add Scheduled Task** icon to start the **Scheduled Task Wizard.** The first page of the wizard is just a welcome page. Click the **Next** button to go on.

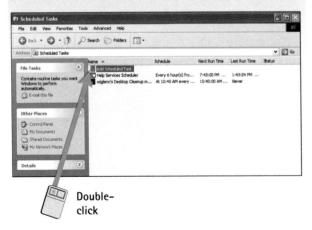

Double-click

3 Choose a Program to Run

Select the program you want to schedule from the list by clicking it once. If you don't see the program on the list, you can try to locate it by clicking the **Browse** button. After you've selected the program, click the **Next** button to go on.

Click

4 Choose When to Run the Program

If you want to change the default name of the task, type a new name in the text box. Choose when you want to perform the task by enabling that option. When you're done, click the **Next** button to go on.

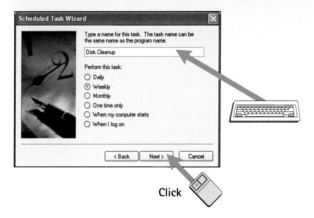

Click

5 Choose a Time and Day

If you chose to run the program daily, weekly, or monthly, you must also specify the time of day to run the program. Type in a time or use the scroll buttons. You must also select the day or days you want the program to run by clicking the appropriate check boxes. Click the **Next** button to go on.

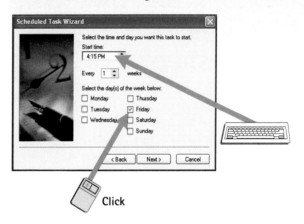

Click

6 Enter a Username and Password

To run a program in Windows, **Task Scheduler** must have your username and password. Type this information into the boxes on this page, and then click the **Next** button to go on.

7 Finish

Click the **Finish** button to schedule your new task. When the specified day and time roll around, the selected program starts and runs with the default settings. If you want the selected program to start using any other settings, you'll have to consult the Help file for the program to see whether it supports changing settings in a scheduled task.

Click

End

How to Use the Windows Troubleshooters

If your computer is on a corporate office network, you are probably fortunate enough to have a network administrator to call when your computer has problems. In a home office situation where *you* are the network administrator, or for a standalone installation, you will be relieved to know that Windows includes a few useful troubleshooters that can help you diagnose and repair problems.

Begin

1 Start Help

Click the **Start** button and then choose **Help and Support**.

Click

2 Open Fixing a Problem Category

Click the **Fixing a problem** subject once to expand it.

Click

3 Choose a Type of Problem

From the list on the left side of the window, choose the type of problem you are having by clicking it once.

Click

4 Choose a Troubleshooter

From the window on the right, locate the troubleshooter you want to run. After you find the troubleshooter you want, **Printing** for example, click it once to start it.

Click

5 Work Through the Steps

Troubleshooters work just like wizards. Each page asks a question. Choose the answer by clicking it once, and then click the **Next** button to go on. Some pages offer steps for you to try to fix your problem. If the steps work, you're done. If the steps don't work, the troubleshooter continues. If the troubleshooter can't fix your problem, it recommends where you should go (Web sites and Microsoft technical support) for more information.

Click

End

How to Get System Information

Often, fixing a problem requires that you find more information about your computer or your installation of Windows than is normally necessary. Fortunately, Windows includes a useful tool named **System Information** that lets you browse all kinds of useful information. Some of this information can be useful to you in determining why something is not working. For example, you can determine whether an existing piece of hardware is conflicting with the new piece you just installed. Much of the information is technical and will be useful when you're speaking with a technical support person.

Begin

1 Start System Information

Click the **Start** button and choose **More Programs, Accessories, System Tools**, and **System Information**.

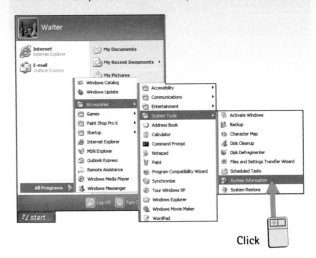

Click

2 View System Summary

The right side of the **Help and Support Services** window that opens contains a brief summary of your system, including the exact version of Windows installed and a snapshot of your basic hardware.

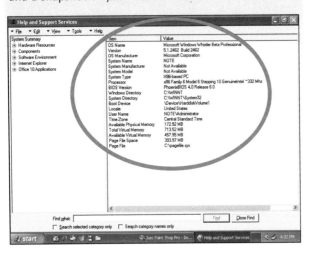

3 View Hardware Resources

Expand the **Hardware Resources** item in the left side of the window by clicking the plus sign next to it. Inside, you'll find various types of resources you can check on. Click any of these resources, such as **IRQs**, to view details on that resource.

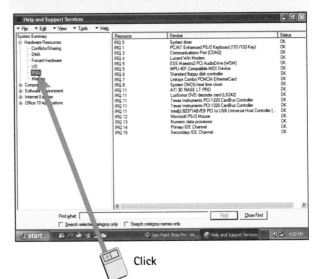

Click

4 View Components

Expand the **Components** item to view details about many of the hardware components on your system. Click any subcategory, such as **CD-ROM**, to view details about that particular component.

Click

5 Access Tools

Many useful tools are available on the **Tools** menu in the **Help and Support Services** window. Some of the tools are not available anywhere else in Windows. A good example is the **DirectX Diagnostic Tool**, which can help you diagnose video problems related to the Windows DirectX drivers.

Click

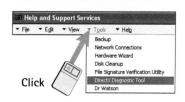

How-To Hints

Printing and Exporting System Information

The **File** menu of the **Help and Support Services** window offers the ability to print and export your system information. When exporting, a text file is created. The entire set of system information (not just the page you're looking at) is printed or exported.

End

9

How to Use System Restore

Windows XP automatically creates system *restore points* at regular intervals. These restore points are basically backups of vital system settings and information. If you make a major change to your system, such as installing a new application or hardware driver, and then discover that the change has caused unwanted side effects, you can return to a previous restore point. The **System Restore** tool is used both to restore the computer to a previous point and to manually create a restore point.

1 Start System Restore

Click the **Start** button and choose **All Programs, Accessories, System Tools,** and **System Restore.**

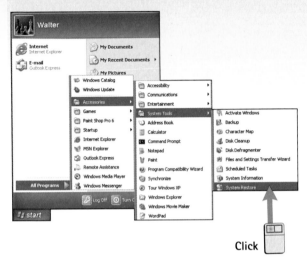

Click

2 Create a Restore Point

Although Windows creates restore points automatically, you can manually set a restore point before you make some change to your system that you think might adversely affect system performance. In the **System Restore** window that opens, select the **Create a restore point** option and then click **Next.**

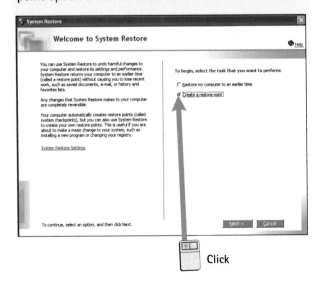

Click

3 Name the Restore Point

Type a name for the restore point that describes it well enough to help you remember it. For example, you might name the restore point after the date, an action you just performed (or are about to perform), or after the fact that you have installed Windows and have everything working the way you want.

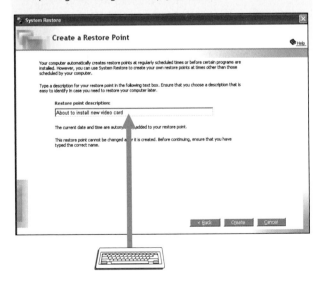

4 Create the Restore Point

When you have named the new restore point, click
Create.

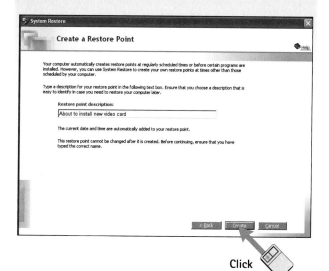

Click

5 Close System Restore

When Windows has successfully created the restore point,
it displays a message to that effect. To return to the
Welcome to System Restore screen shown in Step 2,
click **Home**. Otherwise, click **Close**.

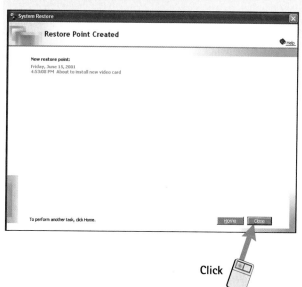

Click

How-To Hints

Restoring a Restore Point

Returning your computer to a restore point is just as easy as setting one. On the initial
page of the **System Restore Wizard**, select the **Restore my computer to an earlier time** option.
The wizard will guide you through choosing the restore point to which you want to return your
system. The necessary files will be restored, your computer will be restarted, and you'll be back
in business in no time. If you use **System Restore** to return your computer settings to a point
before a software installation that went bad, note that **System Restore** just returns your
Windows settings to the restore point—it does not remove the software from your computer. To
do that, use the procedure described in Part 12, Task 2, "How to Change or Remove a Program."

End

How to Compress Files and Folders

Windows XP includes a built-in compression tool. You can compress files and folders to help save hard disk space. While compressed, the items are still accessible. In fact, you probably won't notice any difference between files you've compressed and those you haven't. On large files, however, you may notice that access is a bit slower than normal because of the compression. But if disk space is an issue, you may decide that it's better to have the large file and wait through the file-access hesitation.

Begin

1 Open an Item's Properties

In the **My Documents** or **My Computer** window, right-click the file or folder you want to compress and choose the **Properties** command from the shortcut menu.

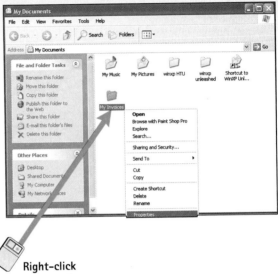

Right-click

2 Open Advanced Options

On the **General** tab of the **Properties** dialog box, click the **Advanced** button to open the **Advanced Attributes** dialog box.

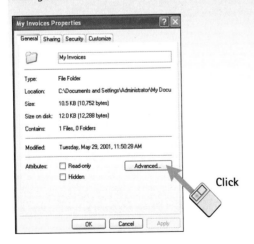

Click

3 Compress the Item

Select the **Compress contents to save disk space** option. Note that there is also an option here that lets you encrypt the item. You cannot use both compression and encryption at the same time.

Click

4 Close the Dialog Boxes

Click the **OK** button to close the **Advanced Attributes** dialog box. Click the **OK** button on the **General** tab of the folder's **Properties** dialog box to close it.

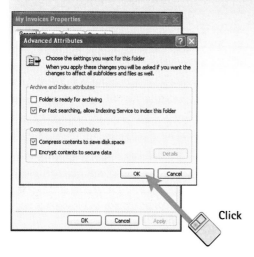

Click

5 Compress Files and Subfolders

A dialog box appears that lets you choose whether to compress only the selected folder or also to compress the files and subfolders within that folder. Choose the option you want and click the **OK** button. The file or folder is compressed.

Click

How-To Hints

Decompressing a Folder

To decompress a folder, simply follow the preceding steps and disable the **Compress contents to save disk space** option on the **Advanced Attributes** dialog box in Step 3.

Visual Indicator

When you compress a file or folder, by default Windows gives no visual indicator that compression is present. To see whether an item is compressed, you must open its **Properties** dialog box and see whether the **Compress contents to save disk space** option is enabled. However, you can tell Windows to display compressed files in a different color: Open the **Control Panel** and double-click **Folder Options**. On the **View** tab of the dialog box that opens, enable the **Display compressed files and folder in alternate color** option.

Sending Compressed Files

If you send a compressed file as an e-mail attachment or transfer a compressed file or folder to another computer using a network or a removable disk, the compression is removed on the copy that is sent. For example, if you e-mail a compressed file to a friend, the file remains compressed on your drive but the attachment is not compressed when your friend receives it.

End

Task

1 How to Add a Program to Your
Computer **248**

2 How to Change or Remove a
Program **250**

3 How to Add Windows Components
from the CD **252**

4 How to Add Windows Components
from the Internet **254**

5 How to Find Out About Your Installed
Hardware **256**

PART 12

Installing New Software and Hardware

*I*f your computer is connected to your company's network, a network administrator is probably responsible for adding and removing hardware and software on your computer. If so, you should definitely take advantage of his or her expertise. However, with Windows XP, adding new hardware and software to your system has never been easier. If you are administering your own computer or network, this part shows you the simple steps for installing your own hardware and software.

Most of the hardware and software you get these days literally installs itself. New programs usually come on CD-ROMs. With Windows XP, you can usually insert the CD-ROM and have Windows find and launch the setup routine for the program, which then walks you through the installation. Windows XP also provides a more hands-on approach to installing software. In the tasks in this part, you see how to perform a manual installation of a program and how to change settings for already-installed software. You'll also learn how to add Windows components from the CD and from Microsoft's Windows Update Web site.

Adding new hardware to a Windows XP computer is not difficult. The hardware itself, whether it is a new CD-ROM drive, modem, or video card, comes with instructions on the physical installation of the device. After the device is installed and you turn on your computer, Windows XP notices that there is new hardware and either configures that hardware for you automatically or asks you for the software that came with the device. Either way, Windows XP handles it all for you. In this part, you will learn how to check the hardware that is already installed on your system. •

Begin

How to Add a Program to Your Computer

Programs—whether they are word processors, spreadsheets, or games—are the reason you use your computer. Almost all new programs today come on CD-ROM. When you insert the CD-ROM into your drive, Windows should automatically run the setup program for you. If this is the case, you won't need to follow the procedure in this task. If the setup process does not start automatically, or if your program is on floppy disk, the following steps show you how to start the installation yourself. If you download a program from the Internet, the setup process is much the same. You'll just have to tell Windows where the files are located. If the program you download is compressed (such as in a ZIP file), you'll have to expand it before installing the program. This process is described in Part 11, "Using the System Tools."

1 Open the Control Panel

Click the **Start** button and then choose **Control Panel**. The **Control Panel** window opens.

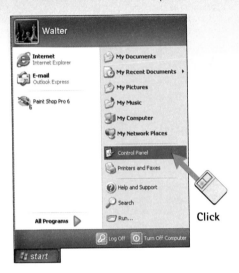

Click

2 Open the Add/Remove Programs Applet

Double-click the **Add/Remove Programs** applet to open it.

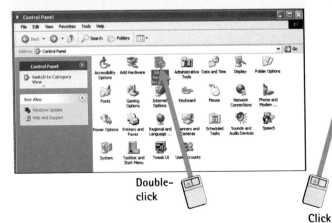

Double-click

3 Add New Programs

Use the **Add/Remove Programs** applet to add, change, and remove programs, as well as to install new Windows components. Click the **Add New Programs** button.

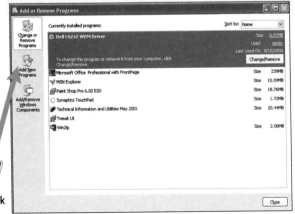

Click

4 Choose CD or Floppy

If programs are available for installation from your network, they will be listed in the window at the bottom of the dialog box (no programs in this category exist in this example). Click the **CD or Floppy** button to indicate that you want to install a program from a disk. This button launches a short wizard that helps you start a program's installation routine. The first page is just a welcome screen. Click the **Next** button to go on.

Click

5 Finish

Windows searches both your floppy and CD-ROM drives for a setup program. If it finds one, the path to the program is displayed for your approval. If you think Windows found the right one, click the **Finish** button to launch the setup program. You can also click the **Browse** button to locate the setup program yourself.

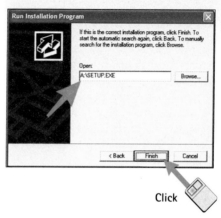

Click

How-To Hints

Installing from the My Computer Window

You can also run a setup program manually without using the **Add/Remove Programs** applet. Just open the **My Computer** window and locate the setup program yourself on the floppy or CD-ROM drive. It is almost always a program named **setup.exe**. If it is not named **setup.exe**, it will be another program with the **.exe** extension. If you can't figure out which program is used to start the installation, check to see whether the folder has a text file that explains the installation process (this file is often named **readme.txt** or **setup.txt**). When you determine the setup program, double-click it to start.

Restarting

Different programs have different installation routines. Some require that you restart your computer after the program has been installed. This is one reason why it is best to save any work and exit any running programs before you install new software.

The Program Files Folder

Your **C:** drive has a folder on it named **Program Files**. Most new programs that you install create a folder for themselves inside this folder that is used to store the program's files.

End

How to Change or Remove a Program

Some programs, such as Microsoft Office, let you customize the installation of the program to include only the components that you want in the installation. You can then add new components later if you want. The **Add/Remove Programs** applet lets you change the installation of a program, and it lets you remove the installation altogether (a process sometimes called *uninstalling* a program).

Begin

1 Open the Control Panel

Select the **Start** button and then choose **Control Panel**. The **Control Panel** window opens.

Click

2 Open the Add/Remove Programs Applet

Double-click the **Add/Remove Programs** applet to open it.

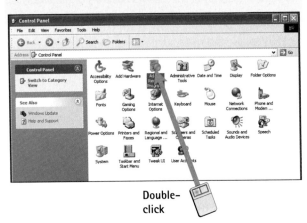

Double-click

3 Select a Program

Choose a program from the list of currently installed programs by clicking it once. Notice that Windows lets you know how much disk space each program takes up and how often you use the program.

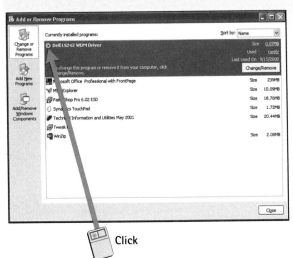

Click

4 Click Change/Remove

Programs that do not let you change the installation show only a **Change/Remove** button. Programs that do let you change the installation show both a **Change** button and a **Remove** button. Click the button that provides the action you want.

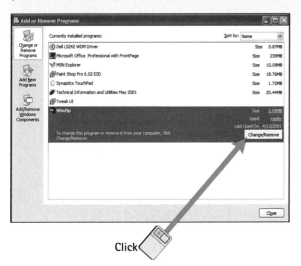

Click

5 Follow the Program's Instructions

Every program has a slightly different routine for changing or removing the installation. Follow the onscreen instructions for the program you are using.

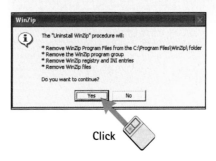

Click

How-To Hints

Be Careful

Some programs automatically go forward with a removal without giving you a chance to confirm as soon as you click the **Change/Remove** or **Remove** button. Be sure that you want to remove a program before clicking either of these buttons.

End

How to Add Windows Components from the CD

Windows XP comes with literally hundreds of components—and not all of them are installed during a normal installation of the operating system. You can add components from the Windows XP CD-ROM at any time after installation.

Begin

1 Open the Control Panel

Click the **Start** button and then choose **Control Panel**. The **Control Panel** window opens.

Click

2 Open the Add/Remove Programs Applet

Double-click the **Add/Remove Programs** applet to open it.

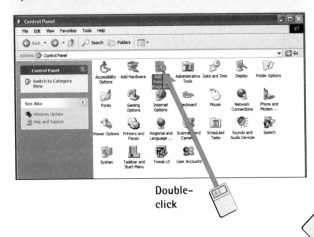

Double-click

3 Choose Add/Remove Windows Components

Click the **Add/Remove Windows Components** button. Windows searches your computer for installed Windows components and then displays the **Windows Components Wizard**. The first screen of the wizard shows a list of the components you can install from the original Windows installation CD-ROM.

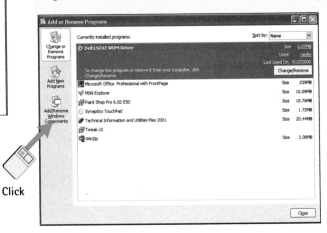

Click

4 Select a Component

Select a component from the list of available components by enabling the check box next to it. Some components have subcomponents that you can choose from. If so, the **Details** button becomes active, and you can click it to see a list of subcomponents to choose from.

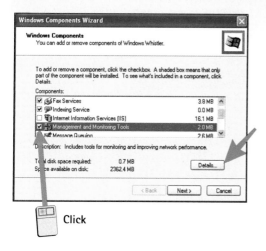

Click

5 Next

After you have selected all the components you want to install, click the **Next** button. Windows builds a list of files that must be installed and copies them to your drive. Windows might prompt you to insert your Windows CD-ROM during this process.

Click

6 Finish

After Windows has installed the components, it lets you know that the process has been completed successfully. Click the **Finish** button to finish. Depending on the components you added, Windows might need to restart your computer.

Click

How-To Hints

Installing Windows

Many components are installed when you initially set up Windows, as described in the Appendix, "Installing Windows XP." When you finish installing Windows, you should always check the installed components using the procedure described in this task to see what goodies you might be missing out on.

End

How to Add Windows Components from the Internet

Microsoft maintains a Web site, named **Windows Update**, that contains the newest versions of Windows components that you can download and add to your system. These components are updated versions of the components that come with Windows as well as new components and updates that Microsoft makes available. If, for some reason, the shortcut to the Windows update site does not work, you can also get there using the address
`http://windowsupdate.microsoft.com/`.

Begin

1 Start Windows Update

Click the **Start** button, point to **All Programs**, and select **Windows Update**. This command launches the Windows Update Web site in Internet Explorer.

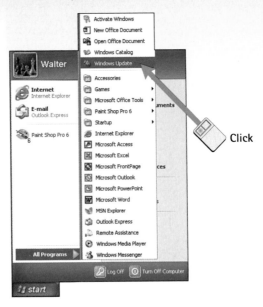

Click

2 Scan for Updates

Click the **Scan for Updates** link. The Windows Update site searches your computer for installed components and then displays a list of components that you can download and install.

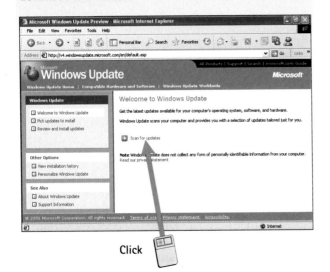

Click

3 Review and Install Updates

Critical updates (bug fixes and security patches) are automatically selected for download. If that's all you want, go ahead and click the **Review and install critical updates** link now. If any other updates are available (such as Windows XP components and driver updates), they are listed in the **Windows Update** list on the left. You can browse categories for other updates to download. Click the **Review and install critical updates** link when you're ready to continue.

Click

4 Choose Components to Update

Scroll down the **Update Basket** window to review the list of updates selected for download. Click the **Remove** button next to any update to remove it from the download list.

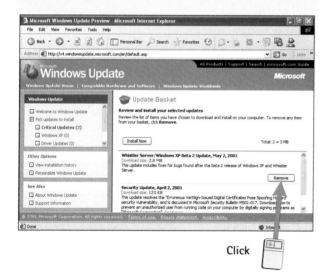

Click

5 Install the Updates

When you are satisfied with the list of updates, click the **Install Now** button to download and install the components.

Click

6 Accept the Licensing Agreement

Before you can download the updates, you must accept the Microsoft licensing agreement. Click **Accept** to continue. The files are then downloaded and installed to your computer. Windows will let you know when the process is finished and whether you have to restart your computer.

Click

How-To Hints

Automatic Updating

Windows can automatically download and install updates when it detects that they are available—provided that you have Internet access. Turn on this feature by opening the **System Control Panel** applet (open the **Control Panel** window and double-click the **System** icon) and switching to the **Automatic Updates** tab. You can have Windows download updates and install them automatically, notify you when updates are available so that you can choose the update time, or disable the service. When automatic updating is active, an icon appears in the system tray to let you know the status.

End

How to Find Out About Your Installed Hardware

Windows uses a tool named the **Device Manager** to help you find out about all the hardware on your system. You can see what is installed, what resources are used, and what devices might be having or causing problems.

Begin

1 Open System Properties

Right-click the **My Computer** icon on your desktop and choose the **Properties** command from the shortcut menu. The **Systems Properties** dialog box opens.

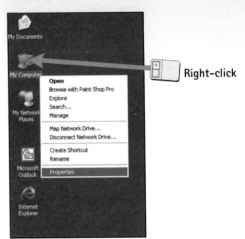

Right-click

2 Switch to Hardware Tab

Switch to the **Hardware** tab by clicking it once.

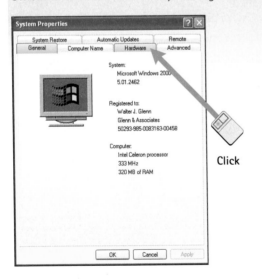

Click

3 Open the Device Manager

Click the **Device Manager** button to open the **Device Manager** window.

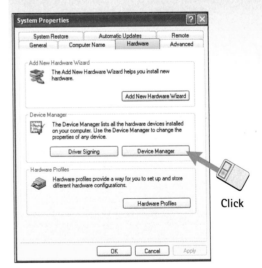

Click

4 Expand a Category

The **Device Manager** window lists hardware categories for the hardware installed on your computer. Click the plus sign next to a category to expand that category and show the actual devices attached to your computer.

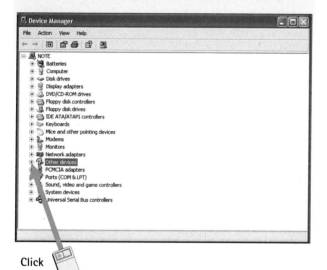

Click

5 Identify Problem Hardware

Devices that are having problems are identified with a little yellow exclamation point. Another type of symbol you might see is a red ×, which indicates a device that is turned off.

6 Open Hardware Properties

You can open a detailed **Properties** dialog box for any device by double-clicking the device's icon. The dialog box tells you whether the device is working properly and lets you disable the device. Other tabs let you reinstall software drivers for the device and view the resources it uses.

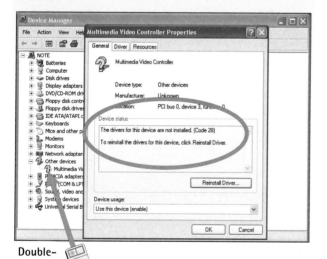

Double-click

How-To Hints

Reinstalling a Device

If you see a device that isn't working, try running the **Add Hardware** applet (you'll find it in the **Control Panel** window). Windows scans your system for devices and presents a list of what it finds. The malfunctioning device should show up in the list, and you can try to reinstall it.

End

Task

1 How to Upgrade to Windows XP   260

2 How to Install Windows XP on a Blank
   Hard Drive   262

3 How to Activate Windows XP   266

4 How to Create Setup Floppy Disks   268

Installing Windows XP

*E*ven though the product itself is far more complex than previous versions of Windows, the installation of Windows XP is much simpler than the installation of previous versions of the program. This is, in part, because the setup routine is smarter and can detect and configure more types of hardware for you. It is also because Microsoft has taken a lot of the decisions out of the setup process.

The installation of the Home and Professional versions of Windows XP do not differ significantly, except that the Professional version offers a few more networking choices. The tasks in this appendix focus on the Professional version, but are virtually identical for the Home version. There are several ways to install Windows XP. The simplest method is to upgrade from another operating system, such as Windows 98/Me, Windows NT, or Windows 2000. In this case, Windows XP takes the place of the old operating system. You can also install Windows XP while keeping an old operating system, such as Windows 98. This is known as a *dual-boot configuration*. When you turn on your computer, you are given the choice of booting to Windows XP or booting to your old operating system. Yet another way to install Windows XP is to install it on a *clean system*—one that has no operating system at all. This is the method you should choose if you build your own computer or if you decide to clear off or format your hard drive before installation. You might also use this method if you put a new hard drive in your computer.

In this appendix, you are introduced to each of these methods of installing Windows XP. You are also shown how to create a set of setup floppy disks to use when installing Windows XP on a clean system. Finally, you are shown how to activate Windows XP and register the software after it is installed. ●

How to Upgrade to Windows XP

Upgrading is the easiest way to install Windows XP. You can upgrade to Windows XP from Windows 95, Windows 98, Windows Me, Windows NT Workstation 3.5 or 4.0, and Windows 2000 Professional. To get started with the upgrade, all you have to do is insert the Windows XP CD-ROM in your computer's CD-ROM drive.

Begin

1 Upgrade

When you insert the Windows XP CD-ROM into your drive, a splash screen automatically appears along with a dialog box that asks what you want to do. Click the **Install Windows XP** button to start the upgrade. If the splash screen does not appear, you must open the CD-ROM and run the **Setup** program yourself.

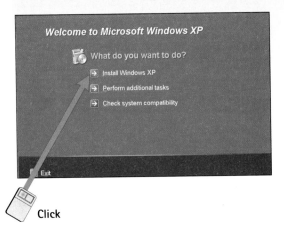

Click

2 Choose Upgrade or Clean Install

From the **Installation Type** drop-down list, choose the type of installation you want to perform. If you choose **Upgrade**, your old operating system (such as Windows 98) is overwritten by Windows XP. Settings you have made in the previous version of Windows and all your software are preserved. If you choose **Clean installation**, Windows XP is installed in addition to your old operating system. You can choose which OS to boot into whenever you start your computer. After you decide which type of installation you would like to perform, click the **Next** button to go on.

3 Accept the License Agreement

You must accept Microsoft's licensing agreement by clicking the **I accept this agreement** option before you can click the **Next** button to proceed with the installation.

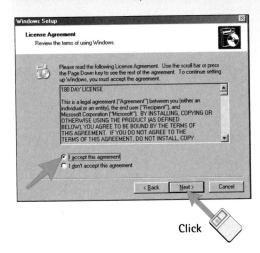

Click

4 Enter the Product Key

Type the 25-digit product identification key from the back of your CD-ROM case and click **Next** to go on.

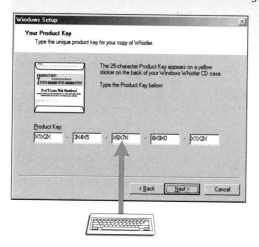

5 Perform Dynamic Update

Microsoft often updates the setup files used to install Windows XP. If your computer has Internet access, the Setup program can download any available updates. Make sure that the **Yes, download the latest Setup files** option is selected and click **Next**.

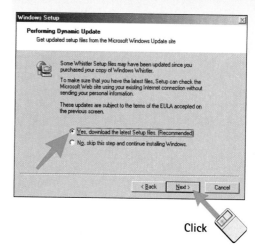

Click

6 Download Updates

From this point on, the upgrade is mostly an automatic process. After the updated files are downloaded, the Setup program will begin examining your system and copying files. During this process, your computer might restart once or twice.

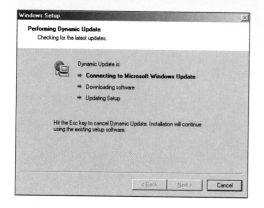

7 Finish the Upgrade

You can watch the progress of the upgrade. Depending on the speed of your computer, the process could take a good bit of time. If it ever seems that nothing is happening, you can verify that the upgrade is still working by watching the progress indicator in the lower-right corner of the screen. If this indicator stops flashing for a long period of time, you should turn your computer off and turn it back on to resume the upgrade process.

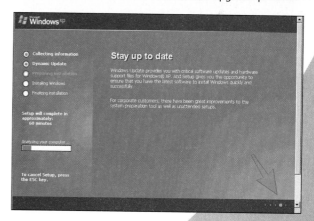

End

TASK **2**

How to Install Windows XP on a Blank Hard Drive

Installing Windows XP on a blank hard drive is a bit more complicated than upgrading from an existing version of Windows. It requires that you have a bootable CD-ROM drive or a set of five setup floppy disks. The procedure for creating the floppy disks is discussed in Task 4, "How to Create Setup Floppy Disks." To begin, insert the CD-ROM or the first of the five floppy disks into your floppy drive and start your computer. If you are using floppy disks, setup asks you for the second, third, fourth, and fifth disks before you can make any other setup decisions.

Begin

1 Choose Setup or Repair

The first decision you are asked to make is whether you want to set up Windows XP or whether you want to repair an existing installation. For more on repairing, see Part 11, "Using the System Tools." To continue with setup, press the **Enter** key.

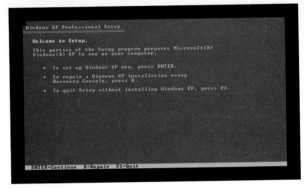

↵Enter

2 Agree to Licensing

To continue setup, you must agree to Microsoft's licensing agreement. Press the **F8** key to continue.

F8

3 Choose a Partition

You must choose the disk partition on which to install Windows XP. Highlight a partition using the up and down arrow keys (in this example, only one disk partition is available). Select the highlighted drive by pressing the **Enter** key. You can also create and delete drive partitions.

↵Enter

4 Format Your Drive

Use the arrow keys to choose whether to format your drive with the NTFS or FAT32 file system. NTFS is more secure, but only Windows XP, Windows 2000, and Windows NT recognize it. Windows 95 and 98 can recognize the FAT system. If your computer will only run Windows XP, you should use NTFS. If your computer will dual-boot Windows XP and Windows 95/98/Me, you should choose FAT32. Other users on the network will be able to access shared files no matter what file system you choose. Press **Enter** when you have made your selection. On the next setup screen, you'll be asked to confirm the format option. Depending on the size of your drive, formatting can take a few minutes.

6 Restart Your Computer

After all files are copied to your disk, your computer must restart. This happens automatically after 15 seconds, but you can also press the **Enter** key as soon as you see this screen. Make sure that you remove any floppy disks before you restart the computer. When the computer starts back up, the Setup program continues in a more familiar graphical interface.

5 Copy Files to Your Disk

The Setup program then copies files to your hard drive. This process can take several minutes.

7 Look for Hardware Devices

After your computer restarts, the Setup program initially spends several minutes looking for hardware devices attached to your computer and preparing the installation. It is normal for your screen to flicker during this process. It is also possible that the Setup program might have to restart your computer a few times. All this happens automatically. You can watch the progress indicator in the lower-right corner of the screen to make sure that the installation is proceeding.

Continued

8 Customize Your Locale

When all the hardware devices on your system have been identified, you are given the chance to customize your locale and keyboard input. The default is for the English language. Click the **Customize** button to change this locale. When you're done, click the **Next** button to go on.

Click

9 Enter Your Name and Organization

Type your name and the name of your company. If you want, you can leave the company name blank. When you're done, click the **Next** button to go on.

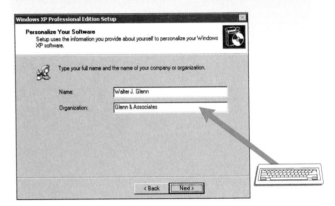

10 Enter Your Product Key

Type the 25-digit product identification number from the back of your CD-ROM case and click **Next** to go on.

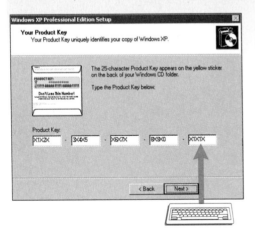

11 Enter a Computer Name and Password

When you install Windows XP on any computer, that computer must be given a name. If you are going to be on a network, this name distinguishes your computer from other computers. Even if you're not planning to put your computer on a network, you must still give the computer a name. A primary user account for your computer is created during installation. This account is given the name **Administrator**. This account is used to change basic computer settings. You can also create additional accounts that other people can use to log in (see Part 9, "Protecting Your Files"). On this screen, you should create and confirm a password for the **Administrator** account.

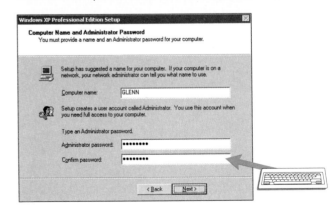

12 Enter the Date and Time

Enter the correct date and time if the Setup program is not reporting it correctly. Select the correct time zone from the drop-down list box. If you want Windows to automatically adjust the system time for daylight savings time, enable that option. Click the **Next** button to go on.

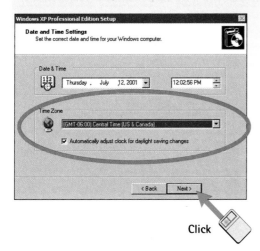

Click

13 Choose Network Settings

The Setup program then installs networking components for your computer. When it's done, you must choose your network settings. Unless you know that custom settings are required for your computer (such as a specific IP address or the names of specific servers on your network), choose the **Typical** option. When you're setting up a home network, you should choose the **Typical** option. You can always change the settings after installation if needed. Click the **Next** button to go on.

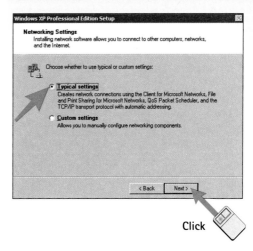

Click

14 Join a Workgroup or Domain

If your computer will be part of a Windows networking domain, choose the **Yes** option. If instead your computer will be part of a workgroup (or will be a standalone computer), choose **No**. Either way, type the name of the domain or workgroup with which this computer is to be associated into the appropriate text box. After you enter this information, the setup program will copy the needed files to your computer, finalize the installation, and restart one more time. You'll then be ready to start using Windows.

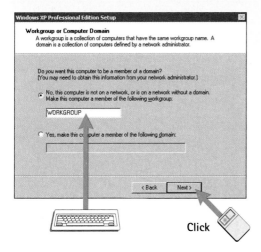

Click

End

How to Activate Windows XP

Windows XP is the first version of Windows that requires *activation*. You must register your copy of Windows over the Internet or by phone if you want to use it for more than about 14 days. The **Activation Wizard** will start immediately the first time you start Windows if you upgraded from a previous version of Windows that had Internet access. Otherwise, you might have to run the **Activate Windows** shortcut located on the **Start** menu to launch the wizard.

Begin

1 Welcome to Windows

The first page of the wizard presents the opportunity to activate your copy of Windows XP. Remember that activation is required and does not send any personal information to Microsoft. You'll also be given the chance to register your copy of Windows XP during this wizard, an optional step that does require personal information.

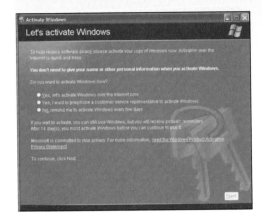

2 Choose to Activate Windows

Make sure that the **Yes, let's activate Windows over the Internet now** option is selected and click **Next**.

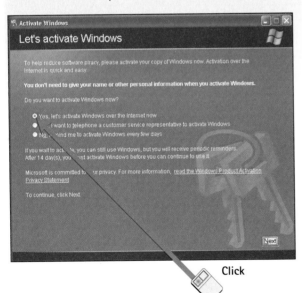

Click

3 Register Windows

During the activation process, you also have the option of *registering* Windows with Microsoft. When you register, you are registering for a warranty; Microsoft will e-mail or mail you information about their products. If you want to do so, choose **Yes, I want to register and activate Windows at the same time** and click **Next**.

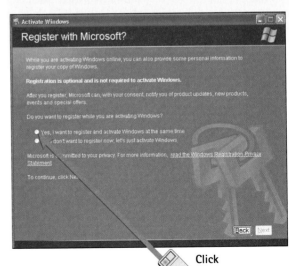

Click

4 Enter Registration Information

If you chose to register, enter the appropriate information in the text boxes. Disable the two check boxes near the bottom of the screen if you don't want to receive advertisements from Microsoft or its partners. Click **Next** to continue.

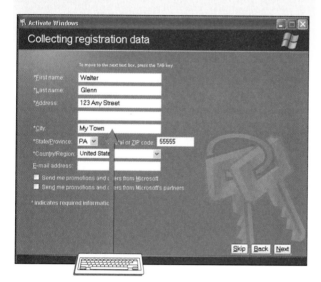

5 Finish

When the activation process is finished, click **OK**. You'll be returned to the Windows desktop.

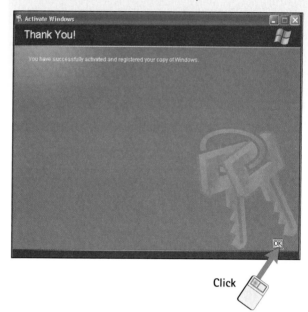

Click

End

How to Create Setup Floppy Disks

If you plan to install Windows XP on a clean system (one without an operating system on it already), you first must create a set of five setup floppy disks. These disks are used to start your computer so that it can recognize your CD-ROM drive and other hardware and install Windows XP. To make these disks, you must perform this task on a computer that has some version of Windows already installed. Insert the Windows XP CD-ROM into that computer's CD-ROM drive and follow these steps.

Begin

1 Browse This CD

When you insert the Windows XP CD-ROM, a splash screen should appear automatically, presenting you with several choices. Click the **Browse this CD** link.

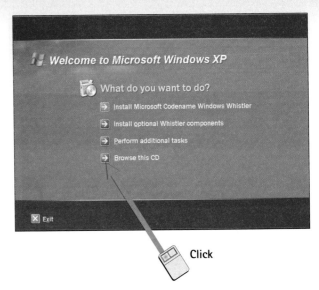

Click

2 Open the BOOTDISK Folder

Double-click the **BOOTDISK** folder to open it.

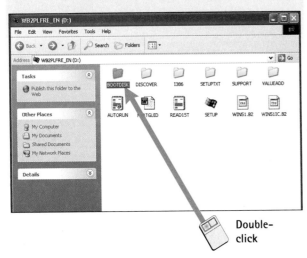

Double-click

3 Start MAKEBT32

From the list of files in the **BOOTDISK** folder, double-click the **MAKEBT32** program icon to start it. A DOS window from which the boot disks will be created opens.

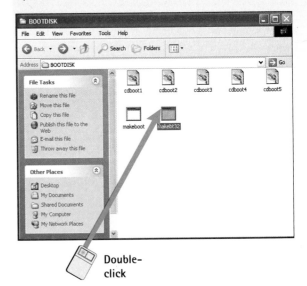

Double-click

Type the Floppy Drive Letter

Type the letter of the floppy drive you want to use to make the setup floppies. This is usually drive **A**.

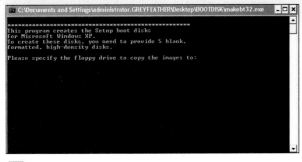

 **Insert Floppy and Press Enter**

Insert a blank, formatted floppy disk into the selected drive and press the **Enter** key. The program begins copying files to the disk, which becomes the first disk in the set. When finished copying, the program prompts you for the next disk and then the next. When the last disk is done, the DOS program window closes automatically.

⏎Enter

Label the Disks

It is important that you label the disks in the order in which they were made. When you use these disks to perform a clean installation as described in Task 2 of this appendix, you must insert the disks in proper order. Use a felt-tip marker to write the disk numbers on the disk labels.

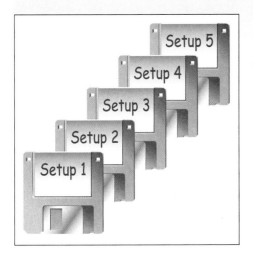

End

Glossary

A

activate   Windows XP requires that you activate your product within a set number of days or you won't be able to continue using it. Activation is a separate process from registration. During activation, a small snapshot of key pieces of hardware on your system is sent to Microsoft. No personal information is required, and none of the hardware information can be used to identify you. In theory, activation prevents people from installing the same copy of Windows on more than one computer—an action that violates the software licensing agreement. *See also* register.

administrator   A user account created during Windows installation that gives full permission to use the computer and modify settings. Administrator is also a title given to a person who manages a computer network or system.

applet   A small program. In Windows, the programs you can access from the Control Panel window (Display, System, and Mouse, for example) are often called applets.

application   A program, such as Microsoft Word, that is separate from Windows.

associate   A document file is "associated with" the program that created it. Files of a certain type (for example, text files with the file extension **.txt**) are associated with the Windows applet Notepad. If you double-click a file to open it, the program associated with that file type launches and opens the selected file.

attachment   A file that is inserted into an e-mail message and sent to a recipient.

Automated System Recovery   A feature of the Windows XP Backup utility, Automated System Recovery backs up certain system files and then creates an emergency rescue floppy disk that you can use to restore your system following a failure.

B

back up   To copy files from your primary computer to separate media (such as a floppy disk or Zip disk) in case the hard disk on the primary computer fails.

boot   To start a computer. During the boot process, the many files that make up the Windows operating system are loaded into memory.

boot disk   A floppy disk that can be used to boot your computer. Boot disks are often used to recover from a system failure or to install Windows.

briefcase   A special folder designed primarily for users who want to transfer files to another computer. The briefcase contains functions for moving and synchronizing files.

browser   A program, such as Internet Explorer, that can display a Web page. Some browsers can display text, graphics, and frames; other browsers can display only text. Popular browsers other than Internet Explorer include Netscape Navigator and Opera.

C

cascade   A way to arrange multiple windows on the screen. The multiple windows are layered, one on top of the other, so that the title bars of all the windows can be seen.

CD-ROM   A type of optical disc that stores up to one gigabyte of data. The setup files for most applications today come on CD-ROM discs.

clean installation   An installation of Windows onto a blank, formatted hard disk. *See also* upgrade.

click   To position the mouse pointer over a file or folder and click the left button on the mouse once. Clicking is used to select files in Windows and to follow a link on the Internet.

Close button   The button with the × on it, found in the upper-right corner of most windows and dialog boxes. Click the Close button to close a window.

collection   A group of associated pictures or video clips in Windows Media Player. Collections are used for organizational purposes.

color depth   The number of colors displayed on your screen. Common color depths include 16 colors, 256 colors, 16,000 colors (24-bit), and millions of colors (32-bit). Change the color depth used by Windows using the Display Properties dialog box.

compression   A way to store data so that it takes up less disk space than normal. Windows XP offers built-in compression that does not require a separate application.

computer name   A name of up to 15 characters given to a computer. On a network, this name helps distinguish the computer from other computers.

Control Panel   A special folder that contains applets used to configure various Windows settings, such as display, mouse use, and sound.

D

decryption   To remove the encryption from a file or folder. *See also* encryption.

defragment   *See* fragmentation.

desktop   The metaphor used by Windows to display your file system. The desktop is the main screen in Windows, on which various icons are displayed.

desktop theme   A coordinated collection of background colors, wallpaper, mouse pointers, and sounds used to provide a unique feel to your desktop.

Device Manager   An application used to control the settings for hardware on your computer. The Device Manager is used to enable and disable hardware devices, as well as to control driver versions and other settings.

disable   In a list of check-box options (as in a dialog box), to remove a check mark from the check box for a particular option. In contrast, you enable an option by clicking an empty check box to place a check mark in the check box.

domain   A way of grouping computers and users in a fairly complicated network. Domains are often used at large companies, where powerful computers called "servers" provide security, Internet access, file storage, and much more to less powerful computers called "workstations." If your computer is on a Windows network, it will either be part of a domain or part of a workgroup. *See also* workgroup.

double-click   To position the mouse pointer over a file or folder and click the left mouse button twice in rapid succession. Double-clicking opens, or launches, a file or folder.

download   To transfer a file from another computer to your own. Downloading commonly refers to transferring a file from an Internet site to your computer.

draft mode   To print a document in a special mode offered by many programs that reduces the amount of ink used during printing and also reduces the quality of the printed document.

dual-boot   A computer on which two operating systems have been installed. When a computer is configured to dual-boot, you are presented with a menu when the computer first starts that prompts you to choose the operating system you want to use.

E

e-mail   Electronic mail messages sent between different users on a network, such as the Internet. Some e-mail systems are configured only on a local network, and e-mail messages can only be sent between other users on the network.

enable   In a list of check-box options (as in a dialog box), to place a check mark in the check box for a particular option. In contrast, you disable an option by clicking a check mark to make the check box empty.

encryption   To translate data into a secret code that only certain users can access. Windows XP provides built-in encryption. After a file is encrypted by a user, only that user can decrypt the file.

Everyone group   A special security group that includes all users of the network. By default, the Everyone group is given read access to all files and folder on your computer that you share with the network. It is best to remove this group and narrow the focus of users to whom you allow access to a resource.

event   An occurrence in Windows, such as when you delete a file or empty the Recycle Bin. An event can also be an occurrence you don't cause, such as when Windows displays an error message. Most such occurrences can be associated with sounds.

Explorer   *See* Windows Explorer.

extension   The three-letter suffix following the dot in a filename. The extension usually identifies the type of file (for example, a **.doc** extension identifies the file as a Microsoft Word document, a **.jpg** extension identifies the file a s a JPEG image file).

F–G

FAT32   A version of the File Allocation Table (FAT) disk format used mainly in Windows 98 and Windows Me. Windows XP can also use the FAT32 file system. When using FAT32, Windows XP cannot use several advanced features, such as encryption and compression. For that reason, it is best to use the NTFS file system with Windows XP whenever possible.

Favorites   A special folder that contains links to favorite Web pages in Internet Explorer.

file   A collection of data that is stored as a single unit on a disk drive and given a name. Almost all information stored on a computer, including Windows itself, is stored as files.

firewall   A system designed to prevent unauthorized access to a computer or an entire network. Firewalls can be hardware-based or software-based. Windows XP comes with a software firewall.

floppy disk   A removable disk that can hold up to 1.44MB of data. Floppy disks are commonly used to transfer information between computers and to back up small amounts of data.

folder   A Windows object that can contain files and other folders. Folders are used to organize storage. (On older, nongraphical systems, folders are called directories.)

format   To prepare a storage medium, such as a hard disk or floppy disk, for writing data. Windows includes utilities for formatting disks.

fragmented   When data is deleted from a hard drive, the data is not actually removed. Instead, it is marked so that it can be overwritten. When new data is stored, it is written to any empty spaces on the drive. These spaces are not necessarily contiguous, which leads to a condition known as fragmentation. Fragmented drives are usable, but can slow down a system. Windows XP includes a defragmenting program that rewrites the data on a drive so that it is contiguous.

H–I–J

home page   The top page of a Web site. The default Web page that loads whenever you open Internet Explorer is also called a home page (it's often called *your* home page).

icon   A small picture on the desktop or in a folder that represents a file or folder. The icon usually helps indicate what kind of file or folder an object is.

Inbox   The folder in an e-mail program to which new messages are delivered.

install   To load software (such as Windows or Microsoft Office) onto your computer. Most programs are installed using a setup program that guides you through the installation step by step. The word "install" is also used to refer to the process of setting up other devices and software configurations on a computer. For example, configuring a printer to work on your computer is often referred to as "installing the printer." Hooking up a new hard drive inside your computer is referred to as "installing the hard drive."

Internet Explorer   The Web browser built into Windows XP.

ISP (Internet service provider)   A company that provides access to the Internet. An ISP might also provide a range of other Web-related services in addition to providing access.

JPEG   A graphics file format that makes use of lossy compression techniques, which means that image quality is degraded when you compress the file.

K–L

lasso The dotted rectangle that follows the mouse pointer when you drag around a group of objects. The lasso encircles the objects and selects all the objects at once.

link On a Web page, a selection of text or a graphic that, when clicked, causes the Web browser to load another Web page.

local area network (LAN) A computer network that spans a relatively small area, such as a single building. LANs can be connected to one another to form a wide area network (WAN).

local printer A printer that is connected directly to a computer. This differs from a network printer that may be connected to a different computer on a network or directly to the network itself.

logon Because it is a secure system, Windows XP requires that you enter a username and password so that it can register you with the network and determine the permissions you have been given on a computer.

lossless compression The condition in which no elements of a picture are lost during compression, resulting in higher picture quality and often larger size of picture files.

lossy compression The condition in which certain elements of a picture are lost during compression, resulting in lower size of picture files but also reduced quality of pictures.

LPT1 The name given to the primary parallel port on a computer. The first printer attached to a computer usually uses the LPT1 port.

M

Makebt32 The program used to make the set of floppy disks used for Windows XP installation. Makebt32 can be found in the BOOTDISK folder on the Windows XP installation CD.

map To create a shortcut to a shared resource on the network by telling your computer to treat the resource as a separate drive on your computer. Because not all programs know how to work with Network Place shortcuts, you can "fool" these programs into working with these shared resources by making them think that the resource is on a different drive on your computer.

maximize To cause a window on your desktop to grow to maximum size, filling your screen.

menu A collection of related commands in a program that is accessed by clicking once on the menu's title.

Microsoft Network (MSN) The ISP and Web service operated by Microsoft.

minimize To cause a window on your desktop to be removed from view. After it's minimized, you can access the window using its taskbar button.

MP3 A compressed audio file format suitable for downloading high-quality audio files from the Web. This has become a wildly popular audio format.

MSN Explorer A simplified Web browser that provides quick access to many MSN-related services, such as Web-based e-mail, calendar, and personalized Web services.

MSN Messenger An instant messaging program, much like ICQ or AOL Instant Messenger, that can be used to communicate directly with another person on a network or the Internet.

My Computer A special folder located on the Windows desktop that contains all the drives (hard disks, floppy disks, CD-ROM, and network drives) available on a computer.

My Documents A special folder located on the Windows desktop meant to hold all documents and personal files you create.

My Network Places A special folder located on the Windows desktop used to browse other computers available on the network.

My Pictures A special folder in the My Documents folder that has special features for viewing and working with pictures.

N–O

network Several computers (and sometimes other devices) that are connected together so that they can share software, data files, and resources. *See also* local area network *and* wide area network.

network drive A shared resource, such as a folder, treated as a drive on your computer. A network drive gets its own drive letter and shows up in the My Computer window.

Network Place   A shortcut to a resource (a file, folder, or a device) on the network. The shortcut you set up to that location works only on your computer; other computers on the network may or may not have the same Network Places you do.

network printer   A printer that is connected to another computer on the network or to the network itself and for which an icon is created in the Printers and Faxes folder on your computer.

newsgroup   An Internet-based forum in which you can participate in threaded discussions.

NTFS   The native file system format used by Windows XP. *See also* FAT32.

object   An item on your screen (usually an icon) that represents a program, file, or folder.

offline folders   Folders that have been marked to be accessible when your computer is not connected to the network. Files in offline folders are periodically synchronized with the actual files on the network.

operating system   A program or group of programs that controls the file system, drive access, and input for a computer. Windows XP is an example of an operating system.

Outlook Express   The e-mail and newsreader program included with Windows XP.

P

parallel port   A port on your computer often used for attaching printers, scanners, and other devices. *See also* LPT1.

parent folder   In a hierarchical list of folders on your computer, the parent folder is the folder *above* (and thus the folder that contains) the folder you are currently in.

path   The description of the location of a file or folder on your computer or on a network. A typical path might include the drive letter, folders, and name of the file (for example, `C:\My Documents\invoice.doc`).

pause printing   To stop a document in the print queue from printing. The document remains in the print queue but does not print until you choose to resume printing. Other documents waiting in the queue continue to print. *See also* restart printing.

peer   On networks where there is no main server, all computers are part of a workgroup and are considered peers that can share their own resources and access other resources on the network.

permission   On a secure system such as Windows XP, users are given specific rights (such as the ability to read or change a file) on objects.

pointer   A small graphic (an arrow, by default) indicating the placement of the mouse on your screen.

print device   In Microsoft lingo, the actual printer hardware connected to a computer is referred to as the print device and the icon in the Printers and Faxes folder that represents the device is referred to as a printer.

print queue   A list of documents waiting for their turn to be printed by a specific printer.

printer   *See* print device.

priority   The status a document has in a print queue. A document's priority governs when it prints related to other documents in the print queue. By default, all documents being printed are given a priority of 1, the lowest priority available. The highest priority is 99. Increasing a document's priority causes it to print before other waiting documents.

product activation   New versions of Windows require that you register and activate the operating system over the Internet or by phone so that you may continue use beyond a short trial period.

product identification key   The serial number found on the back of the Windows CD-ROM case and entered during the installation process that helps identify you as the proper owner of the software.

Properties   A dialog box available for most files and folders that contains various settings relating to the object. You can access this dialog box for most objects by right-clicking the object and choosing the Properties command from the shortcut menu.

publish   To upload a file from your computer to a Web server so that the file is available for viewing on the Internet.

Q–R

queue   A list of the documents waiting their turn to be printed.

Recent Documents   A special folder available on the Start menu that contains shortcuts to the documents you have most recently opened.

Recycle Bin   A special folder on your desktop that temporarily holds files you delete from your computer. When the Recycle Bin becomes full, the oldest files are permanently deleted to make room for new files to be added. You can also empty the Recycle Bin manually, permanently deleting all files inside.

register   During registration of Windows, you provide certain personal information (name, address, phone number, and so on) to Microsoft so that the company can record you as the owner of a Windows license. Registering is optional. When you register, you are eligible for technical support, warranty, and software bulletins; you also may receive special promotions from Microsoft on other products. *See also* activate.

resolution   The dimensions of your screen. Common resolutions include 640×480 pixels, 800×600 pixels, and 1024×768 pixels. You can change the resolution of your screen using the Display applet on the Control Panel.

restart printing   To begin printing a paused document again from the beginning. Restarting a print job can be useful if, for example, you start to print a document and then realize the wrong paper is loaded in the printer. You can pause the document, change the paper, and then restart the document. *See also* pause printing.

restore point   A special backup of system files and settings used by the System Restore application to return your computer to a particular state.

right-click   To hold the mouse pointer over a certain object and click the right mouse button once. Right-clicking an object usually opens a shortcut menu that contains commands relating to the object.

S

scheduled task   A job (such as launching a program or backing up files) defined in the Task Scheduler application to run at a certain time.

screen resolution   *See* resolution.

screen saver   A small program that displays graphics on your screen when the computer has been idle for a certain amount of time. Although designed to prevent images displayed too long from permanently burning themselves into your monitor (a phenomenon that does not often occur on newer monitors), screen savers are mainly used for entertainment and for security in conjunction with a screen saver password.

scroll   To move the display in a window horizontally or vertically to view information that cannot fit on a single screen.

search engine   A Web tool that compiles an index of existing sites and lets your search for pages that contain certain keywords. Some popular search engines are **www.yahoo.com**, **www.google.com**, and **www.altavista.com**

secure system   A computer that can be assigned a password so that unauthorized users are denied access.

select   To click once and bring the focus to an object. For example, in a list of files displayed in an open folder window, you can click a file to select that file. Information about the selected object is frequently displayed.

Send to   A submenu available on the shortcut menu for most files and folders that contains commands for quickly sending files to certain locations, such as the floppy drive, desktop, and My Documents folder.

share   To allow network access to a file or folder on your computer. After you share an object, you can define which users can access the object and exactly what they can do with it.

shortcut   A small file that targets another file on your computer. Double-clicking the shortcut launches the target file.

shortcut menu   The menu available by right-clicking most files and folders. The shortcut menu contains different commands that are associated with the particular object.

Start menu   The menu that opens when you click the Start button at the lower-left corner of your screen. The Start menu provides access to all your programs, special folders, and Windows settings.

standby   When your computer enters a mode in which the power to the monitor, hard drive, CD-ROM drive, and most other elements is turned off or reduced. Just enough power is fed to the computer's memory so that Windows remembers what programs were running and what windows were open. When your computer leaves standby, it should return to the same state it was in before it went to standby.

synchronize   To cause offline files or folders to be in unison with the actual files and folders they represent. Files in either location with newer modification dates replace files with older modification dates.

System Restore   A Windows application that creates restore points (backups of certain system settings) and that can restore Windows to any particular restore point. *See also* restore points.

system tray   The rightmost portion of the taskbar that contains icons representing programs running in the background. The system tray also includes the clock and volume control.

T

taskbar   The bottom part of your desktop that contains the Start menu, Quick Launch bar, program buttons, and system tray.

thread   A group of replies to a single message in a newsreader program such as Outlook Express. When you reply to a message, your reply becomes part of the thread.

tile   A way to arrange multiple windows on the screen. The multiple windows are reduced in size so that some portion of each of them appears on the screen at once. You can tile windows either horizontally or vertically on the screen.

troubleshooter   A special file in the Windows Help program that walks you through steps to take in determining the cause of a problem with Windows. The troubleshooter frequently suggests resolutions to these problems or points you toward more information about the problem.

U–V

uniform resource locator (URL)   The address of a Web page. The URL for a Web page generally includes the type of file (such as `http`), the computer on which the file is located (such as `www.microsoft.com`), the folder on that computer where the file is located (such as `/Windows/`) and the name of the actual file (such as `default.htm`).

upgrade   To install Windows XP over an existing installation of a previous version of Windows (such as Windows 98/Me/2000/NT).

volume label   The name of a disk. When formatting a floppy disk, you can provide a volume label for the disk if you want; alternatively, you can leave the disk unnamed, as most people do.

W–X–Y–Z

wallpaper   A picture displayed on the Windows desktop behind any icons.

wide area network (WAN)   Two or more LANs connected together over a distance. *See also* local area network (LAN).

Web browser   *See* browser.

Web page   A document that is usually one of many related documents that make up a Web site and that is available for anyone to view with a Web browser such as Internet Explorer.

Web server   The computer that serves the contents of a Web site to visitors to that site.

Web site   A group of related Web pages available over the Internet for anyone to view.

Windows Explorer   A tree-based application used to browse the file system on your computer.

Windows Media Player   A program installed with Windows XP that is used to display picture files, music files, and movie files of various formats.

Windows Movie Maker   A program installed with Windows XP that is used to create movie files out of still pictures and recorded video and audio.

wizard   A Windows program that walks you through the steps involved in the installation or configuration of a Windows component or program.

workgroup   A group of computers operating as peers on a network. *See also* peer *and* domain.

Zip drive   A model of disk drive made by Iomega with a removable disk roughly the size of a floppy disk that holds either 100MB or 250MB of data, depending on the exact model. Zip drives have become a popular way of backing up data on home computers.

Index

A

Accessibility Options dialog box, 222-223

accessing system information and tools, 240-241

activating Windows XP, 266

active users, 29

Add Favorite dialog box, 90

Add Hardware applet, 257

Add Printer Wizard, 72-77

Add/Remove Programs applet, 248-249

adding
contacts (Address Book), 109
items to Quick Launch bar, 218
items to Start menu, 216
network places to My Network Places, 134-135
users, 71
Web sites to Favorites menu, 87

Address bar (Internet Explorer), 82

Address Book (Outlook Express), 108
adding contacts, 109
settings, 110-111

Address Book button (Outlook Express), 108

addresses (URLs), 79

Advanced Attributes, 182, 244

advanced search options (Windows Explorer), 35

Alt+Tab key combination, 17

analyzing fragmentation, 234

appearance (desktop), 10-11
arranging windows, 14
changing, 200-201
wallpaper, 198-199

arranging folder icons, 39

ASR disk, 231

associations (files), 113

Attach button (Outlook Express), 114

attachments (e-mail)
etiquette, 115
receiving, 112-113
saving, 113
sending, 114-115

audio
recording, 171
setting volume levels, 192-193
system sounds, 214-215

Auto hide the taskbar option, 208

auto-expanding files, 33

auto-fill feature, 137

Automated System Recovery wizards, 230-231

automatic synchronization, 157

automatic system updates options, 255

automatic tasks, scheduling, 236-237

B

Back button (Internet Explorer), 83

Backup wizard, 226-227

backups
files, 226-229
reports, 227
sessions, 229

BOOTDISK folder, 268

Briefcase (Windows), 146
creating, 146
dragging files to, 147
opening files from, 149
taking it with you, 148-149
updating files, 150-151

browsers
MSNExplorer, 95
Web, 79

browsing
disk drives, 20-21
folder options, 211
folders, 32
newsgroups, 116
Web pages offline, 90-91

buttons
  mouse settings, 204-205
  Outlook Express
    Address Book, 108
    Attach, 114
    Create Mail, 104
    Send/Receive, 106
  Print, 62
  To (new message window),
    109

C

cables (networks), 125

canceling print jobs, 66

cascading windows, 14

CD-ROMs
  adding Windows components
    from Windows XP CD,
    252-253
  installing programs, 248-249

**CDs, copying musical from,
164-165**

changing
  desktop appearance, 200-201
  display settings, 202-203
  logon passwords, 188-189
  mouse settings, 204-205
  Windows XP settings, 191
    desktop themes, 196-197
    screen savers, 194-195
    volume, 192-193
    wallpaper, 198-199

chat
  MSNExplorer, 96
  Windows Messenger
    functionality, 99
    starting, 98

**Clip menu commands
(Combine), 170**

clips (video), 170

clocks, 18

closing programs, 13

collections (movies), 169

color
  changing desktop appearance,
    201
  depth, 202
  setting as wallpaper, 199

Colors dialog box, 93

**Combine command (Clip
menu), 170**

combining video clips, 170

commands
  Clip menu, 170
  File menu
    Import, 168
    New Folder, 107
    Print, 62
    Print Preview, 63
    Save Movie, 171
  Insert menu, 114
  Printer menu, 67
  Start menu
    Help and Support, 238
    *More Programs, Accessories,
    System Tools, Backup, 226*
    *More Programs, Accessories,
    System Tools, Disk
    Cleanup, 232*
    *More Programs, Accessories,
    System Tools, Disk
    Defragmenter, 234*
    *More Programs, Accessories,
    System Tools, Scheduled
    Tasks, 236*
    *More Programs, Accessories,
    System Tools, System
    Information, 240*
    *More Programs, Accessories,
    System Tools, System
    Restore, 242*
    Printers and Faxes, 64

components, 241

compressing
  files, 244-245
  folders, 244-245

computers
  browsing disk drives, 20-21
  finding on networks, 136-137
  locking, 184-185
  shutting down, 28-29

configuring
  folder options, 210-211
  keyboard settings, 206-207
  network permission settings,
    179
  taskbar options, 208-209
  Windows XP, 191, 265
    *accessibility options,
    222-223*
    desktop themes, 196-197
    power options, 212-213
    screen savers, 194-195
    Start menu, 216-217
    system sounds, 214-215
    volume settings, 192-193

**Connection options (Outlook
Express), 111**

**connections (Internet),
130-131**

contacts
  Address Book, 109
  Windows Messenger, 98

Control Panel folder, 191

Control Panel window, 250

copying
  Briefcase to floppy disk, 148
  files, 53
    to Briefcase, 145
    to floppy disks, 57
  folders, 53
  shared files to your computer,
    133
  tracks from CD, 164-165

**Create Mail button (Outlook
Express), 104**

creating
  collections (movies), 169
  e-mail, 104-105
  movies, 168-170

restore points, 242-243
share names (printers), 75
signatures (e-mail), 111

Ctrl+Alt+Del key combination, 7

cursors, blink rate, 207

D

date and time settings, 18

decompressing folders, 245

decrypting files/folders, 183

default printer, 68

defragmenting hard disks, 234-235

Delete key, 51

deleting, 251. See also uninstalling
e-mail, 107
files/folders, 50-51
Recycle Bin, 24
restoring from Recycle Bin, 25
items from Quick Launch bar, 219
items from Start menu, 217
recently-used files, 43
startup programs, 221
temporary files, 92-93

depth (links), 90

desktops, 5
changing appearance, 200-201
displaying icons, 10-11
dragging files to, 46
Recycle Bin, 24-25
screen savers, 194-195
system tray, 18
themes, 196-197
wallpaper, 198-199

Details view, 38-39

digital picture sharing (MSNExplorer), 96

Disk Cleanup wizard, 232-233

disks. See hard disks; floppy disks

Display Properties dialog box, 186-187

display settings, 202-203

documents
printing
canceling, 66
dragging to Printer icon, 64-65
from programs, 62-63
from Windows, 64-65
pausing, 67
priority, 67
restarting, 67
saving, 37

domain-based network permissions
local, 178-179
shared, 180-181

domains, 123

double-clicking files, 8, 42

downloading
Windows components, 254-255
Windows XP updates, 261

dragging, 9
documents to Printer icon, 64-65
files to the desktop, 46
items to Start menu, 216
objects to Recycle Bin, 24

drives, browsing, 20-21

E

editing
files (Word), 41
Internet Explorer settings, 92-93
offline settings, 158-159
Recycle Bin setting, 51
shared files, 141

Effects dialog box, 201

e-mail
attachments
etiquette, 115
receiving, 112-113
saving, 113
sending, 114-115
creating, 104-105
deleting, 107
folders, 107
formatting, 105
forwarding, 107
MSNExplorer, 96
opening, 106
organizing, 107
receiving, 106-107
replying, 107
sending, 104-105
signatures, 111
spell-checking, 105

emptying Recycle Bin, 25, 233

encrypting files/folders, 182-183

Entire Network link, 154

etiquette
e-mail attachments, 115
newsgroups, 121

Everyone group, 180

.exe file extension, 249

expanding threads (newsgroups), 118

Explorer (Windows), 32. See also Internet Explorer; MSNExplorer
files
creating, 36-37
manipulating, 33
opening, 42-43
renaming, 48-49
folders
renaming, 48-49
viewing items in, 38-39

opening, 32
searching for files/folders, 34-35
shortcuts to files/folders, 46-47

exporting system information, 241

F

F1 key, 23

Favorites menu (Internet Explorer), 83, 86-87

File Attachment command (Insert menu), 114

File menu commands
Import, 168
New (Word), 40
New Folder, 107
Print, 62
Print Preview, 63
Save Movie, 171

files, 31
associations, 113
auto-expanding, 33
backing up, 226-227
compressing, 244-245
coping to another drive, 33
copying, 53
creating (Word), 40-41
creating, 36-37
deleting, 50-51
double-clicking, 42
dragging
to Briefcase, 147
to the desktop, 46
encrypting, 182-183
.exe extension, 249
finding on networks, 138-139
moving, 33, 52
offline availability, 152-153
opening, 33
in certain programs, 58-59
recently-used, 42

paths, 31
publishing to the Web, 100-101
recently-used, 42-43
removing recently used, 43
renaming, 48-49
restoring from backups, 228-229
saving, 44
as you work, 45
to Briefcase, 145
floppy drives, 56-57
searching for, 34-35
selecting multiple, 50
sharing, 127, 140-141
shortcuts, 46-47
synchronizing offline items, 156-157
updating in Briefcase, 150-151

finding Web sites, 82
Favorites menu, 83, 86-87
History list, 88-89
Web searches, 84-85

floppy disks
formatting, 54-55
saving files to, 56-57
space concerns, 147
Windows XP setup disks, 268-269

Folder Options dialog box, 158-159, 210

folders, 31
arranging icons, 39
browsing, 32
compressing, 244-245
copying, 53
creating, 36-37
decompressing, 245
deleting, 50-51
e-mail, 107
encrypting, 182-183
making not available offline, 153
moving, 52

offline availability, 145, 152-153
opening, 32
options, 210-211
Printers folder, 64
Recycle Bin, 24
renaming, 36, 48-49
searching for, 34-35
selecting multiple, 50
sharing, 127, 140-141
shortcuts, 46-47
synchronizing offline items, 156-157
viewing items in, 38-39

formatting
drives for Windows XP installation, 263
e-mail, 105
floppy disks, 54-55

Forward button (Internet Explorer), 83

forwarding e-mail, 107

fragmentation, 234

freeing space on hard disks, 232-233

G - H

games, 174-175

grouped Taskbar buttons, 17

hard disks
defragmenting, 234-235
space, freeing, 232-233
Turn off hard disks drop down menu, 213

hardware
Device Manager, 256-257
identifying problem hardware, 257
installing, 247
keyboard settings, 206-207

mouse
   functions, 8-9
   settings, 204-205
networks
   installing, 124-126
   mapping drives, 142-143
system properties, 256
viewing resources, 240

Help and Support command (Start menu), 238

Help system, 22-23

Hibernate option, 29

Hide inactive icons option, 19

History list, 88-89, 93

Home Networking Wizard, 130-131

home pages, 83, 92-93

I

icons
   arranging, 39
   displaying on the desktop, 10-11
   Printer, dragging documents to, 64-65
   shortcut menus, 11
   turning off, 19

idle synchronization, 157

images as wallpaper, 199

Import command (File menu), 168

importing movies, 168

Insert Attachment dialog box, 114

Insert menu, 114

installing
   hardware, 124-126, 247
   printers, 72-75

software, 247-249
   adding components from the Windows XP CD, 252-253
   adding Windows components from the Internet, 254-255
Windows XP, 259
   creating setup floppy disks, 268-269
   networks, 125
   on a blank hard drive, 262-265
   registering with Microsoft, 266-267
   upgrades, 260-261

Internet
   activating Windows XP, 266
   adding Windows components, 254-255
   connections, 80, 130-131
   game playing, 175

Internet Explorer, 80
   Address bar, 82
   changing settings, 92-93
   Favorites menu, 86-87
   History list, 88-89
   Links bar, 82
   loading pages, 81
   Refresh button, 81
   Web sites
      Favorites menu, 83
      finding, 82
      searches, 84-85

Internet Options dialog box, 92-93

Items to Synchronize dialog box, 156

J–K–L

JPEGs, 31

keyboards
   accessibility options, 222
   settings, 206-207

LANs (local area networks), 123

layout (page), 69

left-dragging, 53

licensing agreements (software), 255

links, 81
   depth, 90
   offline availability, 90-91

Links bar (Internet Explorer), 82

List view, 38

local permissions (domain-based networks), 178-179

local printers, 72-75

locating
   computers on networks, 136-137
   files on networks, 138-139

license agreement (Windows XP), 260

locking
   taskbars, 208-209
   workstations, 184-185

logging off of Windows XP, 26-27

logging on to Windows XP, 6-7

logon passwords, 188-189

logon/logoff synchronization, 157

M

Make Available Offline command, 153

MAKEBT32 program, 268

managing
   pictures, 172
   print queue, 66-67

Map Network Drive dialog box, 143

mapping network drives, 142-143

maximizing program windows, 13

Media Guide, 166

memory, 28

messages, 106. *See also* e-mail

Microsoft Office, 250

Minimize All Windows command, 15

minimizing program windows, 13

modifying
Internet Explorer settings, 92-93
settings (printers), 68-69
user accounts, 129

monitors
display settings, 202-203
Turn off monitor drop down menu, 213

mouse
functions, 8-9
settings, 204-205

MouseKeys feature, 223

movies
collections, 169
creating, 168-170
importing, 168
navigating, 163
playing, 162-163, 171
visualizations, 163
volume, 163

moving
files, 52, 57
folders, 52

MSN search engine, 85

MSNExplorer, 94
benefits, 97
e-mail, 96
functionality, 95

MSNMoneyCentral, 96

music
navigating, 163
playing, 162-163
radio stations, 167
recording, 164-165
searching, 166-167
visualizations, 163
volume, 163

Mute option, 192-193

My Calendar link (MSNExplorer), 95

My Computer window
creating files/folders, 36
opening files, 42-43
renaming files/folders, 48-49
shortcuts, 46-47
viewing items in folders, 38-39

My Documents folder, 44-45, 146

My Network Places, 132
adding network places, 134-135
locating computers on the network, 136-137
locating files on the network, 138-139
offline folder/file availability, 154-155

My Programs folder, 12

My Recent Documents option, 42-43

My Web Sites link (MSNExplorer), 95

N

naming
collections (movies), 169
computers (networks), 126
files when saving, 45
folders, 37
printers, 74-75
restore points, 242
user accounts (networks), 128

navigating
disk drives, 21
movies/music, 163
with the mouse, 8-9

network adapter cards, 124-126

Network Places, publishing files to the Web, 101

networks, 123
encrypting files/folder, 182-183
file/folder offline availability, 152-153
finding computers on, 136-137
finding files on, 138-139
hardware, 124-126
Home Networking Wizard, 130-131
installing Windows XP, 125
mapping drives, 142-143
My Network Places, 132-135
naming computers, 126
permissions (domain-based networks), 178-181
printers, 76-77
setting up additional user accounts, 128-129
setting up small networks, 124-126
sharing resources, 127
files/folders, 133, 140-141
Internet connections, 130-131
using offline items, 154
workgroups, 126, 177
workstations, locking, 184-185

New Briefcase icon, 146

New Folder command (File menu), 107

news servers, 116

newsgroups
browsing, 116
etiquette, 121
posts
reading, 118-119
replying to, 119
sending, 120-121
privacy, 119
searching, 117
subscribing to, 116-117
threads, 118-119
viewing, 117

NTFS file, 179

O

Office (Microsoft), 250

Offline Favorite Wizard, 90

offline folders, 145

offline settings, 158-159

online games, 175

Open With dialog box, 58

opening
Device Manager, 256
drives, 20
e-mail, 106
files
from the Briefcase, 149
double-clicking, 42
in certain programs, 58-59
icon shortcut menus, 11
Internet Explorer, 80
menus, 9
My Network Places, 154
New Briefcase, 146
offline folders, 155
print queue, 66
programs, 12-13
Recycle Bin, 24
shared files/folders, 133
User Accounts window, 128
Windows Explorer, 32

Organize Favorites command (Internet Explorer), 87

organizing e-mail, 107

Outlook Express
Address Book, 108
adding contacts, 109
settings, 110-111
buttons
Address Book, 108
Attach, 114
Create Mail, 104
Send/Receive, 106
e-mail
receiving, 106-107
sending, 104-105

P

page layout, 69

paper source, 69

passwords
logon, 188-189
MSNExplorer, 94
screen saver, 186-187
Windows XP logons, 6-7

paths, 31

Pause Printing command (Printer menu), 67

permissions
local (domain-based networks), 178-179
offline, 155
shared (domain-based networks), 180-181

Permissions dialog box, 180

pictures
managing, 172
printing, 173
viewing, 173
as wallpaper, 199

playing
games, 174-175
movies, 162-163, 171
music, 162-163

points, 242-243

posts
newsgroups
reading, 118-119
replying to, 119
sending, 120-121
printers, selecting, 73

Power Options Properties dialog box, 212-213

Power schemes drop down list, 212

Print button, 62

Print command (File menu), 62

Print dialog box, 62

Print Preview command (File menu), 63

print queue
managing, 66-67
opening, 66
pausing, 67
viewing, 66

Printer icon, 64-65

Printer menu commands, 67

printers
default, 68
local, installing, 72-75
naming, 74
network, 76-77
ports, selecting, 73
properties, 63
selecting, 62
settings, 68-69
share names, 75
sharing, 70-71, 127
shortcuts, 65
users, adding, 71

Printers and Faxes command (Start menu), 64

Printers folder, 64

printing
documents, 62-65
canceling, 66
pausing, 67
priority, 67
restarting, 67
options, 63
page layout, 69
paper source, 69
pictures, 173
print queue. *See* print queue
priority, 67
quality, 69
system information, 241

privacy (newsgroups), 119

programs
closing, 13
installing, 248-249
opening files in, 58-59
starting, 12-13, 220-221
switching between, 16-17
Taskbar button, 16
uninstalling, 250-251

properties
hardware, 256-257
offline settings, 158-159
printers, 63
Recycle Bin, 51

publishing files to the Web, 100-101

Q - R

quality (printing), 69

queues. *See* print queue

Quick Launch bar
adding items to, 218
deleting item from, 219

radio stations, 167

Radio Tuner, 166-167

Read options (Outlook Express), 110

reading posts (newsgroups), 118-119

receiving e-mail
attachments, 112-113
Outlook Express, 106-107

recently-used files, 42-43

Reconnect at logon option, 143

recording
audio, 171
music, 164-165
video, 168

Recycle Bin, 24, 50
emptying, 233
modifying properties, 51
restoring items, 25

Refresh button, 81

refreshing Web pages, 81

registering Windows XP installation with Microsoft, 266-267

renaming
Briefcase, 147
files/folders, 41, 48-49
folders, 36
Web pages, 86

replying
to e-mail, 107
to newsgroup posts, 119

reports (backups), 227

resolution (screens), 203

resources (hardware), 240

Restart button, 28

restarting document printing, 67

Restore wizard, 228-229

restoring
files from backups, 228-229
objects from Recycle Bin, 25
restore points, 242-243
program windows, 13

right-clicking objects, 9

right-dragging, 53

routers, 125

S

Save As dialog box, 44-45

Save Attachments dialog box, 113

Save Movie command (File menu), 171

saving
attachments (e-mail), 113
documents, 37
files, 44
as you work, 45
to floppy disks, 56-57
system shutdown, 29

Scheduled Task wizard, 236-237

scheduling tasks, 236-237

screen resolution, 203

screen savers
configuring, 194-195
passwords, 186-187

Search Companion pane (My Network Places), 136-137

Search Companion tool (Internet Explorer), 85

search engines, 85

searching
for computers on a network, 137
for files and folders, 34-35
for files on a network, 138-139
Help system, 22-23
music, 166-167
newsgroups, 117
for Web sites, 84-85

security, 177
changing logon passwords, 188-189
locking workstations, 184-185
screen saver passwords, 186-187

selecting multiple files/folder, 50

Send options (Outlook Express), 111

Send/Receive button (Outlook Express), 106

sending
attachments (e-mail), 114-115
e-mail (Outlook Express), 104-105
files (compressed), 245
instant messages, 99
posts (newsgroups), 120-121

servers. *See* news servers

sessions (backups), 229

setting system volume controls, 19

settings
Address Book, 110-111
printers, 68-69

share names (printers), 75

shared folders, 152-153

shared permissions (domain-based networks), 180-181

sharing
files, 140-141
folders, 140
finding files on a network, 138-139
modifying files, 141
Internet connections, 130-131
printers, 70-71

Sharing dialog box, 70, 140

shopping online, 97

shortcuts
files/folders, 46-47
offline files, 159
printers, 65
Quick Launch bar, 218-219
Start menu, 217

Show the clock option, 209

ShowSounds option, 223

shutting down your computer, 28-29

signatures (e-mail), 111

sizing windows, 14

slideshows, 173

software
installing, 247-249
adding components from the Windows XP CD, 252-253
adding Windows components from the Internet, 254-255
customizing, 250
licensing agreements, 255
uninstalling, 251

Solitaire, 174

Sound Scheme drop down list, 215

Sounds and Audio Devices Properties dialog box, 214

SoundSentry option, 223

space (hard disks), 232-233

speed (mouse settings), 205

spell-checking, 105

Spelling options (Outlook Express), 111

Standby option, 29

Start menu
adding items to, 216
creating folders, 37
renaming shortcuts, 217

Start menu commands
Help and Support, 238
More Programs, Accessories, System Tools, Backup, 226
More Programs, Accessories, System Tools, Disk Cleanup, 232
More Programs, Accessories, System Tools, Disk Defragmenter, 234
More Programs, Accessories, System Tools, Scheduled Tasks, 236
More Programs, Accessories, System Tools, System Information, 240
More Programs, Accessories, System Tools, System Restore, 242
Printers and Faxes, 64

starting
Internet Explorer, 80
MSNExplorer, 94
programs, 12-13, 220-221
Windows Messenger, 98

stock listings, 95

storyboards (Windows Movie Maker), 170

subscribing to newsgroups, 116-117

switching
between programs, 16-17
news servers, 116

Synchronization Settings dialog box, 157

synchronizing
Briefcase, 145
offline items, 156-157
offline options, 159

system information, 240-241

system memory, 28

System Restore tool, 242-243

System Summary, viewing, 240

system tray, 18-19

T

Taskbar button, 16

taskbar settings, 208–209

tasks, scheduling, 236–237

temporary files, 92–93

themes (desktop), 196–197

threads (newsgroups), 118–119

Thumbnail view, 39

tiling windows, 15

timeline (Windows Movie Maker), 170

To button (new message window), 109

tools
  accessing, 241
  System Restore, 242–243

Tools menu, 156

tracks, copying from CD, 164–165

troubleshooting, 238–239
  display Troubleshoot button, 203
  hard disks, defragmenting, 235
  identifying problem hardware, 257

U–V

uninstalling programs, 250–251

updating
  files in the Briefcase, 150–151
  offline Web pages, 91
  Windows components, 255

upgrading Windows, 260–261

URLs (uniform resource locators), 79

user accounts, 6–7
  changing, 129
  selecting type, 129
  setting up, 128

video
  clips, combining, 170
  recording, 168

View workgroup computers link, 154

viewing
  collections (movies), 169
  components, 241
  hardware resources, 240
  items in folders, 38–39
  newsgroups, 117
  pictures, 173
  print queue, 66
  System Summary, 240
  Web pages, 80–81
  workgroup computers, 132

visualizations (movies/music), 163

volume, 19
  movies/music, 163
  Mute option, 192–193

Volume Label box, 55

W

wallpaper, 198–199

WANs (wide area networks), 123

Web browsers, 79
  changing home pages, 92–93
  finding sites, 82
    Favorites menu, 83, 86–87
    History list, 88–89
    Web searches, 84–85

Web pages
  links, 81
  loading, 81
  offline availability, 86, 90–91
  viewing, 80

Web Publishing Wizard, 100–101

Web sites
  Favorites menu, 86–87
  History list, 88–89
  home pages, 83
  navigating, 82–83
  publishing files to, 100–101
  search engines, 85
  searching for, 84–85
  Zone.com, 175

Web tutorials, 81

windows
  arranging, 14
  tiling, 15

Windows Briefcase. See Briefcase

Windows Explorer, 32
  files
    creating, 36-37
    manipulating, 33
    opening, 42-43
    renaming, 48-49
  folders
    renaming, 48-49
    viewing items in, 38-39
  opening, 32
  searching for files/folders, 34-35
  shortcuts to files/folders, 46-47

Windows Media Player, 162

Windows Messenger
  functionality, 99
  starting, 98

Windows Movie Maker, 168–171

Windows XP
  activating, 266
  adding components
    from the CD, 252-253
    from the Internet, 254-255

configuring
  accessibility options,
    222-223
  starting programs on
    Windows startup, 220-221
desktop. *See* desktops
Device Manager, 256-257
display settings, 202-203
Help system, 22-23
installing, 259
  creating setup floppy disks,
    268-269
  on a blank hard drive,
    262-265
  registering with Microsoft,
    266-267
  upgrades, 260-261
keyboard settings, 206-207
license agreement, 260
logging off, 26-27
logging on, 6-7
MSNExplorer, 94
  benefits, 97
  e-mail, 96
  functionality, 95
networks, 123
  My Network Places window,
    132
  setting up additional user
    accounts, 128-129
  setting up small networks,
    124-126
  sharing files/folders, 133
  sharing Internet connec-
    tions, 130-131
  sharing resources, 127
Quick Launch bar, 218-219
security, 177
settings, 191
  desktop themes, 196-197
  screen savers, 194-195
  volume, 192-193
  wallpaper, 198-199
Start menu, 216-217
system sounds, 214-215
taskbar settings, 208-209

Windows Messenger
  functionality, 99
  starting, 98
wizards
  Add Printer, 72-77
  Automated System Recovery,
    230-231
  Backup, 226-227
  Disk Cleanup, 232-233
  Restore, 228-229
  Scheduled Task, 236-237
Word (Microsoft), 40-41
**workgroups, 123, 126, 132,
177**
workstations, locking, 184-185
World Wide Web (WWW), 79

X–Y–Z

**Yes, let's activate Windows
over the Internet now option,
266**

Zone.com Web site, 175